Scripture Animals

Self-portrait of The Rev. Jonathan Fisher, 1824.
Copied, 1838.

Scripture Animals

*A Natural History of the Living
Creatures Named in the Bible*

by Jonathan Fisher

with a Foreword by Mary Ellen Chase

WEATHERVANE BOOKS
•
NEW YORK

With thanks to the Jonathan Fisher Memorial, Inc.,
Blue Hill, Maine, for kindly lending an original
copy, one presented by the author to his
grandson, James Fisher, in 1845;

*James Boorman Fisher's,
from his grandfather,
Jonathan Fisher, 1845,*

and to

Miss Alice Winchester,
former Editor, The Magazine, *Antiques,*
for suggesting its republication.

Foreword

The observation and study of nature was quite clearly a passion with Jonathan Fisher all his days; and this delight through which he might glorify God, instruct the young, and at the same time give himself intense enjoyment, was capable of easy and inevitable rationalization. Since the Bible contained numberless references to animals and since his pen must be dedicated only and always to the blessed purposes of God in the salvation of souls, this combination of duty and pleasure early engaged his mind and energies.

He began seriously to write his *Natural History of the Bible,* the original title of *Scripture Animals,* in 1819, and, according to his Diary entries, he was constantly at work upon it until 1832, when he decided upon its final title. In 1833 he had finished the text and the engraving of its many cuts and in September of that year carried manuscripts and blocks with him to Boston in the eager hope of interesting one among "several booksellers" in its publication. . . .

In November, 1833, he arranged with William Hyde of Portland to publish 1000 copies of his book, and it appeared in the spring of 1834. The entire cost of the edition was $600. Of the 1000 copies issued by Mr. Hyde, Mr. Fisher bought 625 for private sale, and his son-in-law, Capt.

Jeremiah Stevens, rallying nobly to the Fisher standard, purchased 125 copies. The remaining 250 are listed by Mr. Hyde in his account to the author as sold at .60 each to various shops and individuals in the neighborhood of Portland. The parson obviously paid his bill to Mr. Hyde, which for printing and binding amounted to $375, by the later sale of his 625 copies, although he was allowed $130 of that sum for the use of his cuts. Neither Mr. Hyde nor Mr. Fisher made much money on their undertaking, but perhaps the pride of the latter in his book compensated for the loss of monetary gain. Whether or not he disposed of all his copies is not stated, for, since his Diaries closed in 1835, we have only his letters to depend upon for information. In two of these, descriptive of his "western tour" in 1839, he says he sold "while away" 111 copies at .90 each, and, without doubt, in view of his talents as a salesman, he managed to dispose of many more within and without his parish. What Capt. Jeremiah Stevens did with his 125, clearly bought for the honor of the family, remains a subject of amusing conjecture. Perhaps he carried them on his ship and distributed them about his West Indian ports of call!

Jonathan Fisher's evident satisfaction and pride in this last of his books are justified by an examination of it. It consists of 347 pages and is illustrated throughout by woodcuts of the animals described in alphabetical order. Its title page,

Scripture Animals

or

Natural History
Of the Living Creatures Named in the Bible
Written Especially for Youth
Illustrated with Cuts
by Jonathan Fisher, A. M.

is stamped by an illustration which ingeniously combines the branches of trees in order to reveal the profile of the Rev. Mr. Fisher himself. A foreword explains that most of the cuts are copied from the work of various engravers, "Bewick, Mavor, the Cabinet, several Lexicons, and some other works," although a few of them are "from nature." "Of the execution," he says, "I may remark that, not being able to hire them engraved, I have engraved them myself, and having no instruction in the art and but little practice, I can lay no claim to elegance in their appearance." The foreword also justifies the naming of most of the animals in Hebrew and Greek, and some of them in Latin and French as well, by some words descriptive of his own love of languages; and he expresses his hope that the sight of these strange words may "raise a desire in the bosoms of some young persons of natural genius to seek an education."

The charm of *Scripture Animals* (and its charm is undeniable) lies, first of all, in the author's eager and personal description of certain of his subjects. These begin with the *adder,* the *ant,* and the *ass,* and continue through the alphabet in so far as the Bible provides creatures of the initial letters. He is careful to list the number of times each beast is mentioned therein and, unless these are too many as in the case of the *lion* and the *sheep,* the scriptural passages pertaining to it. Once this is done, he proceeds to comment upon the habits of each creature, and now and again he relates personal experiences as the source of his knowledge. When he is writing of the *owl,* which he has drawn from the one found in his woodhouse in February, 1832, he describes the hoots and the sudden screams which have many times startled him on his solitary wayfarings through the woods at night; when he is dealing with the *mouse,* he tells of the great number of field mice in the District of Maine and in Massachusetts in the year 1809, so many that a fox once threw thirteen of them out of his mouth in one gulp! The *pigeon* brings to mind the huge flocks he has seen in Bluehill, which fly at the rate of a mile a minute and which have been killed by thousands. The *caterpillar*, also drawn from nature, recalls one which, while he was in college, he placed in a little box and fed daily with leaves. He watched it spin its cocoon with fascinated eyes and after some weeks saw it emerge as a beautiful moth.

There is charm also in the short poems which follow most of the descriptions. Here, for once, his pleasure in his task softens his moral and religious reflections and results occasionally in some rather captivating lines;

On Behemoth, the Elephant, "a paraphrase from Job":

He sinks the river, which his thrist supplies,
  With fearless leisure; and believes he may
Drink Jordan dry; 'tis little in his eyes,
  While with his trunk he clears his cumbered way.

On the patient Ox, from Isaiah 1:

  He knows his master; ready to obey,
  Is mild and docile, does not often stray.
  Though oft he labors with attending pain,
  How rare to hear him in his toil complain!

On the Bittern:

  The Bittern loves a lone abode,
    And hides from human view.
  And we, to think of Heaven and God,
    Should love retirement, too.

Indeed, he takes such evident joy in this book that he cannot forbear adding an Appendix of animals and fish not, as a matter of fact, found in the Bible, but interesting in themselves: the *haddock*, for instance, and the *rattle-*

snake, to which rum is a fatal poison as it should likewise be to mankind! And lastly, in an essay on Man and his tragic Fall, he finds excuses to write of the Laplanders and the Tartars, who, although they are, of course, depraved and fallen like the rest of us, nevertheless possess old habits of life worthy of description.

Even the somber design of death on the final page—a tombstone with skull and bones, which may have seemed to him a fitting bit of solemnity to offset any possible suggestion of too much delight in his book—cannot dim the life within it. Or the Latin words with which he takes farewell of his young readers:

> *Occumbit Sol, veniunt umbrae*
> The sun sets; the shadows gather.

MARY ELLEN CHASE

Scripture Animals

SCRIPTURE ANIMALS,

OR

NATURAL HISTORY

OF THE LIVING CREATURES NAMED IN THE BIBLE,

WRITTEN ESPECIALLY FOR YOUTH.

ILLUSTRATED WITH CUTS.

BY JONATHAN FISHER, A. M.

He giveth to the beast his food, and to the young ravens which cry.
Psalm 147: 9.

PORTLAND:
PUBLISHED BY WILLIAM HYDE.
1834.

Arthur Shirley.....Printer.

TO THE READER.

THE following articles are submitted to the candor of that public, to whose use they are now presented. In compiling them I have been indebted to Bewick, Mavor, the Cabinet, several Lexicons, and some other works, and to nature. I have endeavored to come to as just a decision as possible respecting the animals intended by the names given in the originals of the Scriptures. In attempting this I have found no small difficulty to encounter by reason of the diversity of opinions among critics upon the subject of the natural history of the bible ; one ascribes the name to one animal, another to another, and the difference of opinion is great.

In the case of domestic animals, and of those wild animals that are more frequently named, the decision has been comparatively easy ; but in the case of some others I have given the figure of the animal, which bears the same name in Europe or America, which is found in the English translation, without venturing to determine to what kind of animal the original name was given. In several articles I have given no figures, because I had no patterns within my reach, nor subjects to sketch from.

As respects the Cuts, a few of them are from nature, but most of them are copied, and generally reduced a little, to bring them conveniently within the compass of the page I have chosen for the work. Of the exe-

cution I may remark, that not being able to hire them
engraved, I have engraved them myself; and having
had no instruction in the art, and but little practice, I
can lay claim to no elegance in their appearance. I
have endeavored to give a true outline; the filling up
must speak for itself.

The work is designed especially to assist young people in gaining a knowledge of the natural history of
the bible, that with what helps they have on other subjects, and from other sources, they may be able to read
that best of books with a good understanding of its
contents. At the close of most of the articles I have
added something in a way of moralizing, or spirituali-
zing, that my young readers may be led to practical and
useful meditations, which may meliorate both heart
and life.

I am aware that the question will naturally occur;
If the work be intended for youth, why are the names
given in Hebrew, Greek, Latin, &c., as well as in
English ? To this I reply, 1. I supposed it likely that
the book might fall into the hands of some, who were
studying these languages, and might help to some critical knowledge of these names, without the labor of
recurring to a number of Lexicons, which they might
not have at hand. 2. I have thought that probably
the sight of these words in other languages might raise
a desire in the bosoms of some young persons of natural genius to seek an education, which might call them
forth into usefulness, when otherwise their talents
might lie dormant for want of excitement. As nearly
as I can recollect the first desire I felt for a liberal education was excited in my own mind, in the ninth year
of my age, by seeing some Greek quotations in the

margin of Hervey's *Theron* and *Aspasio*, which my honored mother had borrowed to read. I wished to be able at some future time to understand a language, which was then altogether unintelligible to me. But, what is more fully to the point, I may state, that the celebrated Professor Lee of England, in a letter to a friend, gives the following account of what led *him* to the study of the languages.

"About the age of seventeen I formed a determination to learn the Latin language; to which I was instigated by the following circumstances: I had been in the habit of reading such books as happened to be in the house where I lodged; but meeting with Latin quotations found myself unable to comprehend them. Being employed about this time in the building of a Roman Catholic Chapel for Sir Edward Smith of Actonburnel, where I saw many Latin books, and frequently heard that language read, my resolution was confirmed."

Thus we see that falling upon a few Latin quotations led the way for the developement of one of the most powerful minds for the acquisition and critical knowledge of language, that modern times have witnessed.

Without further apology I send forth my little book with the desire and prayer that it may be useful to the rising generation, not only for time but also for etenity.

JONATHAN FISHER.

BLUEHILL, JAN. 1834.

1*

EXPLANATION OF TERMS.

Abdomen, the lower part of an insect, joined to the corselet by a thread, or very small waist.

Antler, a prong, or branch of the horn of an animal of the deer kind.

Aquatic, living in, and about water.

Ash-color, a shade of gray, resembling the color of ashes.

Aurelia, often called *butterfly's bottle;* it is the state of an insect between its larva, or worm state, and its perfect, or winged state.

Callosity, a hard, gristly substance, such as is found on the legs of horses, camels, &c.

Carnivorous, applied to such animals as subsist chiefly on flesh.

Chatter, to utter sounds rapidly, and indistinctly, as the black-bird or bob-o'-link.

Chrysalis, the same as aurelia.

Citron-color, greenish yellow.

Clavated, shaped like a club; the feelers of insects, which are largest at the end farthest from the head are so called.

Concocted, partly digested.

Contaminate, to defile, to render impure.

Corselet, the breast of an insect, or that part into which the legs and wings are inserted.

Dormant, sleeping; in a state to appearance lifeless.

Dun-color, between brown and black.

Feelers, slender substances, proceeding in the manner of horns from the heads of insects, with which they appear to feel the objects before them.

Filiform, of a thread like form, as the feelers of some insects.

Flexible, easily bending.

Gallinacious, applied to that order of fowls, which includes our common barn fowls, such as the *hen*, the *turkey*.

Garrulous, talkative ; full of prattle, like the magpie.

Genera, the plural of genus, which signifies a kind, or class of animals, &c. including several species, agreeing in some points, which distinguish them from those of other classes.

Genus, see genera.

Granivorous, usually subsisting on grain or seeds.

Herbivorous, feeding on herbs.

Incubation, the sitting of a fowl upon its eggs.

Insect, a class of animals so called from the latin word, *inseco*, to cut, because they seem to be almost cut off at their waist.

Japaning, varnishing with a glossy black.

Larva, the reptile, or worm state of an insect.

Malicious, ill disposed, inclined to do mischief.

Masticated, made soft by chewing.

Membrane, a thin skinny substance, such as unites the toes of geese, ducks, &c.

Migratory, removing from place to place, as cold, heat, or other circumstances incline.

Olive-color, between yellow and black ; tawny.

Palmated, shaped somewhat like the hand, with the fingers spread.

Pendulous, hanging down as the long ears of some animals.

Pile, a fibre of wool, goat's hair, &c.

Pollen, the small dust in flowers, which renders the seed fruitful.

Proboscis, the trunk of an elephant, and something bearing a relation to it in the case of insects.

Protruding, shooting out, or forward.

Puncture, a small hole, made by some pointed instrument.

Protuberance, a swelling, bunch, or knob.

Sal-ammoniac, a compound of the acid of sea-salt, and of the volatile alkali called, ammonia, from a territory of that name.

Scapular, a feather springing from the shoulder of the wing of a fowl.

Sedge, coarse grass, growing in swamps.

Serrated, notched, after the manner of a saw.

Species, in a loose sense means *sort* or *kind;* in a more strict sense, the whole collection of animals derived from one common pair; and the whole collection of plants that agree in some permanent particulars.

Subterraneous, existing, naturally, under the surface of the earth.

Swarthy, of a dark complexion.

System, a plan, or scheme, consisting of many parts, connected together, and forming one whole.

Tawny, a color partaking of black and yellow.

Torpid, in a benumbed, motionless state.

Transmigration, the heathen doctrine of the passing of the soul after death into the body of some other person, or of some brute animal.

Umber, a yellowish brown color.

Vane, the downy threads of a feather, which branch out from the quill are sometimes called *vanes.*

Virulent, very powerfully poisonous.

Voracity, greediness.

In the following work I have given the pronunciation of the Hebrew and Greek names, as nearly as I could, in Roman letters, and have designated the sounds of the vowels according to Perry's scheme.

ā—as in hate.
ă—as in hat.
â—as in hall.
ē—as in mete.
ĕ—as in met.
ī—as in pine.
ĭ—as in pin.
ō—as in note, and ó—as in whólly.
ŏ—as in not.
ô—as in move, and ò—as in bòok.
ū—as in fume.
ŭ—as in fur.

Where *Hrh*, *Krk*, and *gn* occur, the common reader, if he please, may sound them as *h*, *k*, and the *gn* may be omitted.

SCRIPTURE ANIMALS.

ADDER.

[The figure is from the common American Adder.]

—

A reptile of the serpent kind. The Adder common in North America, is usually from twenty to thirty inches in length, and rather thicker in proportion to its length, than the common striped, or garter snake. On its back it is of a light brown, crossed with broad bars of a different shade, inclining to ash color. Its belly is white, curiously spotted with black and brown. It frequents rocky places, the old walls of cellars, and the ruins of buildings. It does not appear to be venomous.

The name *Adder*, is found five times in the Bible, under four different names in the original.

1. Gen. 49 : 17. Dan shall be a serpent by the way, an *Adder* in the path, that biteth the horse-heels, so that his rider shall fall backward. Here the Hebrew for Adder is (שְׁפִיפֹן) Shefēfon; which both Pagnin and

Buxtorf in their Hebrew Lexicons, suppose to be the *Cerastes*, a viper, with horns, resembling in shape those of a ram. It is so called, from the Greek kĕras, a horn. (*See Viper*.) Some of the Jewish Rabbies derive the name in this place from the Hebrew Shôf, (שׁוּף) which signifies *to bruise*, and is found in Gen. 3 : 15. And thou *shalt bruise* his heel ; applied to the serpent. Others derive it from Shâfäh, (שָׁפָה) *to be high*, or *on a high place ;* because this kind of serpent is supposed sometimes to dart itself down from high places upon those who are passing by. His lying in the path, and biting the horse-heels, agrees with the *Cerastes*, which hides itself in the sand, by the path, and bites the feet of travellers.

The comparison of Dan to this kind of serpent, is supposed to denote the cunning and subtlety of that tribe, conquering its enemies more by craft, than by strength and valor.

Let it be your concern, my young friends, to possess that *subtlety*, which consists in true and innocent *wisdom ;* but detest that *low cunning*, which is disposed secretly to undermine those that rise above it; and shun with care, that *evil speaking*, which wounds, under cover, the reputation of the virtuous.

2. Psal. 58 : 4, 5. They are like the deaf *Adder*, which stoppeth her ear, which will not hearken to the voice of charmers, charming never so wisely. Psal. 91 : 13. Thou shalt tread upon the Lion and *Adder*. In both these places, the Hebrew name is Fĕthĕn, (פֶּתֶן) which some, by an opposition in the sense, derived from Pâthâh, (פָּתָה) *to persuade ;* because this kind of serpent will not be persuaded. Buxtorf and Pagnin both suppose it means the *Asp*, a very poisonous serpent, called in Latin, *aspis*. It is said of this serpent that it cannot

be charmed by any art whatever. It is evident from the concurrent testimony of many authors of different nations, that most kinds of serpents may be charmed. Those, who have the art of charming, by a particular kind of music, will cause them to draw near, like tame and harmless creatures; but when the charming is over, they will hasten away.

The circumstance, that the Asp will not be charmed, has given rise to the idea that it is deaf, and that it stops its ears, the reality of which, in a literal sense, may be doubted; but its refusing to be charmed, gives good ground for the poetic figure of its stopping its ears, and renders it a very fit emblem of those wicked ones, who are so bent upon evil, that nothing will persuade them to renounce it.

> The crafty Adder stops her ears,
>   Nor hears the cunning charmer,
> And wisely thus, because she fears
>   His syren song may harm her.
>
> Happy the youth, who thus bewares,
>   Nor listens to the devil;
> He thus may flee a thousand snares,
>   And shun a world of evil.
>
> But he, who turns his ear away
>   From every faithful warning,
> Must find himself, another day,
>   Consigned to endless burning.

To tread upon the Adder, means to triumph over the most malicious and dangerous enemies. He, who would do this, must be the friend of God, and repose his confidence on the arm of the Almighty.

3. Psal. 140 : 3. *Adder's* poison is under their lips. The Hebrew name is (עַכְשׁוּב) Gnăkhshôv; this also is said by Pagnin and Buxtorf to be a species of the *Asp.* It is so rendered in the Greek translation of the Old Testament, by the seventy. In the Latin translation by Junius and Tremellius, it is *Ptyas,* from the Greek ptūō,

to spit; and is said to be a green colored Adder, which spits its venom into people's eyes. The expression, *poison under their lips,* alludes to the place, where venomous serpents usually carry their poison, which is in little cells, at the roots of several hollow teeth, commonly covered with their upper lip, and not used when they eat.

The Psalmist means here to describe those wicked persons, who utter from their lips those false doctrines, which are ruinous to the souls of men; or those evil slanders, which blast their characters; or those filthy discourses, which contaminate their morals.

4. Prov. 23 : 32. At the last it biteth like a serpent, and stingeth like an Adder. The Hebrew name for adder, in this place, is (צִפְעֹנִי) Tsĭfgnōnē; it is generally thought to mean the *Basilisk,* otherwise called the *Cockatrice,* a very venomous serpent. Junius and Tremellius call it *Hœmorrhois;* a kind of serpent, whose poison causes the blood to start from the veins.

Strong drink, received intemperately, may be compared to the stinging of an Adder, because like poison its intoxicating influence is diffused through the whole system.

If all the venomous serpents in the known world, were collected upon this continent, I doubt whether they would have so pernicious an effect upon the inhabitants, as they actually experience from the intemperate use of strong drink.

> Dear youth, be warned, nor let the sparkling bowl,
>   Tempt your young lips, and drown your mental powers;
>   Will you for pleasure of a few short hours,
> Risk the vast loss of an immortal soul?
>   No, 'tis too much! The poison shun,
>   Nor such an awful hazard run.

ANT.

[The figure is from nature and magnified.]

—

A well known insect. It consists of three principal parts. 1. The head, furnished with a pair of strong nippers, with which it cuts its food; with a pair of feelers, and with prominent eyes. 2 The body or waist, from which proceed six legs, and sometimes a pair of wings. 3. The abdomen, or tail, forming about one third, or half the bulk of the insect. They are of different sizes and colors; some very small, and of a brick red; some larger, and usually black; some very large, and either wholly black, or black with red waists.

Those that are very small, are in many places, very troublesome, getting into honey, sugar, and other sweet things, by thousands, and spoiling them for use. Even the larger ones are not a little troublesome in their intrusions. Some kinds form their habitations in the decaying parts of wood, in which they form their cells in an irregular, but curious manner. Others form their houses under the surface of the ground, and it is amusing to see with what dexterity they bring out the grains of sand in their nippers, while forming their little subterraneous caverns. In some cases they have been known so to multiply, as to drive the inhabitants of a place

2*

before them.   They usually live in families, or little
communities.   When a family removes, as sometimes
they do, they may be seen for some rods on one general
track, some going, and some returning; but those, who
bear their young ones and their eggs, or provisions, will
be seen all tending towards their new habitation. Their
usual food is little worms and various insects.

The Ant is twice mentioned in scripture.   1. Prov.
6 : 6.   Go to the *Ant*, thou sluggard, consider her ways
and be wise, which having no guide, overseer, or ruler,
provideth her meat in summer, and gathereth her food
in harvest.   2. Prov. 30 : 25.   The *Ants* are a people
not strong, yet they prepare their meat in summer.   Its
Hebrew name is (נְמָלָה) Nemâlâ, from (נָמַל)Nâmäl, *to
cut round about*, or *to cut off;* so called, probably, from
its cutting off the parts of its food, which it does with
great dexterity, as I have sometimes witnessed.

The Ant is brought to view by Solomon, as an example for the sluggard; and on account of the activity and
industry with which she employs herself in the summer
season, she is a worthy example.   She is said to provide her meat in summer, and to gather her food in harvest.   This does not absolutely imply that she lays up
food for winter; and it is evident that the Ants in cold
climates do generally, if not universally, lie dormant, or
torpid, in the winter.   Yet the Ants do, what in our
case, would be laying up food for winter; in the time
when their food is to be obtained, they do gather it, and
store it in their cells, to feed upon, when it is not convenient for them to gather it.   When the articles of their
food are most easy to be obtained, then is their harvest
time.

Wise is he, who, taught by this example, does in summer provide for winter; and wiser still is he, who in

the harvest time of this life, provides an inexhaustible store of good things for the life to come.

> Go to the *Ant*, thou sluggard, go,
>   And idly dream no more ;
> See how she toils, while summer smiles,
>   And treasures up her store.
>
> Will spring and seed-time ne'er be past ?
>   Will summer ne'er be gone ?
> Will joyful harvest always last,
>   And life be never done ?
>
> Go to the Ant, thou sluggard, go ;
>   This very day be wise ;
> And spare no pains to have thy gains
>   Well stored above the skies.

APE.
—

THIS is a general name, including several species of animals. 1. The *Ape*, properly so called, having no tail. 2. The *Baboon*, having a short tail. 3. The *Monkey*, having a long, slim tail. All animals of this kind bear a strong resemblance to the human figure, especially in their faces, hands, and feet. The skin of their faces is bare, or nearly so, and often black; and their fingers and toes are furnished with nails, instead of claws. They are generally very mischievous, and full of chatter, and some of them lascivious, thievish, and irritable in their manners.

Of all the species of Apes, the *Ourang Outang* comes nearest to the human figure; and seems to be the first link in the descending chain of gradation below the human. He often walks erect, and is sometimes five or six feet in height, and in color, of a reddish brown, the

face and hands of a swarthy flesh color. He is rarely
found, except in Africa. He feeds upon various kinds
of food; but, like most other Apes, is peculiarly fond of
fruit. In his manners, when tamed, he is more mild,
and less mischievous, than most other kinds. For the
figure, see Satyr, in its place.

Pigmy.   BarbaryApe.

[Figure from Mavor.]

The *Pigmy Apes* are another species; and were looked upon by the ancients, as a dwarfish race of mankind.
They inhabit Africa and Asia the less. They go in
troops, rob orchards and cornfields; and, at the approach
of danger, one who stands sentinel screams, when the
rest run to the mountains. They sit upright, and are
in color, of an olive brown.

[Figure from Bewick.]

The *Gibbon* is remarkable for his long arms, which, when he stands erect, reach the ground; he is about three feet high, of a tawny color, sometimes black; he is of a malicious disposition.

The *Green Monkey* is from the Cape de Verd Islands. He is about the size of a common cat, his face and hands nearly as dark as those of negroes; the hair on the back and outside of the limbs yellowish green, the breast and inside of the limbs, a silver white. He is very snappish and irritable in his manners.

The name *Ape* is mentioned twice in the Bible. 1 Kings 10 : 22. Once in three years came the navy of Tarshish, bringing gold and silver, ivory, *Apes*, and peacocks. Mention of the same thing is made in 2 Chron. 9 : 21. The name in Hebrew is (קוֹף) Kōf, from (יָקַף) Yâkăf, *to encircle*, or *to run round*, it being the general habit of these animals to be skipping and running about with great agility. Their near resemblance to the human form, generally strikes the beholder at first view, with unpleasant feelings. They naturally excite the idea of something monstrous, or deformed, of the human species. But calm reflection may lead us to view in them, the wonderful wisdom of God, who has left no vacancy in his works, but has made the chain of being perfect from the living atom, which sports in the dew-drop, to the highest Archangel.

> Do Apes disgust, because their look and shape
>   Bear such resemblance to the human form,
> While in their actions they are still the Ape,
>   So wild and brutal, that they cannot charm?

> Ye bigger *Apes* of human name and dress,
>   Loose, foppish, vain, in manners much the same,
> Your near alliance to the Ape confess,
>   Till worthier deeds shall prove a higher claim.

ASP.

A very venomous serpent. [*See Adder.*] The name Asp is mentioned five times in the Bible. Deut. 32 : 33. Their wine is the cruel venom of *Asps.*—The Hebrew here is (פְּתָנִים) Pethânēm, from Fĕthĕn. Job 20 : 14. His meat in his bowels is turned, it is the gall of *Asps* within him. Ver. 16 : He shall suck the poison of *Asps.* Isaiah 11 : 8. The sucking child shall play on the hole of the *Asp.* In all these places the Hebrew name is the same, Fĕthĕn, or its plural, Pethânēm. Rom. 3 : 13. The poison of *Asps* is under their lips. The Greek here is ăspĭdōn, the plural of ăspĭs. This the apostle quotes from Psal. 140 : 3, where the English translation has *Adder*, but a species of the Asp is supposed to be meant. Aristotle and others affirm, that the poison of the Asp kills certainly and suddenly.

> The wine of the wicked is death;
>   Their cordials are venom and gall;
> The righteous they kill with their breath,
>   At their feet the poor innocent fall.

But the day of the wicked must come,
  On his head his devices return ;
To drink his own poison his doom ;
  The venom within him shall burn.

O when shall those ages appear,
  When satan, confined in his cell,
Shall leave a new paradise here,
  Where the righteous in safety may dwell ?

The babe on the hole of the Asp
  Shall then without injury play ;
The youth in full safety shall bask
  In the den, where the Basilisk lay.

Dear Saviour, thy kingdom shall then,
  Like a mountain, which reaches the skies,
O'ershade all the kingdoms of men,
  And in glory and majesty rise.

ASS.
[Figure from Bewick.]

THE Ass is an animal of the horse kind, but smaller, and much less elegant in shape ; he has long, large ears, a short mane, and long hairs only on the end of his tail. They are sometimes white, commonly of a pale dun color, with a black stripe running down the back, and another crossing it over the shoulders. In his wild state he is fierce and ungovernable ; when domesticated he is gentle and patient, carries heavy burdens, and contents himself with the meanest and coarsest vegetables

for his food, but is very delicate in his drink.   The *Ass*
was well known, and much used in Judea; even their
nobles and princes often rode upon them.   They are
mentioned many times in the holy scriptures.   The
Hebrew name is (חֲמוֹר) Hrhămōr, which signifies also,
a heap; and they are so called, as some think, from the
heaps, or burdens, of various things, which they carry.
The she Ass in Hebrew, is (אָתוֹן) ăthōn; the young
Ass, (עַיִר) Gnăyĭr; the wild Ass, (פֶּרֶא) Pĕrĕh.

Gen. 49 : 14.   Issachar is a strong *Ass*, couching
down between two burdens.—This indicates that this
tribe should not be warlike, and spirited; but willing
rather to bear heavy burdens of tribute, than to use great
exertions to be free and independent.   To be yielding,
submissive and patient through a spirit of christian for-
bearance, is worthy; to be submissive, through a spirit
of sloth and fear, is base and unworthy.

Numb. 22 : 28.   And the Lord opened the mouth of
the Ass, and she said unto Balaam, what have I done
unto thee, that thou hast smitten me these three
times?—This miracle shows the power of God; it ought
to have led Balaam to consider the evil of his covetous-
ness, and from that moment to resolve explicitly to bless
Israel.   God gave him permission to go to Balak, but
no license to carry with him such a covetous disposition.

Deut. 22 : 10.   Thou shalt not plow with an ox and
an Ass together.—This prohibition might be for several
reasons : 1. To teach decency and symmetry in their
conduct.   2. To teach them to avoid all unnatural mixtures.   3. To teach them simplicity and purity in their
manners.   4. To teach them not to defile the worship
of God with their own superstitions; the ox was a
clean, and the ass an unclean beast.   5. It might be to
impress the idea of the distinction there ought to be
between God's people, and the people of the world;
between saints and sinners.

Job 11 : 12. For vain man would be wise, though man be born like a wild Ass's colt.—This, by a lively figure, teaches that man comes into the world in a fallen, degenerate state. It is a declaration, which should keep all humble.

Zech. 9 : 9. Rejoice greatly, O Daughter of Zion; shout, O Daughter of Jerusalem; behold thy King cometh unto thee; he is just, and having salvation; lowly, and riding upon an Ass; and upon a colt, the foal of an Ass.—This is prophetic of the manner in which Jesus Christ once rode into Jerusalem. Though Lord of heaven and earth, he condescended to ride upon the least honorable of all beasts of burden. This was expressive of his meekness and lowliness, of his condescension and patience.

> Daughter of Zion, lift thy voice with joy;
> Daughter of Judah, shout in thankful praise;
> Let every tongue its sweetest notes employ,
> And one loud concert, all harmonious, raise.
>
> Behold thy King, thy rightful Sovereign, comes;
> *A Saviour just*, the holy name he wears;
> How lowly still, what meekness he assumes;
> An Ass's colt the heavenly Monarch bears.
>
> 'Tis his humiliation. But the day
> Will come, when, armed with his resistless power,
> His glittering arrows shall his voice obey,
> And flaming wrath his stubborn foes devour.
>
> Daughter of Zion, thou, his chosen bride,
> Redeemed, adorned, in robes of glory drest,
> Raised to thy throne, and seated near his side,
> In his kind smiles shall thence be ever blest.

3

BADGER.

[Figure from Bewick.]

—

THE Badger is a clumsy, indolent animal, covered on its body with long, coarse, ash-colored hair; his belly and legs black. In shape, it much resembles the skunk. It burrows in the ground in retired parts of the forest; feeds on roots, nuts, insects and frogs. When attacked by dogs, it throws itself on its back, and makes an able defence with its teeth and claws. When young it is easily tamed, and is very cleanly. It is found in various parts of Europe and Asia. The name in Hebrew translated *Badger*, is (תַּחַשׁ) Tährhäsh, in the plural, (תְּחָשִׁים) Tehrhâshēm. Exodus 25 : 5—And ram skins died red, and *Badger* skins. Ezek. 16 : 10—And I shod thee with *Badger* skins. The seventy and St. Hierome, (Jerome) render the word *purple*, instéad of *Badger*. Pagnin, Buxtorf, and Junius and Tremellius supposed it to mean *Badger*. In Latin, *Taxus*, or *Melis;* in French, *Taisson*. The skins above mentioned, whether we read purple skins, or Badger skins, formed a covering for the tabernacle, above the covering of ram skins. It seems most probable, they were a kind of skins calculated to turn off water. When we read in Ezekiel, according to a literal translation, *I shod thee with Badger*, it seems more natural to suppose that some kind of skin is meant, than a color; admitting Badger skins to be meant, we may gather from this, that it was esteemed valuable and choice for shoes, at least for women.

In the passage above quoted from Ezekiel, God is bringing to view his people under the figure of woman, whom he had taken into covenant with himself, and had arrayed in rich and costly raiment, but who had played the harlot against him.

How often, clad in rich array,
    Some *harlot vile* is seen;
Without, all beautiful and gay,
    But all within unclean.

Let robes of righteousness adorn
    The hidden man, the heart,
The humblest garb we need not scorn,
    We share the better part.

BAT.
[Figure from the Cabinet.]

—

THE Bat is an animal, which seems to hold a middle rank between beast and bird, but is rather to be classed among beasts. Naturalists have reckoned twenty-eight species of them. The common Bat of North America, is in length, from two and a half, to three inches; its wings from tip to tip, from five to six inches. These consist of a naked, thin membrane, extending from the shoulders to the extremity of the toes of the fore feet,

which are very long, then connecting these with the
hind feet.   It has no tail.   Its body much resembles
that of a common mouse, and is covered with soft hair
of the usual mouse color.   In the day time it lies concealed in holes, among old rubbish, &c.   In the night,
it is on the wing, hovering round in an irregular manner,
and seizing moths, flies, &c. which are its principal
food.   It may be caught, by throwing into the air, the
burrs of burdock, made white to attract them.   In winter
they are in a dormant, or torpid state, hanging by their
hind feet, and wrapped in their membranes.

[Figure from Bewick.]

The *Long-Eared Bat*, is in length about one and a quarter inches; length of its ears one inch, spread of its wings
seven inches.

The *Horse-shoe Bat* is so called, because it has a
membrane on the nose, in shape like a horse-shoe.
They are three and a half inches in length, the back of
a dark ash-color, the belly whitish.   They are common
in England, and frequently seen in the salt-petre houses, in quest of gnats.

Ternate   Bat.

[Figure from Bewick.]

—

The most formidable is the *Ternate Bat,* found in South America, Africa, Madagascar, and the islands of the Indian ocean.   They are of the size of the pigeon, or pullet; their wings from tip to tip, measure some-times, above five feet.   At sun-set, they fly from one island to another, in vast multitudes, and return in the morning.   By day, they lodge in hollow trees, hanging together in clusters.   They are fierce, ill-scented, and utter an unpleasant cry.   They are sometimes very fat, and are eaten by the Indians.   They are blood-thirsty, and in South America destroy many cattle, and endan-ger the lives of the inhabitants, when they happen to sleep in the night, in the open air.   Their color is some-times reddish brown, sometimes dusky.   They have teeth like a dog, and a pointed tongue, which they in-sinuate into a vein, and draw the blood, unperceived, till they are satiated.

The Bat is mentioned three times in scripture.   1. Levit. 11 : 19.—The Heron after his kind, the Lapwing and the *Bat.*   This is repeated in Deut. 14 : 18.   The Bat is here reckoned among the animals forbidden to be

3*

eaten by the Israelites. The Hebrew name in these places is (עֲטַלֵּף) Gnătăllăf; the derivation of it is uncertain. The seventy have Nŭkterĭs, signifying, *of the night ;* or an animal of the night. The name is found in the plural in Isai. 2 : 20—Shall cast his idols .... to the moles and to the *Bats.* Moles and Bats, by day, are usually hidden in their holes; they lie concealed. In the day of God's judgment idolaters shall throw their images into those holes, and dark corners, where they may be hidden from view, and may be left neglected, as a cumbrance, while they shall flee for their lives. The day will also come, when idolaters, generally, will throw away their idols, through conviction of their vanity, esteeming them fit to be found only in those neglected places, where moles and bats have their abode.

> Roll on, O God, the happy day,
>   When heathen lands thy name shall own;
> To Moles and Bats shall cast away
>   Their gods of silver, wood, and stone.
>
> Their idols in neglected holes
>   Shall lie, forgotten, in decay;
> While they with gladness in their souls
>   The true Messiah shall obey.

BEAR.
[Figure from Life.]
—

THE Bear is of three or four different species. 1. The black Bear, numerous in the temperate climes of

North America, and in many other parts of the world. Its weight is generally found between one hundred and five hundred pounds. Some of them have rather short legs, and incline to be very fat in the fall of the year. Others are said to have legs longer in proportion to their size, are more inclined to be poor, and are called *ranging* Bears. The common Bear has long, black, rather coarse, and shining hair. He is clumsy in his appearance, but when surprised leaps away with great swiftness. His nose is usually brown, his eyes small, his ears short, and his tail very short. His feet are armed with large, strong claws, the fore paw round, the hind paw long, making a track much like the bare foot of a man. His teeth resemble those of swine. He is dexterous in climbing large trees. He feeds on roots, nuts, berries, fish, &c. and often makes dreadful havoc in corn-fields, and among sheep, and sometimes kills hogs, and horned cattle, and eats of their flesh with great voracity. In Autumn, the fat upon the rump is from four to six inches thick. Taken very young, he may be tamed, and may be taught to perform a variety of odd, amusing tricks; but still retains that ferocity of nature, which renders him a dangerous companion. When winter is about commencing, they retire to their dens, among the clefts of the rocks, in the wild forests, where they subsist upon their fat, till the return of spring. Their skins are very strong, and being dressed with the fur on, are manufactured into muffs, sleigh carpets, and the like. I have seen one, taken in a trap, with a milk-white breast, and have heard of those with white faces. The females are very fond of their young, and will defend them to the last extremity.

2. The *brown* Bear of the Alps. This Bear is said to differ but little from the black Bear, except in size and color, and being more fierce and dangerous.

[Figure from the Cabinet.]

—

3. The *white*, Greenland Bear. This animal grows to an enormous size, his body being sometimes of the bigness of a large ox, and even larger; his shape does not greatly differ from that of the black Bear. He feeds on fish, the carcases of whales, and the dead bodies of men.

4. The *Polar* Bear. He has a long neck and head, and is covered with long white hair; is found only in very cold climates; preys upon seals, fish, and young whales, and will sometimes attack men; he sails about on islands of ice, and swims and dives with dexterity. Their skins are said to measure, sometimes, 14 feet in length.

The Bear, in Hebrew, is (דוב) Dōbv, or Dōv ; perhaps from (דֹּבֶא) Dōbvĕh, *strength*. In Greek, he is called àrktŏs.

The Bear is frequently mentioned in scripture. 1 Sam. 17 : 34. David says, Thy servant kept his father's sheep, and there came a lion and a *Bear*, and took a lamb out of the flock. Ver. 36 : Thy servant slew both the lion and the *Bear*. David adduces this transaction,

not to make a boast of it, but to intimate that he prevailed by trusting in God; and that to him, who should
repose a becoming confidence in the Lord of hosts, the
threatening Goliath would be no more than one of these
beasts, which had been easily vanquished. 2 Sam. 17 :
8. Hushai speaks of David and his men, when retiring
from Absalom, as being chafed in their minds, like a
Bear, robbed of her whelps in the field. From this we
may learn that in Palestine, as well as in other parts of
the world, the Bear had a strong attachment to her
cubs ; and, that if deprived of them, she was very furious.—2 Kings 2 : 24. We read here, of two she Bears,
which came forth out of the wood, and tore forty-two
children, who had dared wickedly to mock the aged
prophet Elisha. This is left upon record, to teach that
youth ought to reverence the aged; and that God is
very angry with those young persons, who make a game
of the bald, or the hoary head, and especially with
those, who mock the aged friends of God.—Prov. 17 :
12. Let a Bear, robbed of her whelps, meet a man,
rather than a fool in his folly. A fool in his folly, here
means a wicked man in the practice of his wickedness.
The wise man teaches that it is not eventually so dangerous to fall in the way of the most savage beast, provoked to its greatest fury, as to fall, before our character
is established, into the company of the vicious and profane; in the former case our natural life is in danger ;
in the latter, the life of our soul is exposed.—Isa. 11 :
7. The cow and the Bear shall feed, their young ones
shall lie down together. This alludes to the very great
peace, and friendship among the inhabitants of the
earth, when the christian religion shall become generally prevalent ; and when the world shall be regulated by
its pure and holy doctrines ; as will be the case, during

those thousand years, while Satan is bound, and shut up in the bottomless pit.—Dan. 7 : 5. And behold, another beast, a second, like a Bear.—This beast in prophetic vision, represents the Medo-Persian Monarchy; this is symbolized by a Bear, because of its cruelty, and because of the great destruction it should make of the lives of men.—Hos. 13 : 8. I will meet them as a Bear that is bereaved of her whelps. In this, God threatens to execute a dreadful vengeance upon those, who forget him, after he has bestowed upon them great favors, and indulged them with peculiar privileges.—The name is found in several other places.

> Children and youth, like Jesse's Son,
>   Your trust in God repose,
> 'Tis thus a victory may be won
>   O'er all invading foes.
>
> Don't vex your neighbors and your friends,
>   Nor drive them from their right,
> Lest, as the Bear her young defends,
>   Provok'd, at length they fight.
>
> Revere the aged; hoary hairs
>   Regard with reverence due;
> Remember how the raging Bears
>   The youth of Bethel slew.
>
> As years advance, the Saviour's cause
>   With glowing love befriend,
> His name divine, his holy laws,
>   With prudent zeal defend.
>
> Ere long the world, reformed shall share
>   His mild and peaceful sway,
> The cow shall feed beside the Bear,
>   Their young together play.
>
> All nations then in bonds of peace
>   One sovereign Lord shall own,
> Envy, and strife, and war shall cease,
>   And love ascend the throne.

BEE.

[Figures from Nature.]

—

THE Bee is of several kinds; the more common are the Humble-Bee, and the Honey-Bee. The latter is probably intended, when the name is brought forward in scripture. The Bee, in Hebrew, is (דְּבֹרָה) Dĕbvōrâh, from (דָּבַר) Dâbvăr, to *speak*, because of the constant hum of their wings. The Bee, in Greek, is Mĕlĭssa.

The Honey-Bee is an insect well known in most parts of the world. It is of three kinds, the queen Bee, the drone, and the working Bee. The queen Bee is the largest, the drone is next in size, the working Bee the smallest. It is generally supposed that but one queen Bee pertains to a swarm. This Bee deposites the eggs for the young swarm. There are a number of drones in a swarm; these are the males, are without stings, and impregnate the eggs. The working Bees are far the most numerous, amounting, sometimes, it is supposed, to fifteen or eighteen thousand in a swarm.   A part of these smooth, and prepare their hive, or dwelling place; a part collect from the fields, the wax, of which their comb is made; a part form this wax into cells; a part bring food for the rest; a few are occupied in standing at the door of the hive, making a constant hum with their wings, perhaps as sentinels.   Their cells are about three fourths of an inch deep, and just of a sufficient size to admit the body of the Bee.   Each cell is of six equal sides, which is the only figure nearly round, which with others, fills the whole space without ' interstices between the cells.   The comb hangs perpendicularly, and consists of two ranges of horizontal cells, so disposed that the angles of three cells on one side of the comb meet together in the centre of the bottom of a cell on the other side of the comb; by this the work is strengthened.   The tiers or ranges of comb, hang parallel to each other, with a space between them, sufficient for two Bees to pass, back towards back, without interfering.

As the cells are formed, the queen Bee deposites in each an egg, which in a few days hatches into a small maggot; this is fed a few days by the laboring Bees, and is then sealed up, with a cover over the mouth of the cell.   At the end of eighteen or twenty days, the young Bee, now come to maturity, pierces its cover, and comes out.   When all the young are discharged, *for the season*, the drones are destroyed by the laboring Bees, the cells well cleared, and the rubbish carried out of the hive.   The care of the working Bees is then to supply their cells with bread and honey for the winter season.   Their bread consists of the *pollen*, or dust of flowers, mixed with honey; and their honey consists of that sweet liquid, in the cells of flowers, which, impregnated with pollen, forms the support, or matter, of the future seed. It is said that Bees are more likely to die in winter, if their bread fails them, than if their honey fails them.

The honey for our use is generally taken from them by suffocating them with the fumes of sulphur, which causes them to fall into a hole, made in the ground, for that purpose, and they are there buried.—It wounds the tender feelings thus to destroy them. In more modern times much honey is taken without destroying the Bees, by means of double hives, one being set upon the top of another. When the upper hive is filled, a slider is drawn out, opening a passage into the top of the lower hive; the door of the upper hive being closed, the Bees pass into the lower, and make a deposite of honey there. When they have done their labor, the under hive is removed, and the upper let down into its place; the under hive then being carried a few rods off, and turned mouth upward, the Bees soon leave it, and retire to the other. This last made comb and honey is very pure, and may be easily taken for use.

When a young swarm leaves the parent hive, it fills the neighboring air with its multitude, dancing on the wing in every direction; by a continual drumming upon a warming-pan, or some other sounding vessel, they are detained from flying away, till the queen lights on a branch of some neighboring tree or bush, when the whole swarm lights upon her, in a cluster of the size of a man's head, or larger; they are then carefully brushed into a hive, prepared for the purpose.

Judges 14 : 8. And behold there was a swarm of Bees, and honey in the carcase of the Lion. This was the carcase of a lion, slain by Samson. The finding of this honey in it furnished him with the subject of his riddle, the explanation of which his espoused wife drew out of him by importunity, and told it to the Philistines, which was the occasion of his slaying thirty men of Ashdod, of whose spoil he took thirty changes of garments, and gave to those, who expounded the riddle. The fact which furnished the riddle, may be accommodated to impress the idea, that what is now an affliction to us, and the occasion of conflict, may, by and by, be a source of sweet satisfaction.

In smiling days, and sunny hours,
The busy Bee from vernal flowers
Sips nectar sweet; and well supplies
His feet with paste, a fragrant prize.

Thus fraught with Flora's balmy stores,
On humming wings away he soars,
Unerring brings his treasure home,
And well secures it in his dome.

Soon to the field again he hies,
From flower to flower, industrious, flies;
And thus in Summer's favoring light
Prepares for Winter's dreary night.

Hence learn, my youthful friends, to weigh,
And fix the worth of every day;
In life's fair prime your stores increase,
That hoary age may pass in peace.

Remember death's cold *Winter* too,
And keep the *Spring* of heaven in view;
With stores of faith and love prepare
The bliss of heavenly Spring to share.

BEETLE.
[Figures from Nature.]
—

THE Beetle is an order of insects, the genera and specics of which are very numerous; in other words, there are many kinds of Beetles, and some of these kinds are again subdivided into a number of sorts. This order of insects is distinguished from the others, by having the wings covered with a *crust* or *case*, under which they are folded up in a very neat and curious manner. They are too numerous to be represented by *cuts* in this work. One or two, however, may be given, which I have drawn from nature; as the *Stag-Beetle*, sometimes called the *Horned Dorr*, and the *Yellow Beetle*.

The name rendered Beetle, in scripture, is found only once, and that in Lev. 11 : 22, where the Hebrew is

(חַרְגֹּל) Hrhărghōl; in the Greek of the 70, it is called ŏfiomākhēs; which seems to mean an insect, which fights the serpent. In the Latin Bible of Junius and Tremellius, it is rendered *Cantharus*, which is the name of one of the several kinds of Beetles. In the common language of this country all kinds of Beetles are called *Bugs*. Respecting the Beetle mentioned in scripture, the more probable opinion is, that the Hebrew word means a species of *Locust*, distinguished from others, by having a bunch on its head and on its tail. It was one of those kinds of insects, which the Israelites were permitted to eat; and I may here remark, that Locusts of several kinds, were anciently eaten by the Ethiopians, Lybians, Parthians, and other nations in their vicinity, and are still eaten in some parts of Africa, and of Arabia, and use probably renders them agreeable and wholesome, however disgusting they may seem to us.

Of the astonishing numbers, both of Beetles and Locusts, it may be said, that while they are very troublesome to man, often making dreadful ravages upon the fruits of the earth; they probably enjoy such a portion of happiness, as is more than a balance for all the suffering which they occasion, and renders it better that they should *be*, than *not be*, notwithstanding they may be reckoned in some respects, as a part of the curse, threatened in consequence of the fall of man.

> The numerous tribes of insects share
>   A little world of good,
> While each can feel, and see, and hear,
>   And taste the sweets of food.
>
> Then let us not o'erlook this race
>   Of creatures, though so small;
> But in their form *His* wisdom trace,
>   Who guides and feeds them all.

BEHEMOTH.
[Figure from Bewick.]

THE *Behemoth*, or otherwise the *Elephant*, is probably the largest and strongest land animal now to be found in the known world. They inhabit the temperate parts of Africa and Asia. Those in Asia are the largest, being, when full grown, from thirteen to fifteen feet high, while those in Africa do not usually exceed eleven feet in height. They sometimes weigh four thousand and five hundred pounds. Their ears are long and pendulous; their eyes small, but expressive; their nose projects in a long proboscis, or trunk, formed of a large number of circular rings of cartilage, or gristle, by means of which they can lengthen or shorten it at pleasure ; it is of a regular taper ; the extremity of it is of a cup form, with two holes, or nostrils in it; on the outward edge of this cup, is a point, like a finger, with which it can untie a knot in a rope, and pick up a very small thing from the ground. With this trunk they gather flowers, herbs, fruits, and other materials of food, which, by bending it inwards, they convey with ease to their mouth. By drawing in their breath, they fill their trunk with water at pleasure, which they either

4*

convey to their mouth for drink, or spout out for amusement. The mouth is furnished with two large tusks, one of which has been known to weigh somewhat more than one hundred pounds. These furnish the *ivory*, of so much value in many kinds of manufacture. Their neck is short and stiff; their legs have a clumsy appearance; their feet are round at the bottom, and spread not beyond the size of their ankles; each foot has five horny risings in the place of toes, but which hardly project beyond the foot itself. Their tail, except in size, much resembles that of swine. Their skin is thick, hard, wrinkled, and naked, except a few scattering coarse hairs, and in color of a dusky brown, like the mud on a hog, that has rolled in the mire, and is dried. Sometimes they are white; these are highly valued, and by some heathens have been worshipped as gods. Before the invention of fire-arms, they were used in war, but they are now employed chiefly for parade, and to bear burdens; and they are capable, in some cases, of carrying four thousand pounds on their back, and one thousand on their trunk. Urged forward, they will travel one hundred miles a day; and with apparent ease, fifty or sixty miles. Their term of life is from one hundred to two hundred years; the female goes with young about two years; when tamed, they do not propagate. They are naturally mild, and when well treated, form a strong attachment to their keeper, but, when much provoked, revenge themselves in a dreadful manner. They are sometimes taken in pits; but when designed to be tamed, they are decoyed by tame females, into enclosures made for the purpose, and are entangled with ropes; and being kept awhile among several tame ones, by chastisement and caresses, are at length brought to obey.

They are considered as the most sagacious of all four footed beasts. In India, they have been employed in launching vessels; this they effect by forcing them into the water with their heads. It is related of one, who was brought to perform this task, that finding the vessel too heavy for him, he withdrew; upon this, his master called out to the keeper, "Take away the lazy beast, and bring another." Upon this he renewed the attempt with such violence, that he fractured his skull, and died upon the spot.

At Adsmeir, an Elephant, being seized with madness, as is sometimes the case, ran through the market-place, and put the crowd to flight; an herb-woman, who had been in the habit of giving him a mouthful of greens, when he used to pass that way, in her haste to escape, left her child behind; the Elephant coming up to it, seemed to recollect himself, and knowing the child of his benefactress, took it up gently, and laid it in a place of safety.

At Delhi, an Elephant passing by a tailor's shop, thrust his trunk in among the workmen; one of them, in sport, pricked it with a needle. At the first puddle of water he met with, he filled his trunk, and on his return, spouted it upon the tailor's work, and ruined it.

An Elephant, which was used to draw the cannon of the French forces in India, was taught to expect a reward for the hard service; but being at a certain time disappointed of it, he was enraged at his *Cornac,* or conductor, and slew him. His wife, being near by, and seeing it, threw her two young sons towards him, saying, "You have killed their father, you may now kill them, and me too." The Elephant stopped, looked mournful, and taking the elder of the two children, placed him with his trunk on his back, and ever after obeyed him, as his Cornac.

The name *Behemoth* occurs in scripture, in Job 40 : 15. There is hardly any reason to doubt but that the Elephant is intended by this name. Some have supposed the River Horse is meant, (see the figure above,) but the description agrees much better with the Elephant. The food of the River Horse is principally fish; but the Behemoth is said to eat grass like the ox, and the mountains are said to bring him forth food. The Elephant does eat grass, and also herbs, leaves, fruits, and tender branches of trees, all which may be found upon mountains. The name in Hebrew, (בְּהֵמוֹת) Bvehāmōth, signifies, according to Rabbi Levi, *The Beast*, by way of eminence. Others, however, suppose the name, which in form is plural, commonly signifying *beasts*, is here used as the singular, and appropriated to this animal, because in size he is equal to a number of ordinary beasts.

God holds forth this beast to the notice of Job, as the chief of his works in the animal kingdom, and calls on him to consider his majesty of size, and the greatness of his strength, that he may be convinced of his own littleness before his Maker; and that he may be humbled for having spoken of God's dealings towards him, with too little reverence, and without becoming submission. This should lead us all to think of God, and to speak of him with solemn awe, and with deep humility of spirit.

I shall close this article with a paraphrase of the description of the Behemoth, in Job 40 : 15 to 24, and a brief remark.

Behold the Behemoth; a ponderous mass !
  He is thy neighbor; *I* have rear'd his frame;
As bullocks do, he feeds on herbs and grass;
  His size and strength thy careful notice claim.

Where lies his strength? 'Tis in his loins confin'd,
  And in his navel. If his tail he wave,
'Tis like a cedar. Folding sinews bind
  His secret parts, and these from danger save.

How are his bones? The *smaller* bones contain
  The strength of brass; the *larger*—these appear
Like bars of iron; your assault is vain,
  He stands unmov'd, you cannot make him fear.

Where is his rank? A chief among the ways
  Of God he stands. But he, who made him so,
When o'er his head his glittering sword he plays,
  With ease can reach him, and can lay him low.

When on the mountains his repast he finds,
  For rugged mountains with his food abound,
The smaller beasts of various names and kinds
  In sportive gambols compass him around.

In grateful shades he lies secure from heat;
  Among the reeds of boggy fens abides;
The spreading grove affords a kind retreat,
  Among the willows of the brook he hides.

He sinks the river, which his thirst supplies,
  With fearless leisure; and believes he may
Draw Jordan dry; 'tis little in his eyes,
  While with his trunk he clears his cumbered way.

Such is the *beast*, my youthful friends, which gave
  To Job a cause in humble dust to lie;
His step majestic, his appearance grave,
  With peaceful mildness beaming from his eye.

Revere your Maker; own his power and skill;
  In dust, repentant, your offences mourn;
Accept a Saviour, who in pure good will
  The pond'rous burden of your guilt has borne.

BITTERN.
[Figures from the Cabinet, reduced and varied.]

—

THE Bittern is a bird of the Heron kind, but rather smaller than the common Heron. Its usual posture of standing, is erect, with the neck stretched up, and the bill pointing upwards. The crown of its head is black; it has black spots on each side of the head, near the angle of the mouth. The general color of its plumage is pale yellow, which is beautifully spotted and barred with black, brown, and grey. It utters a loud, unpleasant note, some resembling the interrupted bellowing of a bull, and may be heard to the distance of a mile. In the former part of the season, especially, it will stand still, till a person approaches very near to it; and when provoked to flight, it moves in a dull, heavy manner. In the latter part of the season, however, it becomes more active, and frequently rises in the air in a spiral course, till it disappears from sight. It inhabits fens, and marshy places; and by day hides among reeds and sedge. It feeds on frogs, insects, and vegetables, and its flesh is esteemed by some a delicacy.

The name, *Bittern*, is found in Isaiah 14 : 23, and 34 : 11, and in Zeph. 2 : 14. In Hebrew, it is (קִפֹּד) Kĭppōdh; the Seventy render it Ekhīnŏs, a *Hedge-hog*. Junius and Tremellius render it *Anataria*, a sort of sea Eagle, which preys upon ducks. In the French Bible it is *Butor*, Bittern. Some have thought it a beaver, some a tortoise, some a kind of swallow, and some an owl.

I have set down these various conjectures, to show my young friends, that a very great degree of uncertainty attends many parts of the natural history of ancient times, the same name being frequently given to very different animals, and neither pictures, nor very particular descriptions having come down to modern times, to enable us easily to decide what animals, &c. are intended.

If the ceremonial law were still in force, it might be of more consequence to know precisely what animals are meant by the names in scripture, but as it is not, nothing of particular consequence respecting faith or practice depends upon this knowledge. In treating of these things we must content ourselves with fixing upon the most probable meaning, leaving others to exercise their own judgment upon the subject.

Isaiah 14 : 23. I will also make it a possession for the *Bittern*, and pools of water. This is a prophetical threatening against Babylon. In the fulfilment of this prophecy, this great city became a hideous quagmire. The animal here named, being connected with pools of water, renders it probable that some aquatic animal is intended. Isaiah 34 : 11. But the Cormorant and the *Bittern* shall possess it. This is a threatening upon Idumea. The name rendered Bittern being here coupled with the Cormorant, or the Pelican, probably some *bird* inhabiting places abounding with water, is intended, and so it is likely to be the Bittern. The Bittern is again coupled with the Cormorant, in Zeph. 2 : 14.—The instruction we may draw from the subject, in connection with which the Bittern is brought to view, is this; that if cities, or nations become excessively wicked, God can easily reduce them to an awful state of desolation ; that he often has done it, and probably will do it again. It becomes every one, then, to shun a course of wickedness, lest he administer to that mass of evil, which may be the ruin of himself, and of the community of which he is a member. In the mean time, if men become so wicked, that they must be destroyed from a place, God can easily replenish it with multitudes of inhabitants of an inferior order.

> The Bittern's posture is erect,
>   Our life should be upright ;
> In all our motives still correct,
>   And heaven-ward in our flight.
>
> In spiral course the Bittern wheeling
>   Mounts up to nether skies ;
> So, while our days away are stealing,
>   May our affections rise.
>
> The Bittern loves a lone abode,
>   And hides from human view,
> And we, to think of heaven and God,
>   Should love retirement too.

BOAR.—[*See Swine.*]

BULL.
[Figure from Bewick.]

THE Bull is the male of the Cow-kind. This kind, though the species of it varies from difference of climate, difference of pasture, and other circumstances, inhabits almost all parts of the known world, except the extremely cold regions of the north. Even the Wild Bull, the Bonasus, the Urus, the Bison, and the Zebu, are supposed to be all of one origin, and of one kind, or of one species, as some reckon them; they all propagate together.

As the Bull becomes the ox by means of early castration, and as the cow is but the female of the kind, I shall treat of them all under one article. The Bull, it is said, was the Ox of Judea, being never altered there, as in most other countries, to fit him for labor. The Bull, carefully educated, is often very gentle, and may be managed without difficulty; but sometimes he is very furious and dangerous; generally he will fight with his antagonist with great obstinacy. In most of the civilized parts of the world, Bulls, except so many as

5

are needed for propagating, are altered usually while
calves; then from about one to three years old, we call
them *Steers*, after that, *Oxen*.

[Figure from Life.]

———

The Ox is usually very gentle; grows to a size much
larger than the Bull; is much taller, has longer horns,
and the hair of his front is much less curled, so that he
seems to be almost another species of animal.   In this
state he is exceedingly useful; he draws the waggon,
the cart, and the plough, and is used for almost all kinds
of draught.   He is very patient in labor.   He is in a
sense, the wealth of the farmer.   When he has labored
from three to nine or ten years old, he is commonly fattened for slaughter; his flesh is then excellent food;
his hide is tanned into leather for shoes, harness, &c.
his horns are manufactured into combs, knife-handles,
&c. his bones are also wrought into knife-handles, and
into buttons; and an oil for japaning, is extracted from
them.   His dung, and also his bones, when powdered,
is excellent manure.   His hair is mixed with mortar for
plastering; from his feet we obtain neats-foot oil; the

size, which comes by boiling them, is manufactured into glue. Candles are made of his suet; his blood is a good manure for fruit trees, and is the basis of Prussian blue.

Cow.   J. F. 1823.

The young Cow, or Heifer, was used in ancient times in Judea, for the draught; but in most countries she is excused from this service, and is kept for her milk, which is for most persons, a very agreeable and wholesome food; the cream, the richer part of the milk, by being churned, produces butter. The milk, being coagulated with rennet, is pressed, and becomes cheese, which, when made of new milk, and well preserved, is a dainty for our tables. The whey, which is pressed from the cheese-curd, is not unpleasant to drink, but is chiefly used for the food of swine.

The Calf, which is the young of the Cow, when we we wish not to raise it, is usually killed when from four to eight weeks old. Its flesh is called veal, and is very pleasant. Its skin forms a soft leather for the nicer kinds of shoes, and for the binding of books. Its stomach affords the rennet, used in cheese-making.

The kind of animal of which I have been treating is so common in the domestic state, that I need not give a particular description of it; but the uses above mentioned are so numerous, and so important, that they ought to excite our thankful admiration of the goodness of God, who so liberally and wonderfully provides for our necessities, and even for our comfort, and for our delight.

The *Bull*, in Hebrew, is called (פַּר) Păr, and also (שׁוֹר) Shōr; the same word is frequently rendered *Ox*. In Jer. 11 : 19, the Ox is called (אַלּוּף) Alôf, *a leader;* being a leader of his kind. In some other passages, the Ox is called (בָּקָר) Bâkâr, which more frequently signifies, *a herd.* It is from a word which signifies *to seek, to inquire after,* probably because the Ox is much sought after by man, or because he seeks to man for food and shelter. The Hebrew for Cow, is sometimes the same as for Ox, and sometimes (פָּרָה) Pârâh.

Psal. 22 : 12. Many Bulls have compassed me about. Christ in this Psalm is brought to view in prophecy, speaking of his condition at the time of his crucifixion. By *Bulls*, we are here to understand the cruel rulers of the Jews, or the fierce Roman soldiers. When we consider this, we ought to be deeply impressed with an admiring sense of what Christ condescended to suffer for sinners.

Isai. 1 : 3. The Ox knoweth his owner and the Ass his master's crib; but Israel doth not know, my people doth not consider. This is a keen, but a very just reproof, from the Lord, of the wilful ignorance and stupidity of those of the human race, who do not know and acknowledge God in a spiritual manner.

> In patient labor through the varying year
> The faithful Ox submits to toil severe,
> To serve his owner; in his meadow feeds,
> Or at his crib receives the meat he needs.
>
> He knows his master; ready to obey,
> Is mild and docile; does not often stray;
> Though oft he labors with attending pain,
> How rare to hear him in his toil complain.

The gentle Cow, that's fed with daily care
Yields to her keeper a delicious fare ;
Her milk, the butter and the cheese supplies,
Which for our tables we so highly prize.

And will not man his bounteous Lord confess,
Who gives the favors his condition bless?
Nor, while he revels on abundant store,
With thankful heart his Maker's name adore?

Shame to the *ingrate,* who would sink below
The very beasts, who their provider know ;
And let the herds, who round their stalls abide,
Reprove his baseness, faithlessness and pride.

Dear youth, from God your comforts all descend,
In thankful praise before him daily bend ;
Hear the kind Saviour ; enter his employ ;
Be meek and lowly ; bear his yoke with joy.

CAMEL.
[Figure from Mavor.]
—

THE Camel is a quadruped fitted by the providence
of God in a very peculiar manner for dry, hot, barren,
sandy countries, and is found principally in Africa, in
Arabia, and in Turkey in Asia. It is in shape, an unsightly creature, having nothing of the graceful majesty
of the horse ; but the want of this is well compensated
5*

by its very great usefulness in the climes, which it principally inhabits.

It has a small head, short ears, a long neck, bending upwards from the breast, a long body, and two protuberances, or bunches, rising on its back; the forward bunch is about twelve inches high, the hinder bunch about eighteen; the forward rises a little back of the shoulders, the hinder a little forward of the hips. These bunches are thickly covered with long, shaggy hair; its tail is long, terminated with a tuft of long hair. On its legs are six calosities, two on each fore leg, and one on each hind leg. Its height, to the top of the highest bunch, is from six to seven feet. The color of the long, coarse hair on the tail and bunches is black, or dusky; the other hair is fine, soft, and of a reddish ash color. The feet of this animal are divided on the upper side, but not on the under side; and the bottom of the foot is covered in a cushion-like manner, with a tough, spongy-like substance, fitted for travelling over burning deserts. It has six cutting teeth in the under jaw, but none in the upper. It feeds on thistles, nettles, cassia, and various shrubs, which, with the addition of a few dates, or a ball of beans and barley, suffice for its nourishment for a long journey. The Camel chews the cud, and besides the four stomachs, common to other ruminating animals, it has a fifth, formed to be a reservoir for water; it holds a large quantity, and before it sets out on a journey it fills it. The water is here kept pure and sweet; when the Camel becomes thirsty, where no water is to be had, by a compression of this stomach it forces out into its upper stomach a sufficient quantity for present use; by means of this, he will travel eight or ten days in succession, in sandy parts, without drinking. In some extreme cases, a Camel out of a company is killed to sup-

ply the famished travellers both with food and drink.
The Camel is of vast use in bearing burdens; by this
means a great part of the trade of Turkey, Arabia,
Egypt, and Barbary is carried on. He kneels to receive
his rider, and also to receive his load, which amounts
commonly to a thousand pounds, and sometimes to
twelve hundred. He is gentle and patient, performs a
journey with expedition, and is cheered forward by music. Though his flesh was forbidden to the Jews, it is
eaten by many others. Its hair is manufactured into
valuable stuffs; Sal-ammoniac is made of its urine; and
its dung is valuable for fuel in those places, where other
fuel cannot be had. The female goes with young
twelve months, suckles her colt two years, and her milk
is a wholesome, nourishing food. In cold regions the
Camel will not propagate, nor can he well endure the
winter of a northern clime.

The name of the Camel in Hebrew is (גָּמָל) Gâmâl,
from a word signifying to *repay;* perhaps because the
Camel so well repays his keeper; its name is much
alike in a number of languages. The name is often
mentioned in scripture. It is first found in Gen. 12 :
16, where Camels are enumerated among the stock of
Abram. In Job 1 : 3, as an evidence of the greatness,
or riches of this upright man, we read that he had three
thousand Camels; these in addition to his other substance must have raised his possessions to a very great
amount.—Of all this, for his trial, he was stripped within a few days. His affliction was very great, but he
came out of it as gold from the furnace. After his trial
he was more blessed, and had greater possessions than
before ; his substance was doubled.

The view of this, my young friends, may lead you to
consider the uncertainty of this world's goods. But if

at any time, you be deprived of them, endeavor to bear the affliction with patience, and to be humble under the mighty hand of God; and in due time he will raise you above all your trials.—The wonderful manner in which the Camel is adapted to hot and barren regions, and his very great usefulness to the inhabitants of such regions, should confirm your faith in the overruling providence of God, and lead you to admire his goodness.—The Rein-deer is not more adapted to the frigid zone, than the Camel to the torrid.

[Figure from Library of Entertaining Knowledge.]

The Camel kneels to take his heavy load,
    And through the desert freely toils along,
Press'd by his driver on the weary road
    With tuneful pipe, or cheerly vocal song.

The thorn, the thistle and the nettle yield
    His scanty food, and in himself he bears
His daily beverage o'er the burning field,
    And his hard lot without repining shares.

Hence learn, dear youth, to labor in your sphere
    With steady hand, though hard your lot may seem;
May smiles from heaven your spirits daily cheer,
    Your toil soon ends, for life is but a dream.

Tho' scant the pittance, which supplies your board,
    A thankful heart can make it savory meat;
Tho' with no wine your cellar can be stor'd,
    Friendship can make your simple beverage sweet.

Live, then contented, tho' a humble cot
    Be here your dwelling, set on things above
Your best affections, then your future lot
    May be most happy in the realms of love.

CAMELEON.

[Figure from Description.]

THIS reptile is reckoned among those, which in the ceremonial law were forbidden to be eaten by the Jews. The name occurs in Leviticus 11 : 30. The Hebrew word rendered *Cameleon* in this place is (כֹּחַ) Kŏährh, which also signifies *Strength*. The Septuagint render it Khāmaileŏn; Junius and Tremellius, render it *Lacerta*, which means *Lizard*. Some have thought that it intends a common toad; some, a Hedge or tree toad; some, a kind of spotted Lizard ; some, a Snail. I think it probable that the word means the *Cameleon*, properly so called; which is a reptile of the Lizard kind, with four short legs, and paws much resembling in shape those of the toad or frog. It has a tail rather flat than round, and quite long, by which it suspends itself from the twigs of trees, &c. Its length, including its tail is about 12 inches. Its skin is soft, but when the creature is at rest, it appears to be full of risings of a bluish grey; the spaces between these are of a pale red and yellow; but seen in different positions its colors are changeable, and assume various tints, like changeable silks ; hence in all ages it has been taken as an emblem of a fickle, unstable mind.

It has been frequently said, that the Cameleon lives on air, perhaps because rarely seen to take any food, or because it keeps its mouth open in breathing. Upon more close inspection it has been found that it feeds on insects; for upon opening it, insects have been found in its entrails.

The Cameleon for living on air
Has had in past ages the fame ;
But insects it seems are its fare,
Its fasting is prov'd but a name.

Some others to fast may pretend,
When from flesh for a while they abstain ;
But vain is their fast in the end,
While their *fish*, and their *sins* they retain.

The Cameleon so oft *does* appear
The tints of its color to change,
That, for minds, which oft whiffle and veer,
An emblem it stands, is not strange

Be it yours, then, dear youth, to decide
With wisdom the way you must run ;
This done, in your course still abide
As steady and true, as the sun.

CANKER WORM.
[Figure from Description.]

THIS name occurs in Joel 1: 4. That which the lo-cust hath left, hath the *Canker-worm* eaten, and that which the Canker-worm hath left, hath the caterpillar eaten. Nahum 3 : 16—The Canker-worm spoileth and flieth away. In Hebrew it is (יֶלֶק) Yĕlĕhk. This in Psalm 105 : 34, is translated *Caterpillar*, and so in Jeremiah 51 : 27. The Seventy render it *Broukhos*, a kind of locust, or grass-worm; and *Akris*, a locust. Some think it a kind of beetle; some, a kind of locust, resembling a hornet.

What we call the *Canker-worm* in this western world, is, when in the *larva*, or caterpillar state, a worm about nine tenths of an inch long; the head of a dusky white or light ash-color, marked on each side, crosswise with two blackish stripes; the back, ash-colored, marked lengthwise with rows of small dark spots, or broken lines. The sides are nearly black, with a pale, or dusky white line the whole length of the body. On the last division, or section of the body there are two white spots; the belly is ash-colored.

These worms are propagated by what is called a *grub*, by which is usually understood the worm in its moth state though more properly meaning its chrysalis state. In the moth state the body of the male is nearly half an inch in length, of a color between ash and amber; the length of its upper wings one and a half inches, ash-colored, with three dark stripes across them, and a dark spot at the tips; the under wings are of a light ash color. The body of the female is about four tenths of an inch long, ash-colored, with a brown stripe running from the hinder part of the thorax, or chest, or from the waist, down the back to the end of the tail. She is without wings, her legs dark, with white joints.

These grubs usually rise from the earth about the middle of March. The females ascend the trees, upon which they intend to deposite their eggs, by the help of their feet; the males resort to them by means of their wings. Their time of pairing commences soon after they rise, and continues eight or ten days. Soon after this the females deposite their eggs in the small cavities of the rough places on the tree; each produces about one hundred eggs; soon after this they die.

After a few days the worm comes forth from these eggs; it is about one tenth of an inch in length, and furnished with ten feet, six forward, four behind. As it progresses from place to place it draws its hindmost feet forward to its breast, bending its body into a loop; then holding by its hinder feet, it extends its body forward to take new hold with its forward feet.

These worms are especially destructive to the apple tree; they are hatched about the time its leaves begin to shoot forth; they seize on their pulpy part, and eat it out, leaving the veins a curious net-work of reddish brown, so that, when they have done eating, the leaves appear like those that are fallen in Autumn, and the whole tree at a distance looks like one that has been girdled, and is become sear.

During their growth they cast their skins two or three times, and they come to their full size in about three weeks. As they move from place to place they leave behind them a silken thread. Strike the tree suddenly, and a multitude of them will be seen suspended from its boughs, each by one of these threads, by which they will again ascend by bending their breast upward, till with the hinder pair of their forward feet they can seize the thread, which they hold, and raising their head again seize on it with their jaws; thus they progress, till they reach the branch whence they fell.

About four weeks after they begin their ravages they quit, and descend the tree, and in different places near the foot of it penetrate the earth from two or three, to six or seven inches in depth, where in about twenty four hours they change into the chrysalis, or grub state, in which they continue, till the warmth of spring brings them forth in the moth state, to deposite their eggs again.

> The apple yields a beverage sweet,
>   Of lively spirit, when mature;
> If us'd with temperance with our meats,
>   It is a cordial pure.
>
> But what will not the race of man
>   Among the fruits of earth abuse?
> The apple beverage, when he can,
>   The tipler will misuse.
>
> But God is angry, when we turn
>   His bounty from its use aside;
> He sends the *Canker-worm* to burn
>   The fruit tree's verdant pride.
>
> Now let the drunkard howl and wail;
>   His empty cups aloud proclaim,
> That God can make his vintage fail,
>   And fill his face with shame.
>
> God's numerous army who can stay?
>   His warriors—each alone but small
> When rank'd by millions in array,
>   The stoutest heart appal.

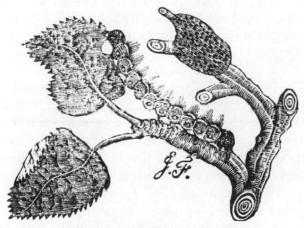

CATERPILLAR.
[Figures from Nature.]

—

THE name, *Caterpillar*, is found in the Bible nine times; in six places it is in the Hebrew, (חָסִיל)

6

Hrhâssēl, from (חָסַל) Hrhâssäl, to consume. In the
Septuagint, Broukhŏs, locust, or grass worm ; and
Erūsĭbē, signifying *rust*. Junius and Tremellius, and
Pagnin and Buxtorf, have it in Latin, *Bruchus*. In the
three other places it is (יֶלֶק) Yĕlĕkk, from (לָקַק)
Lâkkäkk, to lick up ; answering to this, the Septuagint
have Broukhŏs, and ākrĭs, *locust*. Junius and Tremellius, and Pagnin and Buxtorf, have *Bruchus*, or *Melolon-
tha*, a destroyer of honey. Jerome thinks Yĕlĕkk is a
small locust, between the common locust, and the Bruchus, or Caterpillar, creeping, rather than flying. Others think it a hairy worm, such as we call a Caterpillar.
The word Yĕlĕkk in several places is rendered *Canker-
worm*. The passage in Jer. 51 : 27.—Cause the horses
to come up, as the rough Caterpillars ; or more literally,
as the Caterpillar hath raised, or bristled up his hair ;
makes it highly probable that Yĕlĕkk means some kind
of Caterpillar ; a Caterpillar, with his upright bristles,
moving with speed to his prey, may strikingly figure out
a company of horsemen with their spears, rushing into
battle.

The Caterpillar of New England is of several species ;
some thickly covered with bristles, some thinly, but all
having a rough appearance. The figure given is of the
Caterpillar, which infests the apple-tree in the middle
parts of New England ; in the moth state it deposits
its eggs in Autumn upon a twig of the tree, to the number of two hundred and fifty, or more, and cements them
together with a strong glue. In the Spring, while the
leaves of the tree are tender, the Caterpillars burst their
shells and come out not larger than the head of a mus-
lin pin ; they gather upon a leaf, and consume the tender part of it, and then remove to another. They soon
become strong and vigorous, and weave themselves a

silken nest, ten or twelve inches diameter, upon some branch of the tree. Here they repose by night; by day they wander over the tree, eating the leaves of one branch and then of another, pulp, veins and all, to the stem. Some time before they quit the tree, they go down to the foot of it, wander among the grass, return, and ascend it again, leaving each a silken thread on the whole length of his path; which, up and down the tree becomes at length paved with silk; rub this off with your finger for the space of two or three inches, and the ascending and descending Caterpillars, will seem for a little while to be bewildered, groping for their way like a blind man.

When they have come to their full size, as represented in the cut, they leave the tree, and crawl away to convenient places, where they spin around themselves a cone, or cod, and in the midst of it are transformed into the *Aurelia*, or *chrysalis*, sometimes called the butterfly's egg, or bottle, given in the second cut. At the end of about three weeks, it comes forth an umber colored moth, with two yellow bars across each wing. This moth sports itself a while in this new state, then deposites its eggs and dies. The Caterpillar represented in the cut, has a black head and tail, its body is divided into ten segments, or joints; from the three first, next to the head, proceed six black legs; two segments are without legs; the next four have eight legs. Each segment has a brush of yellow bristles, rising erect from the back of it; the middle part of the back is light umber, on each side of it is a yellow stripe. The side of each section is umber, having, towards the belly, a black, oval spot, in the center of which is a round spot of white. A blue stripe runs along on each side of the belly, and there is a narrow, blue ring, round the body between each segment.

Moth.　*Aurelia.*

May 17, 1793, I put a Caterpillar, then full grown, into a box about four inches square, covered on the top with glass; here I fed it daily with fresh leaves from the apple-tree. May 27, it became uneasy, and refused to eat. In one corner of the box I fastened several pegs, in the morning it was enshrouded in its cone, which was attached to these pegs. June 18, it came out a moth, as represented in the cut.—At the time when I took the Caterpillar, I found a bunch of egg-shells, whence a brood had proceeded; counting them, I found the number two hundred and fifty, closely and strongly attached to a twig, as given in the cut.—This kind of Caterpillar feeds chiefly on the apple-tree, cherry-tree, thorn-bush, and rose-bush.

In 1 Kings 8 : 37, Solomon intreats, in his prayer, that if there should be in the land famine, pestilence, blasting, mildew, locust, or caterpillar, &c. God would hear the prayer made towards the holy temple, and re-move the evil. Two things we may be taught by this : 1. That when devouring insects greatly multiply in a land, it is for the sin of the people of that land. 2. That for the removal of such a judgment, the most ready way is to draw near to God in humble, believing pray-er.—In Psalm 105 : 34, we read, He spake, and the lo-

custs came, and Caterpillars, and that without number.
Here, as in Psalm 78 : 46, the Psalmist alludes to the
dreadful plagues sent upon Egypt; this confirms the
account given us by Moses, and at the same time shows
that God can readily so multiply upon us the most contemptible insects, that we cannot stand before them, or
subsist at all, except he be pleased to remove them.
In Jer. 51 : 14, God utters a solemn oath against Babylon, that he would fill her with men, as with Caterpillars; this threatening he accomplished, when Cyrus
marched his army down the empty channel of the Eu-
phrates into the midst of Babylon, and put its inhabitants to the sword.   This may teach us that no human
defence can secure us, when wicked, against the judgments of God.—In Joel 1 : 4, we read, That which the
canker-worm hath left, hath the Caterpillar eaten.—
This was spoken of a dreadful judgment, which fell upon God's peculiar people for their sin; the earth was
stripped of its fruits by the multitudes of devouring insects which were sent upon it.   This may teach us that
no covenant relation to God will shield us from his
wrath, if we persist in sinning against him; yea, the
nearer we are to him in covenant the more angry he is
with us, if we sell ourselves to work evil in his sight.

Caterpillar of the Privet Hawk Moth.

The creeping vermin, feeble in our eyes,
And reptiles base, which men in scorn despise,
Are oft commission'd by a jealous God
To be, for judgment, his tremendous rod.

6*

The Caterpillars, with their bristly mane,
Spread like an army o'er the fruitful plain;
They find an Eden, smiling in its bloom;
They leave a desert; all behind is gloom.

If God be angry, in a thousand ways
He can with ease a mighty army raise;
Nor will disband them, nor remove his frown,
Till man's proud heart in humble dust comes down.

Beware of sin, dear youth, your crimes may turn
The lingering scale, that kindling wrath may burn
Against a nation, thus made ripe for wo,
Till spreading vengeance lay that nation low.

CHAMOIS.

[Figure from Bewick.]

—

AN animal, thus named, is reckoned among the clean
beasts, in Deut. 14 : 5. In Hebrew, it is (זֶמֶר)
Zĕmĕr; Buxtorf, the Septuagint, and Junius and Tremellius, call it the *Camelopard.* The German Jews
call it the *Rock Goat;* Pagnin renders it the same. It
is found only once in the Bible.

The Chamois is of the Goat kind, usually found in

rocky, mountainous places. It is extremely active. Its eyes are round and sparkling; it has two small horns, about six inches in length, rising from the top of the head, inclining forward, then bending backward near their extremities, which are very sharp. On each side of the face there are two black stripes; the rest of the face is whitish yellow. The hair on the body is short; in Spring, ash colored, in Autumn, dun, inclining to black; in Winter, blackish brown. Its hind legs are longer than its fore legs, and bending forward. Its tail is short. Its smell is very acute. It feeds on the best herbage; and on the buds, flowers, and tenderest parts of plants. When it perceives danger approaching, it gives alarm by uttering a sharp hissing through the nostrils, which may be heard at a great distance. As its enemy approaches, it appears in great agitation, strikes the ground with one, or both fore feet; and at length flies with great speed, bounding from rock to rock with great ease, where no dog can follow it. The huntsman, to come near them, must take advantage of the wind, that they may not smell him. They are usually shot with musket balls from behind the clefts of rocks.— Their flesh is good for food; their skin, when tanned, is prized for its softness and warmth. These animals are found in great plenty in the mountainous parts of Switzerland, Germany, and the neighboring countries; they can but ill endure heat, and are rarely found in Summer; to shun the warm rays of the sun, they retire to caverns, to the north side of high mountains, and to the shades of high, spreading trees.

> Be quick your perception of danger, dear youth,
>   And fly from the vicious, who hunt for your souls;
>   As the nimble Chamois
>   From the hunter, so fly
> From those, who would lead you aside from the truth,
>   And trust in that Power, which the tempter controls.

In the choice of the viands your souls to sustain,
  Be nice to distinguish, and cull out the best;
    Like the tasty Chamois,
    Secure a supply
Neither vulgar nor vicious, nor doubtful, nor vain;
  But such as will bear the most critical test.

To the high Rock of Ages keep faithfully near,
  And may its cool shadow you safely defend;
    Like the prudent Chamois
    To the mountains apply,
The mountains of safety, where, shelter'd from fear,
  Your lives may be happy, and peaceful your end.

COCK.
[Figure from the Cabinet.]

—

A domestic fowl, often called the dung-hill Cock. It is not mentioned in the old Testament, but noticed several times in the new. As recorded by each of the Evangelists, Jesus said to Peter, that the Cock should not crow, or should not crow twice, till he had denied him thrice. In Mark 13 : 35, he speaks of the master of the house coming at the cock-crowing. The name in Greek is Alĕktōr, signifying, *from bed*; probably because men used to be roused from bed by the crowing of the Cock.

The Cock is a bird of great courage, and will fight a rival with almost unyielding obstinacy. On this account multitudes in civilized lands have amused themselves with the savage and cruel practice of cock-fighting; a practice which ought never to be mentioned, but in terms of decided disapprobation.

The Cock is the male of the species; the female is called the Hen. The Cock is furnished with a red fleshy comb on the top of his head, and with two wattles of the same color under his throat; his neck is surrounded with a ruff of feathers, very often of a flame color, but not always, the plumage of the bird being very various; this ruff he erects, when angry; his tail is large and circular, usually of a shining black; his legs are each armed with a sharp spur, from one to two inches in length. His walk is stately. His crowing loud and shrill, and may be heard to a great distance. His flesh is a delicacy.

> When the Cock fights, as oft he will,
>   By common instinct led;
> Learn, youth, to meet your foes with skill,
>   Till all your foes are fled.
>
> The foes which chiefly you must fight
>   Are spirits, foul, unclean;
> But arm'd with cunning, and delight
>   To lead the soul to sin.

These meet with resolution, mail'd
    With helmet, sword, and shield,
From God's blest word; when thus assail'd,
    They soon will quit the field.

When the Cock crows, remember him,
    Whose look made Peter feel;
Mourn for your sins, or never dream
    To gain eternal weal.

When the shrill clarion bids you rise,
    Wake up your mental powers,
For meditation learn to prize
    The cheerful morning hours.

COCKATRICE.

THE Hebrew words in scripture rendered by this name
are (צֶפַע & צִפְעוֹנִי) Tsĕfăgn, and Tsĭfgnōnē; Pagnin and Buxtorf suppose it to be the Basilisk, one of
the most venomous of all serpents; said by some to kill
even by its breath. The French bible has *Basilic*; Junius and Tremellius have *Hæmorrois*, a serpent, whose
poison causes the blood to start from the veins. The
Septuagint render the word ăspĭs, an asp. Some think
the horned viper is the reptile intended.

It is found in Isaiah—11 : 8. The weaned child shall
put his hand on the Cockatrice den. This is spoken
in allusion to those peaceful days, when the inhabitants
of every land shall embrace one another as brethren in
Christ; when those nations, now the most savage and
blood-thirsty, will be civilized, and rendered friendly
and benevolent by the transforming power of the gospel.—Isaiah 14 : 29. Out of the serpent's root shall
come forth a Cockatrice, and his fruit shall be a fiery
flying serpent. Under some former kings the Jews had
smitten the Philistines; under Ahaz the strength of

the Jews was broken, and the Philistines rejoiced; but as the Cockatrice is more dreadful than the common serpent, Hezekiah should be more destructive to them, than those that were before him.—Whatever victory we may gain over others, if we are not the friends of God, we have cause rather to mourn than to rejoice; for at length the tide will turn against us.—Isaiah 59 : 5, They hatch Cockatrice eggs, and weave the spider's web. This is spoken of the wicked among the Jews in a time of great declension; their words, their counsels, their plans, were as evil in their tendency, as the eggs of the Basilisk, and as ensnaring as the spider's web to the unsuspecting fly.—Jeremiah 8 : 17. I will send serpents, Cockatrices among you, which will not be charmed, and they shall bite you, saith the Lord. This is a threatening against the wicked Jews. By Cockatrices God here no doubt means cruel, implacable enemies, who would not by any means be turned aside from their work of destruction. The original word is found in Proverbs—23 : 32, where it is rendered *Adder*. Speaking of strong drink, or wine, the wise man says, At last it biteth like a serpent, and stingeth like an *Adder*; (like a Cockatrice, or Basilisk.) Strong drink used intemperately is as a slow, but fatal poison.

> The scorner's words are like a serpent's breath
>   To heedless souls, and listening youth around?
> They kill with painful, everlasting death,
>   Where Gilead's balm is not in season found.
>
> O happy days, when God's resistless power
>   The Crockatrice, the Basilisk shall tame;
> The vilest sinners in that peaceful hour
>   Shall bow submissive to the Savior's name.

Cormorant.

CORMORANT.

—

THE figure is from the Cabinet, and represents the little Cormorant. The Hebrew word rendered Cormorant, in Levit. 11 : 17, and in Deut. 14 : 17, is (שָׁלָךְ) Shâlâkrh, from a word signifying *to throw down*, because it darts down into the water for its prey. But in Isaiah 34 : 11, and in Zeph. 2 : 14, the word rendered Cormorant is (קָאַת) Kââth, from a word which signifies *to vomit ;* because the bird is supposed to vomit up the shell-fish it has taken, to separate the meat from the shells. The former word Buxtorf renders *Mergus*, a diver ; the latter he renders, *Platea*, and *Pelicanus*, a Pelican ; and in Psalm 102 : 6, it is rendered *Pelican*, in the English Bible. For the former word, the Septugint has Kataräktēs ; a bird that descends with impetuosity ; and the Latin and French Bible have a word signifying a *diver*. In the French Bible, the latter word, in Psalm 102 : 6, and in Isaiah 34 : 11, and in Zeph. 2 : 14, is rendered, Cormorant ; but Junius and Tremellius have *Platea*, Pelican.

This variety of rendering, as has been before observed, shows something of the difficulty of translating the natural history of the Bible. Which of the two words, rendered *Cormorant*, has the best claim to be the real Cormorant, I am at a loss to say, but rather think it the former, Shâlâkrh.—The bird usually termed Cormorant, is somewhat more than three feet in length, and four feet in the expansion of its wings, and weighs about seven pounds. The back and coverts of the wings are deep green edged with black, and glossed with blue; the quill and tail feathers dusky, the breast and belly black. It frequents the highest parts of stupendous rocks, hanging over the sea; it is extremely voracious, has a sudden digestion, its smell is rank and disagreeable; it takes its prey from the sea, darting upon it with great swiftness; it takes the fish cross-wise, carries it into the air, throws it up, seizes it by the head, and swallows it, though larger than its neck. In England it was formerly tamed, and trained to fish, with a ring round its neck to prevent its swallowing its prey; it is used in China for the same purpose.

The voraciousness and ill scent of the Cormorant, rendered it very fit that Milton should compare Satan to it, when he sat surveying the beauties of Paradise.

> " Thence up he flew, and on the tree of life,
> The middle tree, and highest there that grew,
> Sat, like a *Cormorant;* yet not true life
> Thereby regain'd, but sat devising death
> To them, who liv'd." [*B.* 4, *l.* 194.]

Under the ceremonial law, the Cormorant was accounted unclean. The bird called Cormorant in Isaiah and in Zephaniah, is represented as inhabiting waste and desolate places. The Psalmist in his affliction, compares himself to this same bird in the wilderness; thus the Kââth in these passages appears to be a bird disposed to retire from the abodes of men, and to dwell in solitary places.

CRANE.
[Figure from the Cabinet.]

—

THE name occurs in Isaiah 38 : 14, and in Jer. 8 : 7. The Hebrew in the former place is (סוּס) Sôs, in the latter, (סיס) Sēs; Pagnin, Buxtorf, and Junius and Tremellius render it *Grus*, a Crane; the French Bible has the same. Harmer thinks the *Hoopoe* is intended. The common Crane is a tall slender bird; its head is covered with black bristles, the back part of it, which is bald and red, distinguishes it from the Stork. The plumage is ash colored; two tufts of feathers spring from the pinion of each wing, which the bird can erect at pleasure. The fore part of the breast, and the quill feathers are black. The Crane in length, is about six feet, its weight, ten pounds.

In the spring season the Cranes arrive in great numbers in the northern parts of Europe and Asia, from the warmer climes of Egypt and India. Their favorite food is corn, that is, grain of various kinds; but hardly any kind of food comes amiss to them. They have been noticed for their social habits, filial and parental affection, and connubial attachment.

In Isaiah 38 : 14, Hczckiah says, as a Crane or a swallow, so did I chatter. This chattering was probably a rapid, mournful, and somewhat incoherent uttering of words, in making complaint before God. The Crane is said to have a loud, sharp voice. In Jer. 8 : we read, The Turtle and the Crane, and the Swallow know the time of their coming; but my people know not the judgment of the Lord. The Crane is a migratory bird.

> Ask now the beasts, and they shall teach,
>   And ask the fowls, and they shall tell;
> The works of nature loudly preach,
>   And say that God does all things well.
>
> The Turtle knows the joyful time
>   When vernal flowers with spring appear;
> The Crane and Swallow change their clime
>   When wintry days and storms draw near.
>
> But thoughtless man o'erlooks the grace,
>   When God the present good bestows;
> Nor in his sufferings will he trace
>   The cause and source of all his woes.

7*

CUCKOW.

THE figure is from Bruce, and represents the Bee
Cuckow.   The name, *Cuckow*, is found among the unclean birds, in Levit. 11 : 16, and in Deut. 14 : 15.
The Hebrew is (שַׁחַף) Shâhrhăf.   Buxtorf says *Æsalon*, or *Larus*, a Merlin, or a Sea-cob.   Pagnin, after
Jerome and the Septuagint, renders it *Larus*, Sea-cob ;
a black small bird inhabiting about the sea-shore, sometimes in the water, sometimes out.   Junius and Tremellius have *Æsalon*.   The French Bible has *Coucou*.
Dr. Shaw thinks it may be the Rhaad, or Saf-saf.—The
Bee Cuckow, the figure of which is given, much resembles in shape and size, the common Cuckow; its
head and neck are brown ; the fore part of the neck
light yellow, darker on each side than in the middle,
where it is nearly white.   The yellow on each side
reaches near to the round part or shoulder of the wing.
The breast and belly are of a dirty white ; the feathers
on the back, and on the outside of the wings, and the
tail feathers are tipped with clear white, increasing with
the length and breadth of the feathers.   The thighs are
dirty white.

'Twas needful once the birds to know,
By law unclean, the Jews to show,
That man by nature wears a stain,
Till Christ shall make him pure again.

The gospel now with clearer light
Shows what is wrong, and what is right,
And holds a Saviour's blood to view,
Man's fallen nature to renew.

DEER.

THE figure is of the Fallow Deer, from Bewick, reduced. There is much uncertainty what animal is intended by the Hebrew word (יַחְמוּר) Yàhrhmôr,
which is found in Deut. 14 : 5, and in 1 Kings 4 : 23,
and which in the English Bible is rendered, Fallow
Deer. Buxtorf says, According to some it is a *Deer*,
according to others, a *Buffalo*, or kind of wild ox. Rabbi Kimchi calls it an animal resembling a large Goat.
Pagnin concludes that it is a Buffalo, or wild ox. The
Septuagint give but one word, *Dorkas*, for the two Hebrew words translated in English, Roebuck, and Fallow
Deer. Junius and Tremellius have *Dama*, Deer.

Supposing it probable that the Fallow Deer may be
intended, I have thought proper to give a sketch of that
animal. The male of the Fallow Deer is called a *Buck ;*

the female a *Doe*. They are somewhat smaller than
the Stag ; they have broad horns, palmated near the
ends ; that is, resembling the palm of the hand, with
the fingers spreading from it. They shed their horns
every year. Their color varies ; they are reddish ; dark
brown ; red, spotted with white ; and sometimes white.
Their tail is short, but longer than that of the Stag.
Their legs are long and slender. The hoof is parted.
They are swift of foot. The Doe has no horns. She
goes with young eight months ; brings forth usually one,
sometimes two, rarely three at a time. Their term of
life is about twenty years. Their flesh is much esteemed for food ; that of the Buck is best from July to Oc-
tober ; that of the Doe, from November to February.
They are kept in great numbers, on the Isle of Great
Britain.

They are naturally timid, putting their confidence for
safety in flight ; but when wounded, or closely shut in,
will fight with considerable obstinacy.

Browse, leaves, and herbs supply
    The Fallow Deer with food ;
A timid race, with speed they fly,
    By worrying dogs pursu'd.

They bound thro' groves and fields
    To lengthen out their span ;
When caught, their flesh a dainty yields
    To feed voluptuous man.

'Tis thus the world around ;
    The lamb, so blithe to day,
By hungry wolf to-morrow found,
    Becomes his favorite prey.

Is then the Lord unkind ?
    Not so ; the general good,
In his unerring plan design'd,
    Is wisely still pursu'd.

Of this we may be sure,
    From all the mass of pain,
Which living creatures e'er endure,
    Still springs superior gain.

DOG.

—

THE different species of this kind of animal are very numerous. It is frequently mentioned in the Bible; the name in Hebrew is (כֶּלֶב) Kĕlĕbv; in Greek Kū-ōn; in Latin, *Canis*. The Shepherd's Dog is commonly supposed to be the common parent of all the rest. To give a particular description of all the varieties of dogs, that now exist, would be an almost endless task, and far exceed the limits I have prescribed for myself. A few of the principal species I shall briefly describe.

[Figure from Bewick.]

—

1. The Shepherd's Dog. He is very useful to those, who tend large flocks of sheep. He is readily taught to guard them against wild beasts with great fidelity and resolution; to prevent individuals of the flock from straying away from the rest; to collect and drive home the flock, at the notice of his master; to drive away intruders from other flocks; and to be a faithful centinal for his master during the night. The Shepherd's Dog was probably much in use in the land of Judea, as the Israelites were, many of them, Shepherds. So in Isaiah 56 : 9, 10, the beasts of the field are called upon to come and devour; and the unfaithful prophets and rulers of the people are called dumb dogs, that cannot bark, sleeping, lying down, loving to slumber. This

should be a serious admonition to the ministers of Christ, to be watchful, and faithful to warn their hearers against the spiritual dangers to which they are exposed.

[Figure from the Cabinet.]

2. The Mastiff. This is a large strong dog; his ears pendulous, lips large and loose, his look somewhat grave and sullen, his bark loud and terrific. He is also useful in guarding the house, garden, and other property of his master. Three Mastiffs have been known to compel a lion to retreat. They were formerly bred in Great Britain, and sent to Rome for the combats of the amphitheatre. But we hope the time is approaching, when not only man will cease to engage in bloody fight with his fellow man; but will also refrain from urging to unnecessary war the beasts of the field.

3. The Bull-dog; so called from his fierceness and courage in attacking the bull. He seizes the bull by some part of the face, and retains his hold, notwithstanding every effort of the bull to shake him off. He was probably designed in the kind providence of God

to be the assistant of the herds-man in managing and subjecting his herds of cattle ; but has been abused for the barbarous, wicked, and cruel sport of bull-baiting ; which ought not to be recollected without abhorrence, and which it is to be hoped will ere long be unknown, except on the page of history.

4. The Cur-dog ; useful also to the herds-man ; generally black and white ; their ears half erect, their bite very keen ; they make their attack at the heels of cattle. Some of them are whelped with short tails.

5. The Greenland or Siberian dog ; has long, shaggy hair, a bushy, curling tail, and a sharp muzzle. They are generally white, but sometimes spotted, and sometimes black. They are trained for drawing sledges ; four are harnessed together, two abreast, and a fifth before them as a leader. A carrier with despatches has been known to perform a journey of two hundred and seventy miles with these dogs in less than four days.

6. The Irish Grey-hound ; the largest of the dog-kind, generally white, or cinnamon color ; of short hair, majestic appearance, and mild aspect. Formerly they were of great use in clearing the country of Ireland of wolves. They are now very scarce.

7. The Grey-hound ; of sharp muzzle, short hair, and long slender legs ; is the fleetest of all dogs, but hunts only by the sight.

8. The Terrier ; a fierce, keen-bitten, hardy dog ; the enemy of all vermin ; mice, rats, weasels, badgers, &c.

9. The Beagle ; a quick scented dog, used in hunting the hare. 10. The Harrier, used also for hunting the hare, from which it has its name ; it is somewhat larger and more nimble than the beagle. 11. The Fox-hound ; quick scented, swift, strong, and very persevering in the

chase ; a dog much valued by the sportsmen in Great Britain. Many years ago two of them chased a large stag about one hundred and twenty miles in less than a day ; at the close of the chase the dogs and stag all died of fatigue.

12. The Old English hound ; is remarkable for his great size and strength. He has a long body, long, sweeping ears, a deep, mellow tone of voice, and exquisite sense of smelling. They are deficient, however, in speed, and are now scarce.

13. The Blood-hound ; of quick scent, swifter than the Old English hound, and generally of a reddish or brown color. Anciently they were used to pursue, and find out thieves and deer stealers ; also to discover the bodies of men, lost on the mountains of Switzerland. 14. The Spanish-Pointer ; is remarkable for his aptness to receive instruction ; is used to find out partridges, pheasants, &c.

15. English-Setter ; is remarkable for his sagacity in discovering various kinds of game, and approaching them with caution.

16. The Newfoundland dog ; a large, web-footed dog ; rather shaggy, tail curling over the back, naturally fond of fish, and swims and dives with ease. He is useful in saving persons from drowning, when fallen into the water. In Newfoundland they are employed in drawing wood for the use of the inhabitants ; three or four of them being able to draw a sled with two or three hundred weight of wood on it.

17. The large, rough Water-dog, is web-footed, of long, shaggy hair, swims easily, is used in hunting ducks, and other water fowls; and is some times kept on board vessels to recover things dropped overboard. 18. The large Water Spaniel; is strongly attached to his master, receives instruction readily, and obeys promptly; his hair is beautifully curled, his aspect mild; he is fond of water, and swims well, and is useful in hunting water fowl. 19. The Springer; lively, active, and pleasant, unwearied in the pursuit of his game, such as woodcocks, snipes, and the like. 20. The Pyrame dog, generally black, with reddish legs, and a red spot above each eye. 21. The Shock dog; a little creature, almost hid in the abundance of its hair. 22. The Comforter; a little good looking dog, kept sometimes by ladies; but is snappish and noisy. 23. The Turn-Spit; a dog whose assistance has been formerly much used in turning the spit in roasting meat. He is frequently spotted with black upon a blue grey ground; he has sometimes the iris of one eye black and the other white. 24. The New Zealand dog, somewhat resembles the Shepherd's dog, and is the common food of the inhabitants in many of the South Sea Islands, and is fattened with vegetables for that purpose.

These are some of the principal varieties of dogs. They all intermingle one with another; they readily become attached to man; their attachment is often very strong; correction for their faults increases their attachment; they are very sagacious; their hearing is quick, and generally their sense of smelling. They bark at strange dogs, howl at certain musical notes, and when they have lost their master. When they have committed a theft, they slink away with their tail between their legs; their common food is flesh; they drink by lapping with their tongues. These are some of their common characteristics.

In Exodus 11 : 7, God says, that *against any of the children of Israel shall not a dog move his tongue.* This alludes to the common practice of dogs to bark at passing strangers; and the import of it is, that God will effectually secure from harm those, whom he sees fit to defend, and those that put their trust in him. David in Psalm 22 : 16, personating the crucified Saviour, says, *Dogs have encompassed me ;* by this he means his wicked persecutors, who were around him like furious dogs around their prey. This is strikingly expressive of the enmity of the heart of natural men against holiness, and of the condescension of Christ in sustaining such reproach, while suffering for our sins. In Prov. 26 : 11, the wise man says, *As a dog returneth to his vomit, so a fool returneth to his folly.* This alludes to the very common practice of sinners to return to their vile, abominable courses, after being outwardly reformed, but not converted, in a season of revival of religion; at the same time it is strongly figurative of the loathsome, and detestable nature of sin ; and hints at it, as a thing from which we ought to turn away with disgust. In Isaiah 56 : 11, the unfaithful watchmen of Israel are called *greedy dogs, that never can have enough.* This points out, and condemns those rulers and teachers, who hold their places not from any regard to the good of others, but through an avaricious desire of gain. In Rev. 22 : 15, it is said *Without are dogs ;* by dogs are here meant those wicked ones of the human race, who for their evil, persecuting, and impure conduct will be excluded from the kingdom of heaven. My dear young friends, let it be the concern of every one of you not to be found among these forever lost, abandoned sinners.

For various use in every different clime
   The Dog is form'd; the species varying still
By casual mixture thro' the lapse of time,
   But all soon yielding to the human will.

One guards the flock, the shepherd's faithful friend;
   Hard by his master night and day he lies.
The house, the barn another well attends,
   And at the thief with daring courage flies.

One gives the wolf, or surly bear the chase,
   Smells out their haunts, and mingles deadly fight.
With hart or stag another winds the race
   From early dawn till shades of rising night.

Some chase the fox, or start the timorous hare;
   Some hunt the pheasant, or the partridge spring;
Some, when the fowler kills his watery fare,
   The duck or whistler to their master bring.

Some the fierce bull with cruel courage teaze;
   With bite severe the beast to madness drive,
Man to amuse! How can such sports as these
   The most benighted, savage state survive!

Some turn the spit, the toilet some attend;
   Some, tiny things, the lady's lap their bed,
Amuse her leisure; some the way befriend
   Of lonely traveller through the evening shade.

Some, where cold mountains rear the snowy peak,
   Each devious path with careful scent explore,
The tir'd lost peasant, sunk in drifts, they seek,
   And to his friends the lifeless corpse restore.

Some from the water—kindly form'd to save,
   When other help avails not,—safely draw
The helpless drowning; from a watery grave
   Redeem its victims; such is nature's law—

Such, rather say, through all his earthly woes
   To cheer and comfort most unworthy man;
Such are the favors, which our God bestows,
   With millions more in his unerring plan.

DOVE.

[Figure from Life.—The Common Dove.]

—

THIS beautiful and harmless bird is frequently mentioned in the Bible. Its name in Hebrew, is (יוֹנָה) Yōnâh; it comes from a word signifying to *oppress ;* the dove being much oppressed, and often pursued and seized by birds of prey. We first meet with the name in Gen. 8 : 8. Speaking of Noah, it is said, He sent forth a dove from him to see if the waters were abated from off the face of the ground. The name in Greek, is Perĭstera. By the name Yōnâh, we are probably to understand the tame pigeon, often called the dove. This bird in its wild, and more natural state is called the Stock-dove; it is of a bluish ash color, the breast dashed with a fine changeable green and purple ; the sides of its neck with shining copper color; its wings are marked with two black bars, the back is white, and the tail barred near the end with black. As its name imports, it is the origin of all the beautiful variety of the tame pigeon. The dove in its domesticated state is gentle, timid, harmless, peaceable, loving to its mate, and neat in its food. It is the emblem of simplicity, love, and innocency. Its plumage is very various ; some are of a snowy whiteness. Its form is elegant, its cooing plaintive and affectionate. Its food is principally grain of various kinds. It lays two eggs at a time, and breeds almost every month in the year, by means of which it multiplies very fast, especially, if well fed. In Persia and Egypt they constitute a good measure of the riches of the husbandman. They feed their young from their crops, the young ones thrusting their bills into their mouths, and taking thence their food.

The male and female take turns in sitting on their eggs. They are used in some countries to carry letters, which are fastened under their wings. Their sight is keen, their eyes are beautiful, their hearing quick, and they are quick in their motions, and swift in their flight.

They are reckoned in the ceremonial law among the clean birds, and were, with the Turtle-dove, offered in sacrifice by divine direction. As the Son of God, on account of his innocency and gentleness, as well as for his being offered in sacrifice for our sins, is called in scripture a Lamb ; so, to give us an idea of purity, mildness, and innocence, the Spirit of God in descending upon the Saviour at the time of his baptism, assumed the form of a Dove.

Another kind of Dove is called the Ring-dove ; it is about eighteen inches in length, and has a semicircular line of white on the back part of the neck. It builds its nest on trees, and refuses to be domesticated.

8*

[Figure from the Cabinet.]

Another kind of Dove is the Turtle; its Hebrew
name is (תּוֹר) Tōr; so called, it is said, from the
note it utters. We find it first mentioned in Gen. 15:
9—where Abraham is commanded of the Lord to take
a heifer, a she-goat, a ram, a turtle-dove, and a young
pigeon; the beasts were divided and parts set over
against parts, the birds were set over against each other
without being divided; when a burning lamp was
made to pass between the parts in confirmation that
God would give to Abraham's seed the land of Canaan.

The Septuagint for *turtle*, has Trūgōn, from a word
which signifies to murmur; the name alludes to the
note of the turtle. The Latin Bible has *turtur*. The
turtle is about twelve inches in length, its back is ash
colored, the breast light orange; on each side of the
neck is a black spot tipped with white.

It is very shy, breeds in the most retired places, feeds
on a variety of vegetable substances, and is very faithful in its attachment to its mate.

If the ant may teach us labor,
  To instruct us how to love,
We have yet another neighbor,
  'Tis the friendly, faithful Dove.

Constant, harmless, gentle, tender;
  If her habits well we mind,
Her example fair may render
  Us affectionate and kind.

See her eye, how bright and winning,
  Sign of what her passions mean;
He, who gave the world beginning,
  Has pronounc'd the turtle clean.

Mark her form, how neat and graceful,
  Gloss'd with crimson, green, and gold;
Mark her manners, mild and peaceful,
  Mending still, as you behold.

When the ark of Noah grounded
  On the lofty mountain's height,
Still with watery deeps surrounded,
  Then the raven took his flight.

Far he went, and lonely roving,
  His late shelter now he spurn'd;
But the dove, more kind and loving,
  To her host again return'd.

'Mong the types of absolution
  Turtles hold a noted place;
Teaching how the soul's pollution
  Yields before a Saviour's grace.

When the Holy Ghost descended
  To declare the Son of God,
Then the turtle's form attended,
  On the Saviour's head it stood.

Fair, but lowly, as the myrtle,
  Spreading o'er the world around;
Chaste and constant, as the turtle,
  May the church of Christ be found.

Crocodile.

DRAGON.
[Figure from Mavor.]

THE Hebrew word rendered Dragon, is (תַּנִּים, or תַּנִּין) Tănnēm, or Tănnēn. The word frequently occurs in the Old Testament. In Gen. 1 : 23, Job 7 : 12, and Ezekiel 32 : 2, it is rendered *Whales*. In most of the places where the word is found the Crocodile is probably intended; and this may be the case even in those, where it is rendered Whale. In Ezekiel 32 : 2, for instance, Pharaoh is compared to a Tănnēn, which troubles the water with his feet; as the whale has no feet, we may believe the Crocodile is meant, which has feet, and is found sometimes on land, and sometimes in water. The Septuagint renders the word eight times by Drăkōn, *Dragon;* three times by Seīrēn, *Siren;* twice by Strouthŏs, *Ostrich;* and by several other words, and four or five times omits to translate it. As it is well known that the Crocodile inhabits the Nile, and its banks, and as Pharaoh, king of Egypt, is called Tănnēn, it is likely that this word especially means Crocodile, but may perhaps be used in some passages, for some other animal in some respects resembling this.

When we read in Deut. 32 : 33, of the poison of dragons, it seems natural to suppose that some kind of venomous serpents is intended; and by some the dragon has been called a fierce, winged serpent. But the Hebrew word here rendered poison, usually means anger, fury; so the passage might be rendered, *the fury of Crocodiles*. Believing that this animal is generally intended by the word *Dragon*, in the Old Testament, I shall give some description of the Crocodile. He is sometimes more than twenty feet in length, and five feet in circumference. His legs are in shape like those of the common lizard, the fore legs much resembling the arms of a man; his head is long, his nose sharp, and his eyes small, compared with his size. His tongue is short, and most of the way fixed to the under part of his mouth. His body is covered with a hard shell, marked both ways with seams. The upper part of his tail is furnished with a kind of rough scales, projecting like saw-teeth; but as he can bend it at pleasure, as the tail of a serpent, what is said of Leviathan, as a crooked serpent, in Isaiah 27 : 1, may apply to this animal. His back is of a dark brown, his belly of a whitish, citron color; his sides are ornamented with large spots of both these colors. The female lays her eggs in the sand to be hatched by the sun.

The Crocodile abounds in the Nile, the Niger, and the Ganges, and in other great rivers of Asia and Africa. The Alligator may be considered as the Crocodile of America, and the Cayman the Crocodile of the Antiles.

In upper Egypt the Crocodile is very destructive; it lies in wait near the brink of the Nile, seizes its victim with a spring, and drags it into the water. It will master even the tiger. The natives of some countries kill it for the sake of its flesh, which to them is pleasant food; and some also eat its eggs. The Ichneumon and Ibis eagerly devour both its eggs and young; and even the parent Crocodiles destroy many of their own young.

In this way kind providence prevents the multiplication of an animal, which otherwise might desolate whole regions of country.

In Job 30 : 29, Job calls himself a brother of Dragons; this he did perhaps on account of his solitary state; being forsaken of most of his friends; or on account of his cries of distress; for the crocodile is fond of solitary places, and is said to utter a howling cry over its prey, and when fighting with an enemy.

In Psal. 91 : 13, it is said, the young lion and the dragon shalt thou trample under feet. From this we may gather that the dragon was a very formidable animal, and abiding sometimes at least upon land; and so probably the crocodile is intended. It further teaches that those who put their trust in God will finally triumph over their most powerful enemies.

In Micah 1 : 8, the prophet says, I will make a wailing like the dragons; from this it appears that the animals here alluded to uttered a wailing, or howling noise.

By the great red dragon, brought to view repeatedly in the book of Revelations, we are to understand **Pagan Rome**, swayed and managed by the prince of the devils in its persecutions of the christians; or rather the prince of the devils himself.

Among the sedge and reeds of Nile
Oft lies conceal'd the crocodile;
   Among the proud a king.
The tamer beasts that come to drink,
When venturing down the rivers brink,
   He seizes with a spring.

A monster huge, with many a scale,
These are his pride, his powerful mail;
   For these thro' ages fam'd.
With fear inspiring beasts and man,
In scripture call'd leviathan,
   And there a dragon nam'd.

Like him the prince of darkness lies
Conceal'd in things that please the eyes,
 That please the ears and taste;
When heedless youth indulge in sin,
He spreads his arms and draws them in,
 And holds the victims fast.

Look, ere you step, my youthful friends,
The old leviathan intends
 To make your souls his prey;
If once he drag you down to hell,
You must in chains and darkness dwell
 A long, eternal day.

DROMEDARY.
[Figure from the Cabinet.]

—

THE name occurs in the English bible four times. 1
Kings 4 : 28. Barley also, and straw for the horses and
dromedaries. Esther 8 : 10. Riders on mules, camels,
and young dromedaries. In these two passages the
Hebrew is (רֶכֶשׁ) Rĕkrhĕsh, the singular for the plural; according to Buxtorf, a light, swift horse, or mule;
according to Pagnin, a dromedary, or mule, the young
of the mare. The Septuagint has a word meaning
chariots; Junius and Tremellius have a word meaning
posts, or messengers. The English name occurs in
Isai. 60 : 6. The dromedaries of Midian and Ephah; and
in Jer. 2 : 23. Thou art a swift dromedary, traversing

her ways.   In these two passages the Hebrew name is
(בִּכְרָה) Bĭkrhâh, which by more general consent is
supposed to mean a dromedary, or camel with but one
bunch on its back.   It is called in Greek Drŏmas, from
a word which signifies *to run*.

This animal is a native of Arabia, and the northern
parts of Africa.   It is much more numerous, and much
swifter, than what is commonly called the camel.   It is
not near so strong as the camel, and therefore less useful in bearing heavy burdens; but on account of its
swiftness is much used for business, which requires
despatch ; being able day after day to travel ninety or
one hundred miles a day.   It needs neither whip nor
spur, but is enlivened by singing, or by the sound of a
pipe.   It is mild and gentle, except when in heat ; it is
then furious.   It goes with young nearly twelve months.
The females are usually kept only for breeding.   It
comes to full strength at about the age of six years, and
lives forty or fifty.   They are governed by a bridle fastened to a ring, fixed in the nose.   Except in being
smaller, swifter, not so strong, and having but one
bunch on the back, they differ but little from the common camel.

[Figures from Library of Entertaining Knowledge.]

—

With even, quick, and steady pace
    The dromedary moves ;
And while he runs his lengthened race,
    The tuneful pipe he loves.

Patient, abstemious, thirst enduring,
  Long journies he performs;
His master oft from foes securing
  Amidst the sandy storms.

So should the christian pilgrim run,
  Cheer'd by a Saviour's grace,
Constant and steady as the sun,
  With speed his heavenly race.

Patient in trials, persevering,
  Through all the vale of tears;
Still by his faithful compass steering,
  Till heavenly rest appears.

EAGLE.

[Figure in part from Nature.]

—

ONE figure is from the white headed Eagle, numerous in the eastern part of the United States; the other is reduced from the figure of the crowned Eagle, by Geo. Edwards.

The name Eagle occurs frequently in the Bible. In the Hebrew it is (נֶשֶׁר) Nĕshĕr; in Greek, Aĕtŏs; in Latin, *Aquila.* In the ceremonial law the Eagle is reckoned unclean. There are several species of this bird, differing in size, strength, color of plumage, and

9

other circumstances. The black Eagle, with white head and tail, the figure of which stands at the head of this article, is very common about the eastern shores of North America; it feeds much upon fish; it goes not itself into the water after them, but pursues the fish-hawk, or sea-eagle, till it is obliged to drop its prey, which with the swiftness of an arrow it seizes, before it reaches the ground. It is frequently troublesome by carrying off lambs after they are grown to a considerable size.

Another species is the black-backed Eagle; this is very destructive to deer, it seizes them between the horns, and beats them with its wings, till at length they are worn down, and become an easy prey. Its body is of a deep brown, upon the upper part of its tail it has a white stripe, or band.

The Earne is another species of Eagle. It is common in Scotland, and inhabits the north of Europe and Iceland. It flies rather heavily; it feeds on fish and seals, which it seizes from the surface of the water. It feeds also on land animals. The head and neck are of a pale ash-color, the body and wings are of the color of ashes, clouded with brown.

Of the Sea-Eagle, see under Osprey.

The Golden Eagle is another species. He is large and strong; his length is three feet; the spread of his wings more than seven feet; his legs are short but large, being about an inch in diameter: they are covered with feathers to the feet. He carries off a hare, lamb, or goose with ease; he builds his nest on the highest part of high rocks; it is six or seven feet in breadth, made of strong sticks, covered with reeds and rushes; the young are in the middle, on the borders are its provisions. In Kerry, a county in Ireland, during a scarce summer, it is said a poor man supplied his family with provisions taken from an eagle's nest; and to delay the flight of the young eagles he clipped their wings.   Another man in Ireland, however, lost his life by means of robbing an eagle's nest.   The nest was on an island in the lake of Kilarney; as the man was swimming from the island with the young eagles, the old ones perceived him, and fell upon him with their beaks and talons, and soon despatched him.   The color of this eagle is dark brown, clouded with a deeper shade of the same.

The figure which here follows is that of the crowned eagle from the coast of Guinea, Africa.

[Figure from George Edwards.]

This is a bird of majestic appearance; the back, tail, covering of the wings, and quill feathers are dark ash color shaded with dark brown.   The back of the neck, and the top of the head, dark brown, spotted with black. Round the eye, and under the throat, white, spotted with reddish brown and black. Middle part of the breast, light, reddish brown; sides and lower part of the breast the same, barred and spotted with black. The feet bright yellow. The legs covered with feathers of dusky white, spotted with black. Beak and claws black.

Of the Eagle in general it may be said, that his sight is very keen, his hearing quick, his courage great, his flight the highest of all birds, his beak hooked, his claws long and sharp, and forming nearly a semicircle. He is very strong, his descent upon his prey is very swift. He is among birds what the lion is among beasts.

The most interesting texts of scripture, respecting the Eagle are the following : Exodus 19 : 4, How I bare you on Eagles' wings, and brought you to myself.— Some historians report that the Eagle does actually take her young upon her back, and fly from her nest with them to teach them to fly ; or to compel them to do it when they are of sufficient age. This is confirmed by that in Deut. 32 : 11, 12, As an Eagle stirreth up her nest, fluttereth over her young, spreadeth abroad her wings, taketh them, beareth them on her wings ; so the Lord alone did lead him, and there was no strange god with him. The description here is so particular, that it leaves hardly room to doubt, but that Moses and the children of Israel were acquainted with Eagles, which thus received their young upon their wings, and bore them on their backs in their flight. The young Eagles, when aloft in air might be compelled to leave their parents, and fly short distances, and then might be received by their parents again. The figure is beautiful to point out the care, discipline, and tenderness of the true God towards his peculiar people, Israel. Prov. 23 : 5, Riches certainly make themselves wings, they fly away as an Eagle towards heaven. The Eagle, though near by us now, may within a few minutes be soaring towards the sky beyond the ken of sight. Riches may be now in our possession; within a few hours they may be entirely gone from us. Ezekiel 1 : 10, They four also had the face of an Eagle; this is spoken of the cherubim, the more immediate attendants of the throne of Immanuel. The face of an Eagle may denote spiritual sagacity, heavenly affection, and great speed in fulfilling the divine commands. Micah 1 : 16, Enlarge thy baldness as the Eagle. The Israelites are here called upon to cut off their hair in token of mourning for their children, who by and by should be gone into captivity. Bald as the Eagle; Bruce describes an Eagle in Abyssinia, under the name of the golden Eagle, which is very large, and the crown of its head bald; the allusion might be to this species of Eagle, or to some other bald Eagle; unless the Eagle in general in moulting sheds his feathers more suddenly than other birds, and is then bald by the means. Psalm 103 : 5, So that thy youth is renewed as the Eagle's.—Rejecting evidently fabulous traditions concerning the Eagle, I think it probable that there is here allusion to the extraordinary vigor, which the Eagle retains to a great age. Matt. 24 : 28, Wheresoever the carcase is, there will the Eagles be gathered together. This relates to the time, when Jerusalem should be encompassed with the Roman armies, which bore the figure of an Eagle for their standards.

> The Eagle's eye, though small, is bright,
> And strong and piercing is his sight;
> Be thus, dear youth, your mental view
> To look each worthy object through.

9*

'Tis gravely said the Eagle's ear
Is quick each passing sound to hear;
When worthy truths are urg'd on you,
Be quick, my friends, in hearing too.

For courage bold the Eagle fam'd,
The king of birds is rightly nam'd;
We too need courage, when the foes
Of God and man our course oppose.

When the swift Eagle seeks the sky,
His flight is urg'd sublimely high;
So when we turn our thoughts above,
Sublimely high should rise our love.

FERRET.
[Figure from Bewick.]
—

THE name occurs but once in the Bible. In Hebrew, it is (אֲנָקָה) Anâkkâh; Buxtorf calls it *Attelabus*, a kind of locust without wings. The Septuagint has Mūgālē, a Shrew-mouse, or a Weasle-mouse. Jerome follows the Septuagint. The name in Hebrew signifies a loud groaning, or whining. It is variously rendered; but as the Ferret seems likely to be intended, I have given a figure of that little animal.

The Ferret is reckoned among unclean reptiles in the ceremonial law. It is said to be originally a native of Africa. From Africa it was brought into Spain to reduce the number of rabbits with which that country abounded. It has been employed in various parts of Europe, for the same purpose; but cannot well endure the cold of northern climes. The female breeds twice a year, and goes six weeks with young.

The color of the Ferret is a pale yellow, its length about fourteen inches, that of the tail five inches ; it has a sharp nose, round ears, red and fiery eyes. It has a fetid smell, and a voracious appetite. Its thirst for blood is such, that it has been known to kill children in the cradle.

The Madagascar *Weasel*, and the *Nems* of Arabia may be considered as varieties of this species.

Each living creature has its foe ;
The Ferret keeps the rabbit low ;
   'Tis wisely so ordain'd ;
Else would the number of each race
To such amount at length increase,
   It could not be sustain'd.

Still by the unerring will of heaven
To every creature, too, is given
   The means of self-defence ;
On earth, in water, and in air,
Each species still retains its share
   Of what the heavens dispense.

To rear their kind, to taste their food,
This is the brute creation's good,
   Nor is their being vain ;
While days, and months, and years, a feast
Is given to reptile, bird and beast,
   Their death's a transient pain.

FISH.

[*See Appendix, after the article Woodcock.*]

FLEA.

[Figure from the Cabinet.]

—

THIS is a well known troublesome insect. Its Hebrew name is (פַּרְעֹשׁ) Pärgnōsh, 1 Sam. 24 : 14, or
15, in some copies. After whom dost thou pursue?
After a dead dog, after a single Flea! 1 Sam. 26 : 20.
The King of Israel is come out to seek a Flea. The
Septuagint has Psŭllŏv; the Latin name is *Pulex.* This
insect when full grown is rarely ¼ of an inch in length;
it has a smooth skin of a bright chesnut color, and of
such tenacity that it is not easily broken. Its legs
are formed for leaping; and are so very elastic, that it
can spring two hundred or three hundred times the
length of its body. Its eggs are deposited in the fur of
animals, or upon blankets; after four or five days a very
small worm bursts from them, and feeds upon the oily
substance, which may adhere to the bed-clothes or to the
fur; then it spins itself a silken shroud, in which it lies a-
bout a fortnight, and then comes forth armed with those
fearful powers, by means of which it punishes the indolence of the sluttish, and often breaks the rest of the
cleanly, especially in habitations newly built, and yet
unfinished, and surrounded with woods and brush.
When the bed-room is well finished and kept clean, and

the bed-clothes frequently washed, and changed, the troublesome invader commonly retires.

When David speaking of Saul's persecution, compares himself to a Flea, he means that Saul ought to feel himself above pursuing one so unworthy of his notice, and one in himself so feeble. Should the king of Israel degrade himself so much, as to come out with an army to chase a butterfly ?

> Let your pursuits, my youthful friends,
> (Whate'er success your toil attends,)
>   Be noble in their aim.
> Then if your enterprise shall fail,
> Nor wisdom, art, nor strength avail,
>   'Twill not degrade your name.

Horse Fly.

FLY.

[The Figure of the Tsaltsalya is from Bruce, the others from nature.]

—

THE name of this insect in Hebrew is (זְבוּב) Zĕb-vôbv, Septuagint, Mŭia, Latin *Musca*. The Hebrew name is found in Isaiah 7 : 18. The Lord shall hiss for the Fly that is in the uttermost part of the rivers of Egypt. In the plural it is found in Eccles. 10 : 1. Dead Flies cause the ointment of the Apothecary to send forth a stinking savor. In Psalm 78 : 45, and 105 : 31, the Hebrew is (עָרֹב) Gnârobv; Buxtorf and Pagnin render it *a mixed multitude of insects.* The Septuagint according to Jerome rendered it koinŏmŭia, the *common Fly ;* but the common copy of the Septuagint, has Kŭnŏmŭia, the *Dog Fly.*

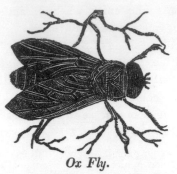

Ox Fly.

The Fly pertains to a very numerous order of Insects, distinguished from other orders by being without stings, and by having two, and only two wings, and two club formed balances behind each wing, which are of much use in directing their course, when flying. The figures given are of the common window Fly, the horse Fly, the ox Fly, and the Tsaltsalya, all of natural size. The Tsaltsàlya is also called the *Zimb*, and is thought to have been the principal among the mixed multitude of Flies, which were sent upon Egypt.

Of the flies most numerous in New England there is besides the common window Fly, a species about one fourth larger, but otherwise much resembling it, which in warm, wet seasons multiplies exceedingly, and is very troublesome. In warm mornings in Autumn the windows next the sun are sometimes darkened with them. There is another species about the same size, of a dark, glossy green, not very numerous, but quickly guided by its exquisite sense of smelling to fresh meat, fish, &c. upon which it deposites its eggs, called fly blows, in abundance. Another species, about one third the size of the window fly, is very troublesome in the dairy room, depositing its eggs in every little crevice it can find in the best of cheese. The Horse Fly, the figure of which is given, and also another species still smaller, and beautifully variegated in its colors, are, in hot weather a great vexation to horses. The Ox Fly in some seasons during part of the Summer is so numerous and blood thirsty, that both neat cattle and horses almost run mad, through the severity of their bite. The Gnat is a very minute fly, of keen and poisonous bite.

Tsaltsalya.

The Tsaltsalya is rather larger than the honey bee, has a stiff hair, or bristle about one fourth of an inch in length projecting from its upper lip, and two from its lower lip; it is covered with brown hair, or down, it inhabits the moist, rich lands about the Nile, and the southern coast of the Red Sea. As soon as its buzzing begins to be heard, at the commencement of the rainy season, the inhabitants of these parts are soon in motion with their flocks and herds for the sands of Beja, till the danger of the insect is over.

The Elephant and Rhinoceros to shield themselves from its bite, roll themselves repeatedly in mire, which, drying upon them forms a coating impenetrable to these insects.

One of the idols worshipped by the Canaanites was called *Baalzebub*, which means *lord of the Fly*; because it is supposed that this idol protected them against Flies. The name was afterwards given by the Jews to the prince of the devils.

> God has his armies at command,
>   Which, though of meanest size,
> By numbers waste a guilty land,
>   And darken all the skies.
>
> The louse, the locust, and the *Fly*,
>   Which, single, none would fear,
> Once made thy land, O Egypt sigh,
>   Among thy plagues severe.
>
> When Pharaoh's proud and stubborn heart
>   Refus'd to give the word,
> And let the chosen tribes depart,
>   And serve their rightful lord ;
>
> God spake, and lo the mingled swarms
>   Came buzzing on the wing ;
> The dreadful plague the land deforms,
>   And terrifies the king.
>
> He pleads, and God the plague removes ;
>   His heart is hard again ;
> The case of Pharaoh plainly proves
>   The power of sin in men.
>
> 'Till God the stubborn heart renew,
>   It will to sin return ;
> Its chosen way it will pursue,
>   Tho' wrath forever burn.

FOWL.

A general name for winged, feathered animals, but more usually appropriated to those of the larger kinds.

FOX.

[Figure from Bewick.]

—

The name of this animal occurs in Scripture ten
times; seven times in the old testament, three times in
the new. In Hebrew it is (שׁוּעָל) Shôgnâl; from the
same root comes a word signifying the hollow of the
hand; and a word signifying a narrow path, as among
the vines of a vineyard. The Fox may have received
his Hebrew name from the circumstance of his being
fond of holes, which are as narrow paths. The name
in Greek is Ἀλῶπēx; in Latin, *Vulpes*; in French, *Re-
nard*. There are several kinds of this animal, as 1.
The Grey-hound Fox, which is the largest, and found
on the mountains and high lands of England and Scotland. It is of this Fox that I have given the figure.
2. The black fox, the fur of which is valued very highly. 3. The cross fox, inhabiting the north parts of
Asia, Europe, and North America. Its fur is also very
valuable; and it has its name from a line of black, running down the back, which is crossed by another over
the shoulders. 4. The Arctic-fox, inhabiting countries
bordering on the frozen ocean. It feeds principally upon the lemings, or marmots, of Lapland. This fox is
of an ash color in summer, and white in winter; it is

smaller than the European fox, its nose sharp and black, its ears short, its fur of but little value.

5. The cur fox, which is the most common. Its eyes are of a lively hazle color, and very expressive; it is generally of a tawny red, mixed with ash color; of a light yellow under the belly, the fore part of the legs black, and the tail tipped with white. The fox is noted for his cunning; he is very destructive among poultry; is fond of grapes and of honey; will feed also upon mice and serpents; and in the chase he is very fleet.

A fox in England was once pursued fifty miles in one day without being taken.

Each pair of foxes generally has a hole, or burrow, either made by themselves, or taken from the badger in countries where that animal is a native. The female goes six weeks with young, and brings forth once a year, about the month of April, and from three to six at a time; for these a bed is prepared in her hole. The young may be easily tamed, and are very playful, and very mischievous. The fox will breed with the dog; and the mongrels are valued for driving cattle, and for destroying mice, rats, &c.

The fox is nearly two years in coming to his growth, and will live to about twelve or fourteen years. He sleeps much by day, and roves in quest of food by night. When he sleeps, he lies in a circular form like a dog, and sometimes lays his bushy tail over his head.

The attachment of the fox to its young is very strong. In the county of Essex, near Chelmsford, England, a female with one cub was pursued by a gentleman's hounds with the utmost speed, her regard for her cub was such, that she seized it in her mouth, and fled with this burden several miles; at length, exhausted and attacked by a mastiff in a farm yard, she dropped her cub at the farmer's feet, who saved it from the mastiff; and the mother was then so fortunate as to preserve her own life.

We first read of the fox in scripture in Judges 15 : 4, where we have the account of Samson taking three hundred, tying them two and two by their tails, and putting a fire brand between them, and letting them loose in the corn fields of the Philistines. Dr. Shaw, Bochart, and some others have expressed an opinion, that these were not strictly speaking foxes, but Jackalls, an animal much resembling the fox, and of which I have here given a figure from Bewick.

The leading reason of this opinion is, that Jackalls were numerous in those regions, and foxes not. On the other hand, as the same word is uniformly used in the original, wherever the fox is mentioned in the old testament, and is uniformly rendered in the Septuagint by the Greek word signifying *Fox;* also as foxes are known to be fond of grapes, and as we read in the Songs of Solomon, song 2 : 15, take us the foxes, the

little Foxes, that spoil the vines, for our vines have tender grapes ; there is somewhat strong reason to believe
that the Fox, and not the Jackall, is intended.   If Foxes in later times were not numerous, like the Jackalls,
they might have been far more numerous in the times
of Samson ; and it is probable that he employed many
persons in collecting these Foxes.—The idea of some
that *sheaves* are intended, instead of Foxes, is so incon-
sistent with the scope of the passage, that it hardly
needs a serious refutation.

In Nehemiah 4 : 3, or 3 : 35, as in the Hebrew bible, we find Tobiah, the Jews' enemy, saying in a way
of scorn of the wall of Jerusalem, If a Fox go up, he
shall even break down their stone wall.   In the issue,
however, this despised wall proved too strong for the
enemies of God's people.   Many at the present day
look upon the efforts of christians to reform the world
with as much contempt, as Tobiah did upon the wall
of Jerusalem ; but these efforts will so prevail at length,
that they will either renounce their enmity against
Christianity, or will be greatly vexed, and mortified.

In Psalm 63 : 10, David says of his enemies, they
shall fall by the sword, they shall be a portion for
Foxes.   This may be considered as prophetic of the
final destruction of the enemies of the church of God.
They will fall by the sword in such numbers, and in
such a friendless condition, that they will remain unburied upon the ground, to be food for the beasts of the
field, and the fowls of the air.   To be the confirmed
enemies of God must be exceedingly dreadful.

When we read in the Song of Solomon, Take us the
Foxes, the little Foxes, that spoil the vines, for our
vines have tender grapes ; the spiritual idea seems to
be this : That the teachers of God's people should be

discreet, industrious, and persevering to guard them against the plausible errors, which subtle deceivers will endeavor to instil into their minds, which, not timely checked, will endanger all the fair promise of holy fruit in the rising generation.

When in Lamen. 5 : 18, we read of Foxes walking upon Mount Zion, it gives us a lively picture of its desolation. In the place where the city was, the land grew up with wild plants, and formed such a retreat, as was the delight of Foxes, which fed upon the vermin among the ruins. In Ezekiel 13 : 4, the prophets of Israel are compared to Foxes. This intimates that they were selfish and artful. Their object was to enrich themselves with the spoils of the people, and in this they manifested much cunning.

In Luke 13 : 32, Christ calls Herod a Fox. This he does, no doubt, from a knowledge of his crafty policy to serve his own private interest, while professedly maintaining the cause of the Jews. Many rulers of modern times, could their hearts be seen, might without doubt be fitly called Foxes.

When in Matt. 8 : 20, and in Luke 9 : 58, Christ says, Foxes have holes, and birds of the air have nests ; but the Son of man hath not where to lay his head ; he gives us a striking intimation of the poverty and suffering to which he condescended to subject himself for our salvation ; and at the same time admonishes those, who think of being his followers, to count well the cost in the first place ; and to expect that in this world they shall have trials, and sustain many evils for his sake ; that, being thus prepared, they may not abandon the cause, after having espoused it.

10*

Artful and cunning, full of guile
   The treacherous Fox is found ;
So many a statesman with a smile
May hide that policy awhile
   Which spreads a blast around.

To feed himself, and shun the snare,
   Which his own life exposes,
This is the subtle Fox's care ;
With this may many a priest compare,
   As well his life discloses.

But there are priests and statesmen too,
   As cunning Foxes, wise,
Whose aim is friendly, just and true,
In all they say, in all they do ;
   And such the world should prize.

To be like these may youth aspire,
   For this their minds well storing ;
At heaven's high altar's holy fire
May they to warm their hearts desire,
   Still heavenly aid imploring.

The birds have nests, the Foxes holes
   To shelter and to rest them ;
But he, who came to save our souls,
What vast affliction o'er him rolls,
   What furious storms opprest him.

His love-invincible prepares
   For all who trust and fear him,
A place of rest from all their cares,
Where subtle demons with their snares
   Can ne'er be lurking near them.

FROG.

[Figure of the speckled Frog, from Mavor.]

—

The name of this animal is found in Scripture four-teen times; in Exodus 8, eleven times; in the Psalms twice; in Rev. once; and in each case in the transla-tion it is in the plural number; in the original it is once in the singular number. In Hebrew it is (צְפַרְדֵּעַ) Tsĕfărdăägn; some derive the name from two Hebrew words, which together may signify *The knowledge of the morning;* but Pagnin thinks this derivation more curi-ous than solid; and supposes the word to be Egyptian. The name in Greek, is Batrakhos, which may signify, to utter a rough sound. The name in Latin, is *Rana;* in French, *Grenouille.*

The Frog is a small four-footed animal, which nat-urally sits in a squat posture upon the folded hind legs, supporting its body about half erect by its fore legs. It has a lively eye, rather pleasant than fierce. It is of different species and different colors.—Those I shall notice are, 1, The small, light brown Frog; this is about three inches in length. 2. The speckled, yel-low-sided Frog, four or five inches in length. These two kinds are generally found in the Summer season in long grass in moist places; they leap with great agility, and when first started, they spurt from behind them a *jet* of water. The design of this is probably to assist them in escaping from the snake, when about to seize them.

[Figure from Life.]

3. The Common Frog. This is somewhat larger than the last mentioned; on the back it is of a muddy green color; about the head and sides of a brighter green, spotted with small black specks. This kind is very frequently found on the margin of fresh ponds, pools, and small collections of water, especially where the bottom is muddy. They often sport themselves in the water, as well as at the brink of it. This kind feeds on common flies, butterflies, &c. which come to the water's edge to drink. They move towards the little insect with the utmost caution, till within due distance, then give a sudden leap, and seize it in an instant. I have frequently amused myself in seeing them in this

manner take their prey. 4. There is another species of Frogs from five to seven inches in length, which is most commonly found on the margins of fresh ponds, and is called the Bull Frog. Its hoarse croaking in the evening is almost terrifying, and may be heard at the distance of more than a mile.

The Frog usually progresses by leaping, to which motion its form is peculiarly adapted. They are excellent swimmers. They are a part of the food of the raven, also of the pickerel and the serpent. When pursued they endeavor to conceal themselves by stirring up the mud at the bottom of the water into which they leap.

In France and some other countries, the loins and hind legs of frogs are eaten by the peasants, and esteemed agreeable and wholesome food. When the mild weather approaches in the Spring, they, and especially the toads, make the pools and marshy places resound in the evening, with their various notes, some of which are very shrill. This music is disagreeable to some, but cheering and pleasant to others. Early in the Spring they deposite their spawn, which consists of a succession of black eggs in a string of slime somewhat resembling a string of glass beads. The young are of an oval shape, with a slender tail, which assists them in swimming, but they are without legs till towards the latter part of Summer, when their legs appear, and their tails are soon after dismissed.

They are a harmless reptile, if reptiles we may call them ; and they have been known to remove in an army from one pond to another.

Frogs were one of the ten plagues sent upon Egypt, to let Pharaoh and his people know that there was a God in heaven superior to all his idols ; and a God able to avenge himself upon his enemies by armies of creatures, in themselves most despicable.

After Moses and Aaron at the command of God had brought forth armies of Frogs upon the land of Egypt, we read in Exodus 8 : 7, that the Magicians did so with their enchantments, and brought up Frogs upon the land of Egypt.   Commentators differ in their ideas how these Frogs were produced.   To me it seems probable that these magicians had communion with evil spirits, and that these evil spirits at the desire of the Magicians, drove up those Frogs from the river, which came in seeming obedience to their enchantments.   This is ascribing no more to wicked spirits, than what they did, when they impelled the swine into the lake of Tiberias. Pharaoh wished for some pretext to excuse himself from obeying the commandment of God, and God suffered him in this to have his wish, and suffered Frogs to be produced in such a manner as to blind his eyes and harden his heart.   It is dangerous to wish for an excuse to neglect duty.

When in Rev. 16 : 13, we read of three unclean spirits, like Frogs, coming out of the mouth of the beast, of the dragon, and of the false prophet, it is probable that we are to understand false, impure, mischievous principles, emanating from the devil, and from the secular and the ecclesiastical power of Rome, in its antichristian state, and instilled into the minds of multitudes, to stir them up against the friends of God.

> The Frogs, when at peace by the pool or the lake,
>   Are harmless, and social, and cheer the dull night
> With croaking, and peeping, and sounds which they make,
>   To express their keen sense of delight.
>
> But once, when commanded to stray from their home,
>   The scourge of proud Egypt's inflexible lord,
> In armies by thousands and millions they come,
>   And invade both his bed and his board.

How cold in his bosom by night they must feel;
 On his table how filthy, disgusting and vile !
His heart seem'd relenting, tho' harden'd like steel,
 And his prayer gain'd him respite awhile.

He returned to his folly, his heart froze again ;
 He refus'd to let Israel retire from his land,
'Till the judgments of God, to the number of ten,
 Brought the proud, cruel monarch at length to a stand.

The Frogs are an emblem of spirits unclean,
 Who fill with dark poison the bosoms of kings ;
The fruit of delusion, how awful it seems,
 When to fight the last battle its armies it brings.

On the mounts of Megiddo the hosts of the slain
 Will be food for young eagles and wild beasts of prey,
Then soon will commence the Messiah's wide reign,
 And earth will be blest with a long happy day.

GIER EAGLE.

[Figure from Bruce.]

THE name is found twice in the Bible ; 1. In Lev.
11 : 18. 2. In Deut. 14 : 17. The name in Hebrew
is (רָחָם or רָחָמָה) Râhrhâm, or Râhrhâmâh. Buxtorf has *Merops* and *Pica ;* Bee-eater, and Magpie.
Pagnin has, *Porphirio, Cygnus, Pelecanus, Pica ;* Plover,
Swan, Pelican, Magpie. Junius and Tremellius have
Merops, Bee-eater. But after consulting Buxtorf, Pagnin, and the Septuagint, we shall find ourselves wholly

at a loss to decide from them what bird is here intended.

I think it in measure probable that the Gier-Eagle here mentioned is a kind of *Vulture*, of small size but little larger than the *Rook*, or *Crow*. It is found in some places in the south of Syria, and in Barbary, but most frequently in Egypt, and about Cairo, and called by Europeans, *Poule de Pharaone*, Pharaoh's Hen. It is remarkable for parental affection. Bruce calls it *Rachamah*, and the description he gives of it is in substance as follows : the point of the beak is very sharp and strong ; it is black for about three fourths of an inch from the point, then covered with a yellow, fleshy membrane, which clothes also the fore part of the head and thoat ; this membrane is wrinkled, and has a few hairs on it ; the nostrils are large and open, and it has very large ears covered by no feathers. The body is wholly white from the yellow membrane to the tail. The large wing feathers, six in number, are black ; the smaller three, iron grey, lighter towards the middle, and partly covered by three others of the same color, but still smaller. The thighs are covered with down-like feathers ; the legs are a dirty white, inclining to flesh color. It has three toes forward, and one behind, with black claws. It generally goes single, and sits and walks on the ground. It delights in the most putrid carrion. It is one of the birds reckoned in the ceremonial law unclean.

For parental affection the Rachamah's fam'd,
And the parent, who lacks it, deserves to be blam'd.
But few of the birds, or the beasts can be found,
That do not with love to their offspring abound.

'Tis a pity that man, who with power of reflection,
And reason is furnish'd, should want this affection.
When justice shall call him, and urge its strict claim,
The conduct of brutes will condemn him to shame.

Would you, my dear readers, be tender and kind?
If e'er to be parents and masters designed,
To masters and parents be loving and true,
And think of your Maker's rich favors to you.

GLEDE.

I find it so difficult to determine of what species the bird so called is, that I have given no figure of it. The name is found but once in Scripture, and that in Deut. 14 : 13. The name in Hebrew is (רָאָה) Râáh, from a root signifying *to see;* meaning probably some quick sighted bird. The Septuagint has *Vulture;* Junius and Tremellius, *Cornix*, a Crow; French bible, *Vautour*, Vulture; Buxtorf has *Cornix*. Pagnin speaks of it as a bird of the vulture kind, white, and less than the common Vulture. Bochart supposes it to be a sharp-sighted bird called Ox-eye. Others have other conjectures. The greater probability seems to be, that it was a small white Vulture. It was one of the birds unclean to the Israelites.

While the meaning of names of some beasts and some birds
    Found in Scripture is doubtful and hard to be trac'd,
We have cause to rejoice that so plain are the words
    In which the great truths of salvation are plac'd.

The former allow us in some speculation;
    The latter demand our implicit belief;
Our hope here may anchor without hesitation;
    From fears and from doubtings we here find relief.

GNAT.—[*See Fly.*]

GOAT.

[Figure of the He-Goat from Bewick, that of the She-Goat from Life.]

—

This animal in the ceremonial law was reckoned in the class of clean beasts. It is frequently mentioned in the bible. Its name is first found in the singular number in Levit. 3 : 12. It is there in Hebrew (עֵז) gnär. The name is found again in Levit. 4 : 24, it is there in Hebrew (שָׂעִיר) Sâgnêr, signifying a *He-Goat*, so called from its long, rough hair. The name in Greek is Aix, and also Khĩmarŏs. The Scape-Goat is called in Hebrew (עֲזָאזֵל) Gnăzâzāl ; which from the derivation may signify, *a wandering Goat.*

She Goat.

The Goat is an animal found either in the wild, or domestic state, in most parts of the world. In some parts it is a very useful animal, yielding milk, meat, and clothing. It is playful and capricious; it delights in mountainous regions, and springs fearlessly from cliff to cliff with surprising dexterity. It feeds on mountain herbs, leaves, buds, and the bark of trees. In gardens it is mischievous. The flesh of the Goat is wholesome food, that of the kid a dainty. The female goes with young five months, and generally brings forth two at a birth. Her milk is sweet, nourishing, and in measure medicinal, and is much used in Wales, and in some other places, with good effect, by consumptive people. The Goat would be much more generally prized, than it is, were it not that the sheep in most regions is still more useful, and has superseded the use of the Goat.

In Lev. 16 : we read of two Goats being brought forward for the sin-offering; one was to be sacrificed, to be a type of the death of Christ to atone for sin; over the head of the other, called the Gnăzâzāl, or wandering Goat, the sins of the people were to be confessed, and the Goat then sent away into the wilderness, to show that through the sacrifice of Christ the sins of believers will be removed entirely from them.

In Daniel 8 : 21, we read, The rough Goat is the king of Grecia, (kingdom of Javan,) and the great horn between his eyes is the first king.   Here the name for Goat in the Hebrew, is (צָפִיר) Tsâfĕr, derived from a word which signifies, *to fly away*, or to be early in the morning.   The name with the adjective signifies a *hairy He Goat;* and it well represents the rapid and terrifying conquests of Alexander, the first king of Greece. The wonderful precision with which the three great monarchies, the Medo-Persian, the Grecian, and the Roman, are predicted in the book of Daniel, may well put to the blush that infidel, who is disposed to reject the inspiration of the scriptures.   Men may exclaim against the credulity of christians, and boast of their own skepticism, and of the strength of their minds; but it must be a stretch of credulity far beyond what christians are chargeable with, to believe that uninspired men could guess so accurately of the fate of nations and kingdoms, for centuries to come, as the prophets must have done, if they were not inspired.

In Matt. 25 : Christ compares the wicked to Goats, while the righteous are compared to sheep; the comparison is judicious; for Goats in their habits are vicious and lascivious; but sheep on the other hand are so mild and patient, that they are accounted the emblem of innocence.

The Goat was once offer'd for sin,
  A type of a Saviour to come,
Whose blood should our consciences clean,
  And prepare for a heavenly home.

O'er the head of a Goat were confess'd
  The transgressions of God's chosen sons ;
The Goat then-alive was releas'd,
  And far through the desert he runs.

So Christ has the sinner assum'd,
  And our sins on himself he has borne ;
By the Spirit of grace, then, illum'd,
  To the Lord in true faith may we turn.

But if we reject such a friend
  As Messiah has made himself known,
Like vile Goats we ourselves in the end
  Must bear our transgressions alone.

How great is Immanuel's day,
  When his friends from his foes he will sever,
And send unbelievers away
  To dwell in fierce torments forever !

WILD GOAT, OR IBEX.
[Figure from Bewick.]
—

JOB 39 : 1—Knowest thou the time when the wild
Goats of the rock bring forth ? The Hebrew word for
Wild Goat, in this place, is(יָעֵלָה) Yăgnlâh, proba-
11*

bly from Gnâlâh, *to ascend*, because these Goats are fond of climbing the highest precipices.

These Goats are natives of the Pyrenees, the Alps, the Carpathian mountains, and many districts of Asia. Their agility in bounding from rock to rock is surprising ; the hunting of them is difficult. They are expert in eluding the chase of men, dogs, and beasts of prey ; and when closely pursued, will throw themselves down steep precipices, and by falling on their horns escape unhurt ; on this account, though they have many enemies often making war upon them, they continue to be very numerous. The general color of the Ibex is brown, mingled with a little grey ; its beard is black, and it has a black stripe running the length of its back ; its belly and thighs are light colored, like the common deer. The horns of the Ibex are from two to three feet in length, falling backwards in a curve towards the rump, and are almost all their length surrounded with prominent rings.

We may close this article with a brief notice of the Goat of Syria, and of the Goat of Angora ; the Goat of Syria is reckoned by some to be a species of the Goat of Angora ; it is somewhat larger than the common Goat ; it has long, silky hair, of a reddish, or Fox-color; it is distinguishable by its long, pendulous ears, which reach nearly to the ground, and are sometimes troublesome to it in feeding, so that their keepers cut off one of them. Their horns are short and black. They are driven in herds through the streets of Aleppo, for the purpose of supplying the inhabitants with milk.

The Goat of Angora is clothed with long, white, glossy hair. The stuffs manufactured of this hair afford the inhabitants a profitable trade, and are known by the name of Camblet.

GRASSHOPPER.
[Figure from Nature.]

—

THE Grasshopper is a very common, well known insect. The name is found in Levit. 11 : 22, Eccl. 12 : 5, and Isaiah 40 : 22, where in Hebrew, it is (חָגָב) Hrhâgâbv, rendered *Cicada* by Buxtorf and by Junius and Tremellius, which may signify either Grasshopper, or Locust. The Septuagint renders it ākrĭs, Locust. In Num. 13 : 33, the Hebrew is the same. In Judges 6 : 5, and 7 : 12, it is (אַרְבֶּה) ărbāh, where Buxtorf and Junius and Tremellius have *Locusta*, the Locust. So in Job 39 : 20, and Jer. 46 : 23. In Amos 7 : 1, the Hebrew is (גֹּבַי) gōbväi, Locustæ, for (גֹּבִים) gobvēm. Nahum 3 : 17, (גֹּבָי גּוֹב כְּגוֹב) Kĕgōbv gōbväi, as the Locust of Locusts. Here Junius and Tremellius have *Prasocuris*, a green worm, preying upon leeks.

The insect generally known by the name of Grasshopper, is of the Locust kind, and is of several species. That most common in New England, when full grown is one inch and three-fourths in length; its head has some resemblance to that of a sheep without the ears; from the front of it proceed two feelers about half an inch in length ; its whole body is covered with a kind of crust, or shell, like a coat of mail, but not so hard as that of the common bug, or beetle ; its wings are about an inch in length, covered with a thin, semi-transparent crust. Its abdomen, or part of the body below the waist, consists of six or seven successive rings, and is terminated with a sort of double spade ; it has six legs ; the two hindmost when extended are about an inch and a half long, admirably fitted for leaping to a great distance, even without the help of its wings ; when its wings are used the distance is increased ; and before a strong wind it will sometimes proceed several miles at one flight. Its general color is green, its breast pea-green, its back of a muddy green approaching to black ; its hind legs below the middle joints are nearly red. Its mouth is furnished with sharp nippers, with which it preys upon almost all kinds of grass and green herbs. It is said to be furnished with two holes under the wings, through which, by emitting wind it makes its chirping sound.   When the Grasshopper first appears in Spring, which is sometimes earlier, and sometimes later, according to the state of the weather, it is about the size of a common flea, and of a whitish color; as it increases in size, it becomes of a rusty brown, and at length green. During the progress of its growth it bursts its shell, like some other insects, and comes forth in its most perfect shape.   When caught, it quickly besmears the fingers with a substance resembling molasses.   In the course of Autumn the female with the little spades at the end of her body forms small holes in the ground, in which she deposites her eggs ; these she cements together with that red, glutinous matter, which she emits from her mouth, and leaves them for the warmth of Spring to hatch them.

These insects are sometimes so numerous in New England, that they almost produce a famine for the flocks and herds, and do much injury to grain and garden sauce. In some Springs, when the young brood has come forth in multitudes innumerable, a cold, and an abundant rain succeeds, of some days' continuance, and destroys most of them. This is to be accounted a merciful providence. When they are numerous, they may be seen just at night, in the cold days of Autumn, *camping* upon the sunny side of fences in great multitudes; when it is warm in the morning they *flee away.*

There is another kind of Grasshopper, not so common, of an iron grey color, in their general appearance, with longer wings than those of the common grasshopper, and whose wings when expanded are like a miniature yellow fan, with a black stripe near its border; and another kind much resembling these in appearance, which make a snapping with their wings, when they fly. Of these two kinds there are but few, and they are peculiar for sporting along before a person, when walking in the street, and the former of the two kinds for making a shuffling noise with their wings a few feet from the ground. It seems as if their Maker intended by these their little arts to call the notice of man to the skill displayed in their formation.

> When the earth in the spring season feels
>   The beam, which its bare bosom warms,
> The Grasshoppers burst from their shells,
>   And cover the ground with their swarms.
>
> Sometimes they are spar'd, and they prove
>   A scourge for the sins of the land;
> Sometimes does their Maker remove
>   The scourge with his merciful hand.
>
> Sometimes in such swarms they abound
>   They strip the green fields of their bloom;
> The earth seems in mourning around,
>   And its face has the features of gloom.

When age and infirmities meet
  To swell a man's burden of care,
A Grasshopper adds to the weight,
  And makes it still harder to bear.

But O, the blest season is near,
  When sin shall no longer prevail;
No grasshoppers then shall we fear,
  To cause the fair harvest to fail.

HARE.

[Figure from Bewick.]

THE name is found in Levit. 11 : 6, and in Deut. 14 : 7, in each place it is in Hebrew (אַרְנֶבֶת) ärnĕbvĕth; the derivation is uncertain; some however, think it is from ârăbv, to *ensnare*, because the Hare is often taken with snares.   Pagnin and Buxtorf agree in rendering it *Lepus*, the *Hare*.   The Septuagint has in one place *Khoirogrullios*, the *grunting Hog*; in the other place dāsūpous, the *Hairy foot*, meaning probably the Hare. Junius and Tremellius have *Lepus*, the Hare.

This animal is found in the list of those forbidden in the ceremonial law.   It is feeble and very timid; somewhat larger than the Rabbit, rather smaller than the domestic cat.   In Summer it is of a reddish brown; in Winter, in cold climates it becomes white, which is evidence of a kind care of providence over the creatures, for their security; the hare on this account is less easily distinguished from the snow.   It has long ears, moveable in various directions, that it may hear the slightest sound of approaching danger. It has prominent eyes, that it may readily see on all sides its pursuers. Its hind legs are quite long in proportion to its size, and furnished with strong muscles, enabling it to leap with great velocity, and giving it a peculiar advantage for ascending rising ground. Its tail is but an inch or two in length; its feet are covered with soft hair, and the hind ones are long and broad, supporting it, like snow-shoes, on the soft snow. It is generally lean, but its flesh is pleasant, and it is pursued by men, dogs, foxes, and birds of prey; the cat and the weasle also lie in ambush for it, so if it were not for its prolificness, and the several ways provided for its safety, the race would soon become extinct. The female goes thirty days with young; they breed three or four times in a year, and bring forth three or four at a litter. Their fur is used in the hatter's business. They are found in almost all countries from the equator to the poles. The Hare when started sometimes eludes its pursuers by its circular and mazy course; sometimes by hiding in a thick bush or hedge, sometimes by leaping into the water, and swimming to a bunch of rushes, sometimes by creeping into a hollow tree. In the day time they sleep in their coverts, by night they ramble for their food. They may be tamed, but do not form a strong attachment; and are disposed to return to natural wildness, whenever they can gain their liberty. Occasionally to take a Hare for food is innocent : to hunt them in mere sport, as many have done, is a species of barbarity, which I desire my dear readers ever to avoid.

As the poor, timid Hare, when pursu'd in the chase,
  Flies fleetly, and doubles her course,
So we, when the tempter our souls would disgrace,
  May succeed more by wisdom, than force.

As the Hare is all eye, and all ear to perceive
  What of danger is lurking around;
So we, when our foes by their arts would deceive,
  Should both prayerful and watchful be found.

When we see how our Maker provides for the weak,
  And makes feeble creatures his care,
To him for protection we daily should seek,
  Nor doubt but his favor to share.

HART.
[Figure from Bewick.]

The name *Hart*, is found eight or nine times in the
bible. We find it in Deut. 12 : 15, where the Hebrew

is (אַיָל) ăyyâl; as if it were a wild ram, the Hebrew for ram being, (אַיִל) ăyĭl, and both from a root, or primitive word, signifying strength, fortitude, &c. In all the other passages the Hebrew is the same. The Septuagint has ĕlāfŏs, which signifies a *Hart* also, and is derived from two words which signify to draw out serpents.

The Hart is otherwise called the Stag, and is the male of the Red Deer; the female is called the Hind.

The Stag is of a reddish brown color, with a dark stripe down the back of the neck; he is of an elegant form, fitted to bound very lightly through the forests.

His horns the first year are but a knob, covered with a sort of downy skin, like velvet. The second year the horns are straight and single; the third year they have each two branches, called antlers; the fourth year three, and so on, till they have six or seven on each horn; the number afterwards is uncertain. They shed their horns every year about the last of February, soon after which the new horn begins to appear, which grows up rapidly, and is soft, and covered with a hairy skin, with blood vessels to afford nourishment to the horn. After the horns are come to their growth, they soon begin to harden, when the skin falls off, leaving furrows in the horns, where the blood vessels were. Their horns come to their hardness and beauty about the last of July; then they quit the thickets of their retirement, and range the forests with great ardor in quest of the females; it is then dangerous to meet with them; and if two stags meet, their contest is violent, and continues till one or the other is vanquished, and quits the field, leaving the other in possession of the female.

The eye of the Stag is very beautiful and sparkling,

12

his hearing quick, his sense of smelling acute. At the least noise he raises his head, erects his ears, and listens with great attention, and if he perceives an enemy approaching, he flies off as fleetly as the wind. He is pleased with the sound of the shepherd's pipe, and is sometimes allured by it to his destruction. His food consists of leaves, grass, and the twigs of trees. The term of his life is estimated at from thirty five to forty years. Though naturally timid, when he cannot retreat he will make a bold defence. It is said that William, the Duke of Cumberland, once shut up a stag and a tiger in the same inclosure, when the Stag made such a bold resistance, that the Tiger was constrained to retire.

The female of the Red Deer is called the Hind ; she goes with young eight months and a few days ; and usually brings forth but one at a time, which is called a Fawn. She hides her young with the greatest art and caution, to preserve them from beasts of prey, and from the Stag himself, who is a dangerous enemy to them, and would destroy them, if he should find them.   The Hebrew for the Hind in Scripture is uniformly (אַיָּלָה) ăyyâlâh, the feminine of ăyyâl.

The Hart, and of course the Hind, is reckoned in the ceremonial law among the clean beasts.

In Psalm 42 : 1. David says, As the Hart panteth after the water brooks, so panteth my soul after thee, O God. When two Harts have had a furious contest with each other, their thirst for water is extreme, and without doubt it is very great, when they have become heated in the chase, and yet have not time to stop and quench their thirst. David was well acquainted with circumstances of this nature, and draws from them a strong figure to express his exceeding great desire to have intimate communion with God. O, if young persons in general were as earnest for communion with God, as David was, it would presage much good to the rising generation.

In Isaiah 35 : 6, God by the prophet says, Then shall the lame man leap as a Hart, and the tongue of the dumb shall sing. This probably has reference to the time of the propagation of the gospel, when many that were literally lame were healed, and leaped for joy at the mercy received, and many that were literally dumb, had their speech restored, and uttered unfeigned praise to God; when many also were healed of their spiritual lameness, and became active in the service of God; and when many, who before had no heart to praise him, were constrained to sing aloud of his salvation.

In Psalm 18 : 33, David says of God that he made his feet like Hind's feet, and set him upon his high places; this may probably allude to the fleetness of the Hind in escaping from danger, and to the ease with which she ascends high mountains. David when pursued by Saul, was constrained to flee from place to place, like the hunted Hind, but he always escaped him; and at length was established on mount Zion, when Saul, and nearly all his house were cut off. This should encourage all, when in the faithful discharge of duty, to maintain a steady confidence in God, though envied and persecuted by all those around them.

In Proverbs 5 : 19, Solomon exhorts the husband to let his consort be to him as the loving Hind and the pleasant Roe. It appears from this that a strong attachment had been observed to subsist between the Hart and the Hind; and from this example he would enforce the duty and advantage of strong, steady mutual attachment between husband and wife. Such an attachment, if general, would prevent a world of evil.

> With elegance of form and branching head,
> 　With feet for flight, with mild yet sparkling eye,
> The Stag appears; no animal of dread,
> 　But quick to notice, and from danger fly.
>
> Yet to retain his chosen, favorite Hind
> 　He holds fierce contest, and is nobly brave;
> And e'en the Tiger, with the Hart confin'd,
> 　Has been compelled the battle ground to leave.
>
> Press'd in the chase the panting Hart desires
> 　With burning thirst to find the cooling stream;
> So pants for God the saint, and so aspires
> 　The holy soul to quench its thirst in him.
>
> When Christ appear'd, he made the lame to leap,
> 　The dumb spake plainly, and his praises sung;
> The quicken'd feet with ease ascend the steep
> 　Where duty calls, and vocal is the tongue.
>
> Strong is the affection 'twixt the Hart and Hind;
> 　Strong be the love where plighted hands are given,
> Fair friendship's chain their wedded souls should bind
> 　In one on earth, nor yet be loos'd in heaven.

Dove Hawk.

HAWK.

ONE figure is from nature; the other called Ger-Falcon, is from the Cabinet. The name is found in the

Bible in Levit. 11 : 16, and Deut. 14 : 15, also in Job
39 : 26; in each place the Hebrew is (נֵץ) Nāts, perhaps from Nătsâh, to *fly ;* because the Hawk is a bird
of swift and easy flight, and often in a spiral course ascends very high in air.   The Septuagint has Hiĕräx,
the Latin is *Accipiter.*   It is reckoned among the unclean birds.   It is of various species.   The figure given
from nature is of a hawk in size between the Hen-
Hawk, and the Pigeon-Hawk; I have ventured to call
it the *Dove-Hawk.*   Its length was thirteen inches, its
breadth, when the wings were closed, three and a half
inches.   The crown of its head was flat, its breast nearly ash color, spotted with reddish brown ; its back of a
dark iron grey, spotted with dark brown, approaching
black.   Down its wings were two rows of feathers of
greyish brown, tipt with white.   The quill feathers
dark grey, barred with dark brown ; the tail of a light
reddish grey, crossed with four bars of dark brown, the
thighs covered to a little below the knee with long,
downy feathers ; the legs yellow, the beak black.

Gerfalcon. J.F.

12*

The figure from the Cabinet represents a species of Hawk, called the Ger-Falcon; hawks being all of the Falcon tribe, they are called Falcons from the Latin *falx*, a *hook* or sickle; because of their hooked beaks, and long, sickled-shaped talons, or claws. The Ger-Falcon is the largest of the kind, and but little inferior to the eagle. It has a quite flat head; some have a yellow beak, and white plumage, marked with dusky lines, bars and spots; some are nearly white; some are ash color, with black spots much in the shape of a heart, and their beak of a dark blue. They are very bold and fierce; the female is somewhat larger than the male. In ancient times this Falcon with some others of the tribe, was trained to catch hares, partridges, and quails; the training of them required much time and patience; but almost every man of note had his Falcon, with a small silver plate fastened to his leg, with the owner's name inscribed. In the time of Edward III. it was felony to kill a Hawk, and to steal their eggs was punished with imprisonment for a year. But customs change with times and the improvements in the arts. Falconry is now generally gone into disuse; I shall not therefore attempt to describe the manner of training these birds for service.

In Job 39 : 26, we read, Doth the Hawk fly by thy wisdom, and stretch her wing towards the south? The design of the blessed God in this appeal was to excite reflection in the mind of Job upon that folly in which he had presumed to find fault with any of the divine dispensations. God would lead him by looking at the works of creation, and at the wonderful form and instincts of various animals, to perceive that the wisdom of his Maker must infinitely surpass his wisdom; and by means of perceiving this he would have him believe and acknowledge that God must be wise and good in those things which in themselves might seem dark, mysterious and unpleasant. From this record all who read it should learn to confide with full submission in the wisdom and benevolence of all the divine operations.

Who gives the Hawk his length of wing for flight?
Who gives his eye its strength for piercing sight?
Who gives him skill in spiral course to rise
On daring pinions to the nether skies?
Who bids him seek, when wintry days draw near,
Those southern climes, where milder breezes cheer :
Who gives him courage to invade his prey,
And strength to bear the victim, seiz'd, away?
Have we, mere creatures, as ourselves we are;
We, whose dull vision cannot reach afar?
We, whose most skilful hands can only ape
Our Maker's works by giving outward shape
To lifeless matter, which is lifeless still,
And must be so, in spite of all our skill?
No! Let us blush, and feel, and frankly own
In power and skill Jehovah reigns alone.
In his broad hand the whole creation lies;
No drop nor dust escapes his piercing eyes;
As seen in heaven, by angels understood,
His plan is wisdom, his design is good;
And all his works will in some future day
His grace and glory to his saints display.

HERON.
[Figure from Mavor.]

—

THE name is found in the list of unclean birds, in
Lev. 11 : 19, and in Deut. 14 : 18. In Hebrew it is
(אֲנָפָה) ănâfáh ; for this Buxtorf has *ardea*, signifying
the *Heron*. Junius and Tremellius have the same. The
Septuagint has Khărădriŏs, a bird which makes its
abode in the neighborhood of ditches, and other excava-
ted places; which may answer to the Heron. Pagnin
names eight or ten different translations, which various
interpreters have given to the word. *Heron* seems as
likely to be the right name as any. The original is
from the same root, as the word which signifies *face*, or
countenance ; and the long beak of the Heron gives him
a formidable countenance. The species of Herons are
numerous. The common Heron of Great Britain is
three feet in length, and five feet in the spread of its
wings, and yet it weighs but little more than three lbs.
Its body is ash colored, its head and neck white, spot-

ted with black, with a crest of long, black feathers on the back part of the head ; its beak is about five inches long, and its legs very long. It is exceedingly voracious and very destructive to the tenants of brooks and fish pools. It has been known to devour fifty fish of considerable size in one day. For the purpose of holding its slippery prey the middle claw of the foot is serrated, has teeth like a saw. It is usually seen standing alone by the sides of ponds and brooks, waiting for its prey, which, when it comes near, it seizes with a quick and sure grasp. It often wades to the depth of its legs in water, and there stands, waiting the approach of those fish upon which it feeds. In early times it was among the sports of the Britons to take Herons by the help of the Falcon ; one of these birds was taken in Holland, which, by a silver plate fastened to its leg, appeared to have been taken by a Falcon forty years before. They build their nests on high cliffs, and on large, high trees, and each nest usually contains five or six large, pale green eggs.

> The Heron is form'd for his place and his prey,
>   To seize and hold safely the smooth, finny race.
> All creatures the laws of their instinct obey,
>   And their Maker's wise hand in this instinct we trace.
>
> The long, slender leg, and the long pointed beak,
>   Adapted to wading and seizing their food,
> *Design* in their Maker most sensibly speak,
>   And say in plain language, *his purpose is good.*
>
> Let us range through all nature, and carefully weigh
>   How each part is adapted to other parts near ;
> The result then perceiving, with truth we may say,
>   The marks of vast wisdom and kindness are here.

HIND.—[*See Hart.*]

HORNET.
[Figures from Nature.]

—

THE name of this insect is found three times in scripture; it is first found in Exodus 23 : 28: I will send *Hornets* before thee. Here in the translation it is plural, but in the original it is singular, and is (צִרְעָה) Tsïrgnâh, corresponding with a word signifying *leprous*. The poison of the Hornet may cause an affection upon the skin resembling some of the cases of leprosy.

The other passages in which the name is found are Deut. 7 : 20, and Joshua 24 : 12. In the first of the three passages God promises to send the Hornet before the Israelites to drive out their enemies before them. In the second Moses declares that God would do it. In the third God declares that he had done it in the case of the two kings of the Amorites.

The Septuagint has Sfēkīas, signifying *Wasps*; some kinds of which nearly resemble Hornets. Junius and Tremellius have *crabronem*, the Hornet; the French Bible has *frelons*, meaning the same.

Some have thought the *Hornet* mentioned in Scripture to be the *Tsaltsalya*, or *Zimb*, a very troublesome fly, which abounds in Egypt, in the interior of Africa, and sometimes in Palestine; but I see no sufficient reason for this supposition. Buxtorf and Jerome call it the *Hornet*; the Targum call it the *wasp*.

The Hornet is an insect of the wasp kind, and among the largest of the kind; the Hornet of New England is in length about three quarters of an inch, in breadth one quarter, exclusive of its wings. It builds its nest of the very small fibres of decayed wood, such as are started from its surface by rain. These it fastens together with some kind of glutinous matter, which resists the action of water. The parts of its nest, thus constructed, consist of a course grey paper of considerable strength.— The Hornet usually begins its nest by forming a small cord, of an inch or two in length, attached to a twig of some tree or bush; at the lower end of this it forms several cells, with their cup downwards; in each of these an egg is deposited. When the young of these come to maturity, additional cells are made, which are covered with a sort of canopy, or cap, of the same material with the cells.

When the first comb is as large as they intend, they commence a second story, underneath the first, and suspended from it by a cord; this comb is usually larger than the first, and below this there is sometimes a third and a fourth story, all of which are well covered with their grey paper; and their nests are sometimes extended to a size larger than a man's head, somewhat in the shape of an egg, with the small end downward. Near the small end is a round hole, which is their common entrance.

The general color of the Hornet is a clear, shining black; its face is chiefly white; round the extremity of its tail are three white circles, broken with several black spots. In shape it bears much resemblance to

the honey bee; still more to the yellow wasp, and is
armed with a sting, by means of which it injects a virulent poison. When disturbed in its nest, it is bold
and furious; after being provoked, they will come several rods with a swiftness much like a bullet, and will
strike a person in the face with a hard blow, piercing
it at the same instant with their sting, the pain from
which is sometimes almost intolerable.

In the time of Moses God caused these insects to be
so much enraged against the Amorites, that they fled before them, and left their land in possession of the Israelites; or they were so disconcerted by them, that they
fell an easy prey to Israel.

The Historian *Elian* mentions the expulsion of the
Pharselites, from about the mountains of *Solima*, by
wasps. Wilson informs that when *Sapores*, a king of
Persia, beseiged a Christian city, his elephants and
other beasts, being stung by Hornets, became so unruly,
that his whole army fled.

From these sketches we may learn that it is a vain
thing to think of fighting against God; when it is needful for the safety of those, who trust in him, he can, by
means of feeble insects, defeat the most powerful armies.

We should learn also both to fear and to trust the
power of God, who never wants for expedients, either
for the destruction of his enemies, or for the protection
of his friends.

> Arm'd with a sword of keenest point,
>   This bath'd in venom strong,
> The Hornet, rous'd, assails his foe,
>   Nor is the contest long.
>
> Both man and beast, the strong and weak,
>   Alike his courage tries;
> Fearless himself, he fills with fear,
>   And each opposer flies.

When Canaan's race was ripe in sin,
  And doom'd by heaven to fall,
The Hornet sent, in armies flew,
  And drove them great and small.

Let youth betimes their trust repose
  In their Creator's power;
And base defeat will shame the foes
  That would their souls devour.

HORSE.
[Figure from Bewick.]

THE name of the Horse occurs in scripture very frequently. In Hebrew it is (סוס) Sôs; in Greek, Hĭppŏs; in Latin *Equus*.

As a noble, generous, and brave animal, and one that is calculated to surprise us by his swiftness, to charm us by the gracefulness of his shape, to excite our admiration at the majesty and stateliness of his steps, to animate us by his ardor and courage, and to win our esteem by his various usefulness, the Horse is without a rival.

In war the Horse appears proud and daring; in the race he is fleet and emulous; in the chariot he is lofty;

under his rider he is diligent and careful ; at the common draught he is resolute and patient. To his constant master he is kind, docile, and obedient.

Horses were not much used by the Jews till after the days of David ; asses and mules were their principal beasts of burden. In the time of Solomon they began to multiply. That prince brought vast numbers of them from Egypt. If there be not a mistake in the transcribing, a mistake easy to be made, he had forty thousand stalls for Horses ; see 1 Kings 4 : 26. In 2 Chron. 9 : 25, the parallel place, we read four thousand stalls. If there be not a mistake, the stall in one passage may mean a stable containing ten apartments, each for one Horse, and each called a stall in the other passage. In this multiplying of Horses he transgressed the instructions given for the kings of Israel, in Deut. 17 : 16, in which God forbids them to multiply Horses, and also to multiply wives ; in both these particulars Solomon offended, and as a fruit of it he lost, in the days of his successor, the larger part of his kingdom. This should teach us that no human policy can avail us, as a substitute for strict obedience to the commands of God.

In almost all ages Horses have been used sometimes for war, sometimes for the race, and sometimes for the chase, in which occupations it is to be hoped they will not be used much longer. They have also been used, and may continue to be used with profit and pleasure, both to convey our persons from place to place, to labor in the draught, to bear burdens, and to till our lands. In return for this service we ought to use them kindly, to feed them well, and to beware of overloading them. The merciful man regardeth the life of his beast, says the scripture. The same sacred oracles assure us, in the mean time, that *a Horse is a vain thing for safety.*

Many a person through vain confidence, or foolish daring, has lost his life by a Horse.

The Horse is found in almost all countries; but the warmer climes, luxuriant with fresh feed, are most congenial to his nature. In some parts of Africa he appears in his grandeur; the most elegant, fleet, and persevering Horses are found in Arabia, and are conveyed thence to various parts of the world to improve the breed of Horses. These Arabian Horses are brown, their manes and tails short, and the hair of them black and tufted. South America abounds with wild Horses, the offspring of such as were conveyed thither by the Spaniards.

The Kalmuc Tartars are said to hunt down their wild Horses with a hawk, which fastens upon the forehead of the animal, and so torments and embarrasses him, that he soon yields to his pursuers.

In 2 Kings 23 : 11, we read that Josiah took away the Horses that the kings of Judah had given to the sun, at the entering of the house of the Lord. Some of the Jewish Rabbies inform us, that these Horses were brought every morning, and attached to chariots dedicated to the sun, of which we read in the same verse. This devotion of horses and chariots to the sun was a species of idolatry practised by Armenians and Persians, and probably was derived from them by the Jews.

We have a short appeal from God to Job, concerning the Horse, in chap. 39 : 19—25 inclusive. I will attempt a paraphrase.

Owes the brave steed his conquering strength to thee?
  His neck with thunder has thine arm array'd?
Like a poor locust wilt thou make him flee?
  He bounds, he snorts,—be thou thyself afraid.

He paws the valley, glories in his might;
  Goes forth to meet the armies in array;
He mocks at fear, nor yields to coward flight,
  Nor from the jav'lin turns his breast away.

The rattling quiver gives him no alarm;
  The glittering spear, the sounding shield he scorns;
The space before him fades as by a charm,
  When full of rage in his fleet course he burns.

The valley thunders, while he bounds it o'er,
  Nor does he deem it is the trumpet's sound;
Hah! Hah! he saith, amidst the trumpet's roar,
  And smells the battle, while it thunders round.

HORSE-LEECH.
[Figure from Nature.]

THE name of this reptile is found but once in scripture; it is in Prov. 30 : 15, The Horse-leech has two daughters, crying, give, give. The name in Hebrew is (עֲלוּקָה) Gnălôkkâh. Junius and Tremellius have *Hirudo*; Buxtorf and Pagnin have the same, and also *Sanguisuga*; both signifying Horse-leech.

Though the name of this animal is found but once in scripture, there is such a correspondence in Lexicons and translations, that I doubt not but that the Leech is intended. This reptile is said to be of four kinds; the *Horse-leech*, the *Snail-leech*, the *Broad-tailed-leech*, and the great *brown Leech*, which alone is said to be of use in extracting blood. The brown Leech is the most common in New England; it is of different lengths, from one to four inches, resembling a flat worm of many narrow, successive rings, by means of which it can lengthen and shorten itself. Its back is a dark brown, its belly in part red, sprinkled with many small black spots, less than mustard seeds. Its mouth is said to be

13*

of a triangular form, with three sharp teeth, with which it pierces the skin; over the punctures, thus made, its lips are closely placed, and it sucks out the blood with great force, and is not readily removed till it has filled itself. They bring forth their young alive. When applied for the drawing of blood, they should be taken out of water an hour or two before used; and if they do not readily adhere, the part may be rubbed with sugared milk, or blood. They are most readily found in the margin of fresh ponds.

This reptile appears to have the power of suction at the tail, as well as at the head, by means of which it can fix itself somewhat firmly to the inside of the glass vial, in which it is sometimes placed. This power of suction at either end might suggest the idea of two daughters, though it draw blood only by the mouth. But the idea which Agur probably intended to illustrate was the insatiableness of avarice, through which oppressors devour the poor and needy; their thirst for gain constantly cries, give, give; nor will they rest, till they have drawn the last drop from the veins of their victim.

Dear youth, in early life inure
   Your souls to feel for others' wo;
Mark what the suffering poor endure,
   And let the milk of kindness flow.

Scorn to deserve the oppressor's name,
   Detest that avarice, which still cries
Give, give; nor knows to blush for shame,
   Till at its feet the needy dies.

Be 't your's in ripening years to hear
   The poor man's blessing, and to share
The widow's smiles, to wipe her tears,
   And orphans' praises for a crown to wear.

Regard the stranger's and the Red-man's right,
   Nor vex the helpless in their lawful claim;
Your name in heaven will then be fair and bright,
   Blazon'd on records of immortal fame.

KID.—[*See Goat.*]

LAMB.—[*See Sheep.*]

LAPWING.
[Figure from Mavor.]

THE name of this bird is found but twice in the Bible; first in Lev. 11 : 19; next in Deut. 14 : 18. The name in Hebrew is (דוּכִיפַת) Dôkrhēfáth, which Buxtorf calls *Gallus Sylvestris*, or the Cock of the woods. Junius and Tremellius have *Attagen*, which may be rendered a *Woodcock*, or *Snipe*. The Septuagint has ĕpŏps; Pagnin has *Upupa*, rendered *Hoopoo*, *Houpoo*, *Hoopoe*, or *Lapwing;* the French Bible has Huppe; from among this variety of names and opinions, it is difficult to select any one, with confidence that it is the right. That

the Hoopoe is intended I think rather probable ; this is
a bird of passage, found in different parts from the north
of Europe to the south of Africa.   It rarely continues
long in any place, even in mild climates.   It feeds on
insects, especially such as are found in manure and filth
on the ground.   It builds its nest in hollow trees, and
in ruins, and lays six or seven eggs for a brood.   The
smell of its nest is very offensive, but it makes amends
for this, in part, by its beautiful plumage ; the breast
and belly are white; the back, wings, and tail are barred with black and white, and on its head it has a tuft
or crest, of a double row of feathers, from an inch and a
half to two inches in length, which it can erect and
spread at pleasure ; these feathers are tipt with black.
Its beak is long, slender, and a little hooked.   Its name
Hoopoe, is said to be given it on account of its note.
The Turks called it by a name signifying, *The Messen-
ger Bird ;* and the Swedes considered its appearance
ominous of war.   It is about the size of a Thrush.

> The Hoopoe charms not by the scent of its nest,
>   Nor is nice in the choice of its meat ;
> But scarce can we fail to admire its fine crest,
>   And its plumage, so gay and so neat.
>
> The Maker of all has so temper'd each part,
>   Of the world he in wisdom has made,
> That where one thing is wanting, by infinite art
>   Its loss is by others repaid.
>
> Let none, whose complexion is freckled or brown,
>   Complain that of beauty they fail ;
> Their voice may be sweet, they may teach by their frown,
>   Or by wisdom and virtue prevail.

LEOPARD.
[Figure from Bewick.]

—

THE Leopard is mentioned in Scripture eight or ten times ; the name in Hebrew is (נָמֵר) Nâmār, plural Nămarēm. We find it first in Solomon's Song, 4 : 8. *from the mountains of Leopards.* Septuagint, Pàrdalis. The Leopard is a swift, cunning, and fierce animal, much resembling the Panther, but rather less, and his skin of a livlier yellow ; he is equally voracious and cruel, and more difficult to tame. They are about four feet in length. Their yellow skin are diversified with a multitude of small black spots, in circular groups ; and when well dressed is much valued for its beauty.

Leopards abound in the interior of Africa, and in the more southern parts of Asia, from Arabia to China. They make great havoc among the herds on the plains of Lower Guinea, where the Negroes take them in pits, slightly covered with bushes. Their flesh is said to be white as veal, and well tasted.

Besides the more common Leopard, there is another species, with a small head, and short ears, called the *Hunting Leopard.* It inhabits India, where it is tamed, and trained for the chase of Antelopes, Jackalls, &c.

It is carried in a wagon, chained and blindfolded, till the game is seen; it is then let loose, and winds its way artfully, till near the animal, and then leaps upon it with several long, sudden bounds. If it fail in the first attempt, it gives up the chase for that time, and returns to its master.

From the frequent mention of the Leopard in Scripture, it is probable that they were somewhat common in Judea.

In Isaiah 11 : 6, we read, the wolf also shall dwell with the lamb, and the *Leopard* shall lie down with the kid, and the calf and the young lion, and the fatling together, and a little child shall lead them. It may be reasonably doubted whether the nature of the beasts of the field will ever be so changed, as to admit a literal fulfilment of this passage; but we have reason to believe that a period will yet be witnessed, in which the human passions will be so generally under the control of the principles of the gospel, that this passage will receive a very striking figurative accomplishment. It alludes, no doubt, to the thousand years of the prosperity of the Church of Christ, while Satan shall be restrained from deceiving the nations. In Jer. 5 : 6, in a threatning of judgments upon the Jews for their wickedness, we read, A Leopard shall watch over their cities; every one that goeth out thence, shall be torn in pieces. From this passage we may infer, that the Leopard of Judea sometimes made his attacks upon men, as well as upon the herds and flocks; and further, that destruction by wild beasts was among the evils that God sometimes inflicted upon wicked nations. In Jer. 13 : 23, we read, Can the Ethiopian change his skin, or the Leopard his spots? Then may ye also do good, that are accustomed to do evil. From this it appears that the Leopard spoken of in Scripture was a spotted animal; and the comparison very strikingly illustrates the almost unconquerable force of evil habits; to subdue them, we must almost surmount impossibilities. Let young people take warning from this, and beware how they contract evil habits. In Hab. 1: 8, the Prophet says of the horses of the Chaldeans, that they were swifter than Leopards; this intimates that the Leopard was a very fleet animal; it further teaches, that when God is about to bring judgments upon a nation, he will remove impediments, so that nothing shall hinder their approach. In Dan. 7: 6, we read of a beast, which appeared to him in a dream, like a Leopard, with four wings and four heads. This Leopard was a symbol of a kingdom, or empire; and it referred to the Grecian empire under Alexander; the swiftness of the Leopard, and the added wings represent the rapidity of his conquests; and the four heads the partition of the empire among his four captains.

In Rev. 13: 2, in the visions of John, we read of a beast like a Leopard, which rose out of the sea. This beast was a symbol of a persecuting dominion; it was first the Roman empire in its heathen state. In one of its heads it was wounded in the time of Constantine, when the empire ceased to be heathen; it was healed afterwards, when the empire became Papal; Christian in name, but Heathen in spirit.

Voracious, cruel, cunning, swift and strong,
The savage Leopard holds a name and rank
Not low among the beasts of prey.   His thirst
For blood and carnage fit him well to stand
In holy writ an emblem of a power,
Warlike and fierce, with blood and murder stain'd.
   Dark are his spots; tho' torrid suns assail,
They will not fade, nor yet to water yield,
Tho' long applied.—Such are the spots of sin,
When oft repeated.   Grace, and grace alone,
A Savior's blood applying, will remove
Their deadly stain.   Long has this world,
Blasted by sin, appear'd a field of strife,
Confusion, discord, wretchednes and blood,
Where nations, furious as the beasts of prey,
On nations rush.   But these ungrateful days
Shall soon pass by.   The happy time draws near,
When with the wolf the timid lamb shall dwell,
Fearless of danger; when the kid shall lie
Safe in the Leopard's bosom; when the calf,
The lion's whelp, and fatling shall repose
In peace together, and in harmless sport
A little child shall lead them.   Roll ye suns,
The happy period hasten.

LEVIATHAN.—[*See dragon, and also whale.*]

LION.

—

NOTICE of this animal often occurs in the Holy Scriptures. The name in Hebrew is sometimes (כְּפִיר) Kĕfēr, *a young Lion.* Judg. 14 : 5. Sometimes (אַרְיֵה) ăryāh, a Lion of adult age. Gen. 49: 9. Sometimes (שַׁחַל) Shă-hrhăl, a fierce Lion, of middle age; Job. 4: 10. Sometimes (שַׁחַץ) Shă-hrhăts, a Lion more advanced in age, than the one before named ; Job. 28 : 8. Sometimes (לָבִיא)Lâbvēh, a huge old Lion, but yet in strength. Job. 4: 11. And finally Lăyĭsh, the old Lion, becoming feeble. Isaiah 30 : 6, Septuagint, Lĕōn. The female is called the *Lionness ;* in Hebrew (לְבִיָּא) Lĕbvēyyâh.

The Lion inhabits Africa and the warmer parts of Asia. His abode is especially within the limits of the torrid zone. The largest, full grown Lions are between eight and nine feet in length, about five feet high, and their tail about four feet. The Lionness is about a fourth part less than the Lion. The Lion's head and

14

neck are covered with a long, shaggy mane, which he can erect at pleasure, and which becomes longer and thicker, as he advances in years. The rest of his body is covered with short, smooth hair of a tawny color, which may be well represented by yellow ochre, darkened with a very little lamp-black. The female is of the same color, but has no mane.

The Lion is often called the king of beasts; and, so far as great strength, undaunted courage, majesty of appearance, and dreadfulness to enemies entitles to this honor, it may be awarded him. He is not, however, a cruel animal; creatures of the feebler classes he will sometimes spare, though thrown to him to be devoured, and will defend them, and impart to them of his food. He has sometimes been known to spare men and women, when within his power. He appears to attack rather through the impulse of hunger, than through wantonness. Sir John Gager, who in the year 1546 was lord-mayor of London, when once travelling through a desert in the Turkish dominions, met a Lion, which suffered him to pass unmolested; for this escape he made provision in his will for a sermon to be preached annually on the 16th of November, in commemoration of it.

The courage and strength of the Lion is much affected by climate. In the deserts of Biledulgerid and Zahara, his strength and resolution are terrible; so that a single Lion has been known to attack a whole Caravan, and to make great destruction; on the contrary, the Lions of Mount Atlas are smaller in size, and of much less strength and boldness.

As the habitations of men approach the regions inhabited by Lions, these animals become more timid, so that they are sometimes put to flight by the shouts of women and children.

Such is the fear inspired by the Lion, that all other animals shun him, and some of them even tremble at his roaring, which in the night sounds like distant thunder. He rarely takes his prey in the open field, or in the chase, but obtains it by stratagem; to this end he lies in ambush, flat on his belly, near some foot path, or some spring, or brook to which animals resort to drink; when he thinks them sufficiently near, with one bound he leaps upon them, and secures them. If he fails to reach them, he does not pursue them; but measures his steps back to his covert, and lies in wait again.

Sparrman relates a case of a deviation of a Lion from their usual mode of endeavoring to take their prey. A Hottentot, as he was travelling, perceived that during the day he was followed by a Lion; he suspected that he was waiting for the covert of night to seize him, and cast in his mind how to escape. At length coming to a piece of broken ground, a rising part of which descended on the further side in a precipice, the thought struck him how to proceed. He halted, and as he halted, the Lion halted. He then sat down on the edge of the precipice, till dark; he then slid gently down it a little way, and putting his cloak and his hat upon his staff, raised it up in sight of the Lion, and moved it a little; the Lion, mistaking it for the man, crept near by, and giving a leap at it, was precipitated down the steep, and the Hottentot escaped.

The superior arts and devices of men have greatly diminished the number of Lions from what it anciently was; there being formerly more Lions carried from Lybia by the Romans, in one year, for their public spectacles, according to Dr. Shaw, than could be found, when he wrote, in all that country. Thus have the Indians faded away before the white men. O that it could be said, with equal innocency on the part of the white !

The Lionness goes with young about five months, and brings forth rarely more than two, or three at a litter.   These she secretes in the most unfrequented and inaccessible places ; but if they are discovered, she defends them with the most persevering and dreadful fury.   She suckles them about twelve months, and they are about five years in coming to their full growth.

Lions are sometimes taken in pits, and sometimes destroyed by placing the resemblance of a man, with a number of loaded guns pointing towards it, so that when he springs upon it, by means of cords they are let off, and he receives his death wound upon the spot. They are sometimes hunted with dogs ; twelve or sixteen falling upon him at once will soon dispatch him ; but usually three or four lose their lives in the conflict.

The Lion, taken very young, may be tamed, but is still a dangerous play-thing.   Though not hasty to resent unkind treatment, he will not always bear it.   Labat tells us of a gentleman, who kept a Lion in his chamber, and employed a servant to attend upon him. The servant frequently mixed blows with his caresses. This injudicious course continued for some time.   At length, one morning, the gentleman was awakened by an unusual noise in his chamber, and, drawing his curtains, to his surprise he saw the Lion over the dead body of the man, with his head in his mouth, which he had severed from the body.   Greatly terrified he flew from the room, and, obtaining help, secured the Lion from doing further injury.

That the Lion is a long-lived animal, is evident from the fact, that the great Lion, called *Pompey*, which died in the tower in London, in 1760, had been kept there more than seventy years. And since that time one brought from the river Gambia died there at the age of sixty-three.

The figure given in the cut was taken from the life, from one exhibited in Boston in the year 1794. He was then upwards of three feet high, and seven feet in length, and between four and five years old. He was caught, when a whelp, in the forests of Goree, in Africa.

The Lion is mentioned in scripture more than a hundred times; a few of the instances, only, will be given, and these to illustrate particular subjects.—1. The Lion is used to represent the devil. 1 Peter 5 : 8, Your adversary, the devil, as a roaring Lion, walketh about, seeking whom he may devour. The Lion is a fit emblem of the devil in respect to that cunning, which he uses to take his prey at unawares, and in the strong grasp with which he holds it when taken, and in the sure destruction of his prey, if it be not speedily taken from him. In view of this it becomes all, and especially young persons, to be exceedingly watchful, lest for want of circumspection they fall a prey to this worst of Lions. 2. The Lion is put for imaginary difficulties in the path of duty. Prov. 22 : 13, The slothful man saith, there is a Lion in the way; I shall be slain in the streets. In countries, where the Lion is in the habit of infesting the paths travelled by men, he is a formidable obstacle; but the indolent often raise up in their way imaginary Lions, where there is nothing to injure them, which are as effectual to impede their course, as real Lions would be. 3. The Lion represents a tyrannical ruler, and a persecuting government. 2 Tim. 4 : 17, I was delivered out of the mouth of the Lion. In this the apostle Paul expresses his escape at that time from the persecuting Nero, to fall into whose hands was not less to be

14*

dreaded, than to fall into the paws of a Lion.   In Rev. 13 : 3, speaking of one of the beasts, representing forms of government, which the apostle saw rising out of the sea, he says that his mouth was as the mouth of a Lion. This mouth was the dreadfully destructive power of the Roman dominion.   4. The Lion is used for enemies and evils of various kinds.   Psalm 91 : 13—Thou shalt tread upon the Lion and adder; the young Lion and the dragon shalt thou trample under feet.   In other words the godly, who are here spoken of, who put their trust in God, will at length triumph over all their foes, and surmount all the difficulties that lie in their way to final rest and happiness.   5. The Lion is put for Judah, or the tribe of Judah.   Gen. 49 : 9—Judah is a Lion's whelp; from the prey, my son, thou art gone up.   He stooped down, he couched as a Lion, and as an old Lion; who shall rouse him up?   The tribe of Judah is so compared, because it was a powerful and warlike tribe. When the Israelites, after the death of Joshua, inquired of the Lord, who should go up first against the common enemy, it was answered from the Lord, that Judah should go up.   It was from the tribe of Judah especially that the kings of God's people were raised up; and from this tribe, according to the flesh, Christ came.   6. The Lion is put figuratively for the Lord Jesus Christ. Rev. 5 : 5, Behold the Lion of the tribe of Judah, the root of David, hath prevailed to open the book, and to loose the seals thereof.   When the Lion is taken for an emblem of our divine Saviour, it is in respect to his strength to subdue all enemies under him—in respect to his kingly authority, in which he rules all nations— and in respect to the awful majesty, in which he will appear to the wicked in the day of judgment.

What is this that appears from the forest, that bounds over the desert? He draws near, he stops, he raises his head, he shakes his shaggy mane, he roars, and the distant mountains echo, as with the sound of thunder. He seizes a camel from a travelling company of Hagarenes. They shout against him, they shake against him their staves; he regards it not, he is deaf to their cries. He leisurely rends his prey; they approach him, to assail him with their lances. At the lashing of his tail the ground trembles, his eyes shoot fire at them, his teeth are as the jaws of death. They melt before him, they flee away. He satiates his hunger, he moves off with a stately step; he looks upon the retiring company, as upon grasshoppers, that are hastening away. He returns to his den, he couches down, he sleeps without fear, and who shall rouse him up? What was that, which came from the forest? Surely it was the Lion.

Who is this that appears from the east on a snowy throne, borne by living creatures of shining glory? His eyes are flaming fire, his eyelids as the darting of lightnings; his face is as the noon day sun. His head is as the snow on Lebanon; his robes as the light of the North, when it beams with snow and crimson; his girdle as the band of day break; his feet as polished brass glowing in a furnace; his hands hold the seven stars; his voice is as the roaring of the sea in a day of tempest. He comes to speak to men and to angels their destinies. Who is this that appears from the east on a snowy throne? This is the Lion of the tribe of Judah.

LIZARD.

THIS name is found in the English translation of the
Bible but once.   In Hebrew it is (לְטָאָה) Letââh.
In Buxtorf it is rendered by *Stellio* and *Lacerta*.   Junius
and Tremellius and Jerome have Stellio.   Rabbi Solomon renders it by a word supposed by Pagnin to signify *Lacerta*.   *Stellio* signifies a reptile resembling a Lizard, with spots on his back, as if set with stars, sometimes called an *Evet* or *Newt*.   Lacerta signifies in general a Lizard.   The French bible has *Lesard*, a Lizard.
The Septuagint has Khālābōtēs, not found in the Lex-
icon of Schrevellius ; see Levit 11 : 30.   But Schrevellius has Kālābātēs, a fish resembling a Lizard.   I think
it likely to be some kind of Lizard, which is here prohibited as unclean under the ceremonial law.

The Lizard is a reptile, which if deprived of his legs
would resemble a small serpent, but much thicker in
proportion to its length, than a serpent.   It has four
legs, much resembling human arms in miniature, with
their hands and fingers.

There are numerous species of the Lizard kind, dif-
fering in size, color and habits.   Of the Lizards of
New England some are called *Swifts* and some *Slows*.
Those called Swifts are usually about four inches long ;

their body of a light ash color, striped with black, and their tails blue. They are frequently found under the loose bark of trees, or under loose clapboards of a house, or near some such places, ready to retreat under cover with the quickness almost of lightning, if surprised. One species of those Lizards called *Slows*, is found under stones, and is black, spotted here and there with yellow ; is five or six inches in length, and almost of the thickness of a common man's little finger. These are very slow in their motions. There are others found under stones much smaller, and of different colors. Some found in frog ponds, are small, and nearly of a brick red color.

The *El-adda*, mentioned by Bruce, is six inches in length, near three fourths of an inch in thickness, and of yellowish color, crossed over the back with eight black bands. The figure given in the cut is that of the brown Lizard from George Edwards. Lizards in general feed on insects. The sight of the Lizard is to most persons unpleasant, because of its measure of resemblance to a serpent, between which and the human race there is an unconquerable enmity. But no doubt the Lizard forms a useful link in the chain of being, and enjoys a portion of happiness, which renders its existence to itself a blessing.

> The Lizard, aside from his feet,
>   So much like a serpent appears,
> That a glance at him near where we sit
>   Scarce fails to awaken our fears.
>
> But the reptile—the Swift, or the Slow,
>   Tho' disgusting to us it may seem,
> Is feeble and harmless we know,
>   And to injure us never would dream.
>
> Then let it enjoy, while it may,
>   The pittance its Maker bestows ;
> The laws of its nature obey,
>   And secure in its covert repose.

LOCUST.

[Figure from the Encyclopedia, reduced.]

—

THE name Locust is found in scripture somewhat more than twenty times. We meet with it first in Exdus 10 : 4, where the plague of Locusts is threatened upon Egypt. The name in Hebrew is usually (אַרְבֶּה) ărbāh ; in the Septuagint ākris ; in Latin *locusta*. The Hebrew name is derived from a word which signifies, *to be numerous*, *to multiply*, *to increase ;* which intimates that the Locust is an insect which appears in great multitudes.

[Figure from Riley's Narrative.]

The following sketches of the Locust are collected from Capt. Riley's narrative.

The Locust of Africa is a winged insect, which resembles both in size, and in general appearance, at first view, the largest sized grasshopper of America; but on a close inspection differs from it materially. The shape of his head and face is similar to that of a common sheep, being crowned with two long, tapering protuberances, which turn back like the horns of a goat. He has attached to his muzzle a pair of smellers, or feelers, by the help of which he feels, and gathers up the herbage about him, which he nips off, making a champing noise, like a sheep when eating. He has four wings, and the hinder pair (or under pair) are quite transparent; he has six legs, with two claws to each foot, which are divided something like the hoof of a sheep, but are more spread in proportion to their size, and are pointed. He is stout about the neck, breast and body, the hinder part of which is forked, and armed with a hard, bony substance, by the help of which he can make a hole in the ground.

The largest African Locust is above three inches in length, and nearly one inch in thickness; he has the most voracious appetite of any insect in the world, and devours grass, grain, the leaves of trees, and every green thing with indiscriminate and merciless avidity. They go forth by bands, or flights, and each flight is said to have a king, which directs its movements with great regularity.

Locusts can fly only when their wings are perfectly dry, and when they rise, they always fly off before the wind and fill the air like an immense cloud of thick smoke. When the leader alights upon the ground, all the flight follows his example as fast as possible. They are at times so numerous, that they may be said to cover the whole face of the country; then they devour every spear of grass and grain, even eating it into the ground, dislodging it root and branch; cutting off all the leaves from the shrubs and trees, and sometimes all the bark from tender trees, in a whole province, and that too, in a very short space of time.

The female, a little before the flights disappear for the season, thrusts her hinder parts into the ground up to her wings, first having found a suitable spot of earth for that purpose. Here she forms a cell from one to three inches deep, and from one to two inches in diameter. Having made the sides of the cell strong by means of a glutinous matter, which she has the power of producing, she deposits her eggs, which are blackish and so small as scarcely to be distinguishable with the naked eye. Each cell is filled full, and contains an immense number of eggs. She then seals it over carefully with the same kind of glutinous matter of which the inside of the cell is formed, and covering it over with earth, she leaves it to be hatched out by the heat

of the sun in due time, which generally happens in the
month of January.

Riley states that near Magadore he took upon the
top of a sharp pointed penknife what he judged to be
not more than a thousandth part of the eggs in one cell,
and found them by the help of a microscope to amount
to seven hundred and forty one. I confess I find some
difficulty in crediting this account; it would give, according to Riley's judgment, seven hundred and forty
one thousand eggs to one cell. The number is so extraordinary, and differs so much from general analogy,
in the case of kindred insects, that I think there must
be some incorrectness in the statement.

Riley further remarks, that when the Locust is hatched he crawls out of the earth a little worm of a light
brown color; and the whole cell of them are said to
hatch about the same time. They commence their
march, all going one course, generally towards the north
and west, devouring every green thing that comes in
their way.

In the space of one week they are prepared for their
transformation, when they climb up a stout spire of
grass, or twig, attach their skin fast to it, and by a sudden effort burst the skin asunder at its head, and come
forth a four winged insect, with six legs. After two
or three days they set off in a body, on the wing, and
fly from five miles to a hundred, as the country seems
to please their taste.

Dry, warm summers are favorable to their breeding;
cold, wet ones destroy them in the empire of Morocco,
till they come again from other parts. They deposite
their eggs in the latter part of summer, or in the begin-
ing of the fall months.

The Moors, Arabs, and Jews in Barbary esteem Lo-

15

custs as good food; they fry them in *argan* oil ; their taste is much like the yolk of hard boiled hen's eggs.

Mr. Simpson, Consul at Tangier, stated that in 1814, being at Cape Spartel, where the Locusts covered the whole face of the ground at night, not one was to be seen next morning. After the fog in the Straits was dissipated, he saw the surface of the water covered with the appearance of a reddish scum. Soon after, by the arrival of a vessel from Gibraltar, he had evidence that the appearance. was occasioned by innumerable multitudes of Locusts, drowned in attempting to cross the Straits.

Thus far from Riley.

In the foregoing account Riley states that the Locust s are prepared for their transformation in about one week ; the *Cabinet* states that they continue in their *larva* (their worm) state, about a month, and then prepare for their transformation. This latter statement seems the most probable.

When progressing in the worm state in Barbary, trenches have been dug by the inhabitants, and rows of stubble have been set on fire to arrest their progress ; but the trenches have soon been filled, and the fires extinguished by their multitudes.

Besides the common Locust, there is another kind mentioned in Scripture, called the Bald Locust, in Hebrew (סָלְעָם) Sólgnâm, Lev. 11 : 22. It is rendered by some, *Bombyx*, a Silk Worm. The writers of the Talmud describe it as a species of Locust frequenting rocks; the name being probably derived from a word signifying a rock. Buxtorf speaks of it by the name of *Attelabus*, a species of small Locust without wings. The Septuagint has ättäkēs, an insect, or reptile, which walks upon four legs, and leaps.

In Proverbs 30 : 27, Agur says, the Locusts have no

king, yet they go forth, all of them, by bands. In the narrative by Riley, each band is spoken of as having a king. In the case of Bees, and some kinds of Wasps, it is the fact that each swarm has a king, or rather queen, which is distinguished by its form, being much larger and longer than the others. The meaning of Agur might· be, that Locusts had no one among them distinguished from the rest in appearance, and it is possible that of each band some one might assume the lead, and the rest by instinct follow.

In Nahum 3 : 15, Nineveh is called upon to make herself many, as the Locust ; which confirms the idea that in those regions the Locusts were wont to appear in vast multitudes.

In Rev. 9 : 3, Locusts are represented as coming out of the bottomless pit, which was opened by a star, which fell from heaven. These Locusts are supposed by some interpreters to intend the *Saracens* or *Arabians* who were like Locusts for multitude, and came out of the same regions, and overspread the neighboring nations rapidly in their conquests.

Locusts were one of the ten plagues sent upon Egypt, to constrain Pharaoh to permit the Israelites to depart from his land. For the time they were a dreadful scourge ; but when they were removed, he still hardened his heart, and would not let Israel go. From this we may raise two reflections; 1. That God, when he pleases, can scourge a nation dreadfully by the multitudes of such insects, as, viewed by themselves, singly, are rather contemptible, than formidable. 2. That there needs something besides judgments and afflictions to soften the heart of the impenitent sinner : Though thou bray a fool in a mortar, among wheat with a pestle, yet will not his foolishness depart from him.

Moses, obedient to divine command,
O'er Egypt's fertile, wide extended plain
  Stretched forth his rod, his wonder-working wand,
  When lo, the Locusts, band succeeding band,
Came down like showers of overwhelming rain.

The land, like Eden, ere their march began,
Is left behind them like a fire-swept field;
  Uncheck'd, undaunted by the arts of man,
  From plant to plant, from shrub to shrub they ran,
Till Egypt's honors to their fury yield.

'Know'st not thou, Pharaoh,' to the haughty king,
Exclaim'd his servants, trembling with dismay,
  'Egypt is wasted? Not a verdant thing
  'From all the fields can any mortal bring,
'To show a remnant; all is swept away.'

The haughty monarch feels his heart relent
Just for the moment, and is driven to call
  In haste for Moses; God a west wind sent,
  Before its blast the bands of Locusts went,
And in the Red Sea all their legions fall.

He sees a respite; his unyielding heart
Is hard again; no threatening now avails;
  The wound soon heals, he soon forgets the smart;
  To let God's people from his realms depart,
No fear impels, the plea of Moses fails.

Such is the nature of the human will,
That all expedients, but the power of grace,
  Tho' long apply'd, and with the greatest skill,
  Leave the heart stubborn, unpersuaded still
Sin to forsake, and run the heavenly race.

Louse.

LOUSE.

—

THIS little unwelcome insect is named in scripture only in connection with the third plague, which God sent upon Pharaoh and the land of Egypt, to punish them for refusing to let Israel go out of their land. We find the name first in Exodus 8 : 12, in the Hebrew bible, (8 : 16, in the English) and there it is in the plural number, and written defectively. In v. 15, it is written in full, (כִּנִּים) Krhĭn-nēm. In the Septuagint Sknīfĕs, and Sknĭpĕs; from Sknĭps; explained by Schrevelius as a *fly*, or a little *worm*, of the kind that devours wood. In Latin the Louse is called *Pediculus*, in French, *Pou.*

Pagnin observes that the Hebrews suppose that Lice were really the insects intended in the passage referred to above.

Almost every kind of animal and plant has its peculiar kind of louse. Those that infest the human species are of two kinds, those that make the head their habitation, and those that harbor about the body. The figure given is from the Cabinet, and represents the Louse magnified.

When the magicians in Egypt essayed to bring forth Lice by their inchantments, they failed, and were constrained to acknowledge that their production was by

15*

the finger of God. This may teach us, that however God may suffer deceivers by the assistance of evil angels, or by their own craftiness, to produce seeming miracles, he can easily overwhelm their devices by such exhibitions of his power, as shall throw their lying wonders entirely into the shade.

Lice are troublesome insects to those infested by them; but they have their use in the scale of being. Contemptible as they may seem, God can use them to execute his judgments upon the proudest of men. They are usually the attendants of sloth, negligence, and filth. To those, who will be indolent and filthy, they are a just and daily punishment. But when they occasionally visit those, who are disposed to be cleanly, they stimulate to those exertions to be freed from them, which at the same time increase their cleanliness, promote the neatness of their appearance, and excite their industry. Though the Louse is troublesome to those infested by it, there is not the least reason to doubt but that the good which it enjoys is more than a balance for the suffering it occasions. Mean while it is one link of the almost infinitely progressive scale of being, the entire removal of which would leave a vacancy, which could not possibly be so well filled in any other way.

In Psal. 105: 31, we read, He spake, and there came divers sorts of flies and lice in all their coasts. The Psalm containing this, though bound in the same volume with the book of Exodus, was written long after Exodus, and by another hand; so that the allusions in it to the Mosaic account of the plagues of Egypt in Exodus, do as really confirm that account, as one heathen author confirms the testimony of another heathen author, who wrote before him. This remark applies to many other parts of the bible.

Let thy raiment be wash'd and be clean;
  Let the comb be applied to thy hair;
On all that is on thee be seen
  The marks of a provident care.
Tho' in face and in features the world call thee homely,
Thy dress and thy person at least will be comely.

  The vermin that others infest,
    Nor cease the vile slattern to wound,
Will never deprive thee of rest,
    Nor on thy neat person be found.
Wise industry adds to the worth and the number
Of sweets that the sluggard must lose by his slumber.

MOLE.

—

THIS creeping thing is named, I believe, but twice in scripture. 1. In Lev. 11 : 30. The lizard, and the snail, and the *Mole*. 2. In Isai. 2 : 20. Shall cast his idols to the *Moles* and to the bats. In the first passage the Hebrew is תִּנְשֶׁמֶת Tĭnshĕmĕth, äspälăx, Septuagint —*Talpa*, latin—*Taupe*, French. The same Hebrew word is found in v. 18, among the names of birds, and rendered *Swan*. Some have thought the word in v. 30, means the Dor-mouse, in latin *Glis*. The more common opinion is, that the Mole is intended. In the second passage the Hebrew is (חֲפֹר פֵּרוֹת) Hrhĕppōr-pārōth, signifying, according to some, a *digger of trenches*; others think it should be one word, the two last radicals being doubled to denote perseverance in digging. In this passage the Septuagint has Mātaiois, *vain things.* The Latin and French translators understand the word of *Moles.*

The figure given is from Bewick, and represents the radiated, or star-mole.

The Mole is an animal ranking in size between the rat and the mouse; it is covered with short, fine, glossy fur, in color almost black ; its forelegs differ but little from broad hands, having strong claws, and attached to the body almost without legs. Its hind legs are somewhat longer, but these are short. It has holes for ears, but no outward ears, yet its hearing is very quick; its smelling is said also to be quick. Its eyes are extremely small, and hidden in its fur. The radiated Mole has a fleshy substance protruding from its nose, resembling a little star. The Mole is every way fitted for its mode of life. They subsist upon worms, insects, the roots of grass, and the bark of other roots. Their life is spent almost wholly under the surface of the ground, where they form their warm and soft nest, from which their paths extend in several directions, like so many tubes, and are about one and a half or two inches diameter. They choose a loose, muddy soil for the place of their labors, and dispose of the dirt from their tubes, or holes, by throwing it up every few feet in little heaps, called mole-hills ; these are very troublesome to the farmer. They are so prolific, that were they not destroyed, many of them by the arts of man, and more of them by occasional flooding rains, they would nearly ruin many pleasant meadows.

The female brings forth in spring, four or five at a litter, and for their nests they choose the drier parts of the meadow. It might naturally seem to us that their enjoyment without light can be but small ; but they are usually plump and fat, and this indicates that they enjoy their mode of living, as well as those animals that bask in the sunshine. Their sense of taste and smell may be exquisite, and afford them much delight. Their fur is so soft and glossy, and their skin of such tenacity, that it seems rather strange that it is not more used in manufactures ; but perhaps their · commonness prevents it. Sometimes, however, very fine hats have been made of their fur.

While the common Mole is black, there are others but little darker than mouse color, and others yellow ; and in Siberia there are Moles of a green and gold color.

In the distinction of meats, given to the Israelites, the Mole is classed with the unclean. When we read in Isaiah 2 : 20, of casting idols to Moles and to Bats, the import is probably this ; that when God comes to execute his fearful judgments upon the wicked nations of the earth, they will be so convinced that their idols afford them no help, that they will cast them away into those obscure places, where they will be as much hidden from the common view, as in the day time the Moles and Bats are hidden. Abandoning their idols, their concern will be to hide themselves from the wrath of the Lord.

So sleek and so plump is the Mole
In its dark, subterranean hole,
Engag'd in its humble employment,
That tho' it has almost no eyes,
No doubt, while its labor it plies,
It has a good share of enjoyment.

Let us, my dear youth, by the thought,
While we muse on the subject, be taught,
That tho' humble and low our condition,
We still may have happiness too,
While our wants, and our cares are but few,
And we practice the grace of submission.

What a day it will be to the souls
Of the wicked, when they to the Moles

And the Bats their dumb idols shall throw,
  And themselves in the clefts of the rocks
  Shall hide to escape the dread shocks,
Of the trumpets and vials of woe !

These days of distress will pass o'er,
  Then earth will be shaken no more,
But sinners will turn from their sinning ;
  The tumult of battle will cease,
  The years will roll onward in peace,
Each day with devotion beginning.

MOTH.

THE name of this little insect occurs somewhat frequently in scripture. We find it first in Job 4 : 19.
Crushed before the Moth. Its name in Heb. is (עָשׁ)
Gnâsh, from a word which signifies to *eat,* to *waste
away,* to *consume.* Sēs, Septuagint—*Tinea* latin—
Tigne, French. The figures are from nature, two of
them magnified.

Moth is a name given by naturalists to one division of
an order of the class of insects called *Lepidoptera,* that
is, *scaly-winged.* They differ from butterflies, another
division of this order in several respects ; the wings of
the butterfly stand on its back erect, those of the Moth
generally lie flat, or nearly so ; the feelers of the butterfly are *clavated,* or club-formed ; those of the Moth
are *filiform,* or thread-formed ; the wings of the butterfly are generally variegated with beautiful colors ;

those of the Moth are nearly of one color, much resembling that of brown paper. The butterfly is an insect which sports about, and performs its operations in the day time ; the Moth in the night ; hence appears the wisdom of giving goodly wings to the butterfly, while the effect would be in great measure lost, if they were given to the Moth. The wisdom and goodness of God may be seen in all his works.

The Moth spoken of in scripture appears to be one of the smallest kinds, in length but the fourth part of an inch. Its wings lie over its back, not flat, but obliquely, as the two sides of a common roof. Its feelers are long, its motions very quick, its wings of a light flaxen color.

The worm from which the Moth proceeds, much infests woollen garments that are but little used ; eating a little cavity into them, and forming of the knap its nest in which it lies shrouded during its aurelia state. A multitude of them thus nested in one garment, will nearly ruin it ; and they may be wisely intended to teach us the vanity of laying up treasure on earth ; as every kind of earthly substance is liable to be wasted away, or to be taken from us by violence, or by stealth.

Eliphaz, in the passage already quoted, (Job 4 : 19,) speaks of the human race as having their foundation in the dust, and as being crushed before the *Moth*. This is a striking figurative expression to teach the frailty of man, his liability to be destroyed by the feeblest insect, and the presumption of thinking to set up his wisdom against the wisdom of God, and of extolling his own righteousness. In chapter 13 : 28, Job speaks of man as a garment that is *motheaten ;* this is a fair illustration of his own case, covered with painful ulcers, which

were almost ready to put an end to his life ; it illustrates the case of man, when consuming away with
painful disease.   In chapter 27 : 13, Job speaks of the
wicked man as building his house as the Moth ; the
wicked man in many instances builds up an estate by
taking from the possessions of others in a fraudulent
way ; but at length the man, and his possessions perish
together.   David in Psalm 39 : 11, speaks of God as
making the beauty of man consume away like a Moth ;
that is, like a garment consumed by Moths ; the expression is elliptical ; when God corrects man for his
transgressions he often brings upon him those diseases,
which in a little time cause all his beauty, his come-
liness to fade away, and his strength to fail.   In Isaiah
50 : 9, the prophet says of his adversaries, *the Moth
shall eat them up*.   The prophet is here speaking in the
name of the Messiah ; and the passage teaches that the
enemies of christianity will by degrees fade away as a
garment that is consumed by Moths.   So the enemies of the church of Christ, however strong they may
seem to be for a time, will at length fall before it.   In
Matthew 6 : 19, the blessed Savior admonishes us not
to lay up our treasure where moth and rust corrupt.
Every thing here below is perishable.   If this world be
our all, in a little time we shall have nothing ; as respects us it will vanish away.   Happy is he, who has a
treasure in heaven, and whose heart is there.

> Vain man, with all his pomp and power,
> May fade and wither in an hour.
> If God but look, and on him frown,
> An insect *Moth* can crush him down.
>
> Let man his costly robes prepare,
> And store them up to clothe his heir,
> The busy Moth shall waste the store,
> And time's sharp tooth his robes devour.
>
> Happy the youth, whose care is given
> Betimes to store his wealth in heaven :
> No wasting moth can wing its way,
> Nor thief ascend to realms of day.

Mice.

MOUSE.
—

This is a little animal of which there are several kinds; they are diffused extensively over the earth, and are several times mentioned in scripture. In the plural number they are called *Mice.* The Hebrew name for the *Mouse* first occurs in Lev. 11 : 29, it is (עַכְבָּר) Gnäkrhbâr; Mūs, Septuagint; *Mus,* Latin; *Souris,* French. In Greek, Latin, and English, the name is nearly the same, which is an argument that the animal is very common.

The figures given are of the short tailed field Mouse from Bewick, and of the common Mouse, from the Cabinet.

We may first notice the common Mouse. This inhabits chiefly the house and barn, and subsists on all kinds of grain, and upon bread, cheese, and the like. Its color is well known, much resembling that of ashes, except the belly, which is nearly white. Its fur is soft and sleek; its tail long, slender and naked; its ears somewhat long, and its eyes prominent. Its motions are very quick; its teeth sharp and strong, so that it is often busy in gnawing the edges of boards, &c. to enlarge the crevices between them, and fit itself a passage from one part of the house to another; so that it is difficult to prevent their access to every part of our dwell-

16

ings. They are very prolific, bringing forth several times in a year, and from five to ten at a litter. The young ones are at first naked, but are soon covered, and in about three weeks able to subsist by themselves.

Aristotle shut up a female Mouse in a vessel prepared for the purpose, and supplied it with a sufficiency of grain, and in a short time he found it to contain one hundred and twenty mice. So prolific they are, that were it not for cats, foxes, owls, hawks, weasels, and snakes, who all feed upon them, they would soon overwhelm us, and produce a famine, especially if we take into view the field Mouse in connection with the common mouse. Herodotus informs us that the army of Senacharib, king of Asyria, was once defeated by means of Mice, which in one night so gnawed their harness, and their bowstrings, that they were obliged to retreat with precipitation.

The common Mouse, and one kind, at least, of the field Mouse, is of a quite comely appearance, exhibiting a very pleasant symmetry in its parts, and would not be looked upon with disgust, were it not for its mischievousness.

We may next notice the field Mouse. The more common of these in New-England are the short-tailed field mice. The shape of these is not so beautiful as that of the common Mouse. The color of all of those I have seen differs but little from that of the common mouse, except that it is rather darker, the back being nearly of a slate color. The field mouse described by Bewick is on the back of a reddish brown. The body of the common field mouse is between three and four inches long, its tail between one and two inches ; its eyes are very small, but larger than those of the mole. It works much in cold climes, in winter, under the snow; it makes numerous, and sometimes long paths, or channels between the snow and ground among the stubble and roots of grass, feeding upon roots, and the bark of young trees, sometimes gnawing from young apple trees the whole of their roots, as in some instances I have seen. Sometimes a year occurs in which they greatly abound; then for a few years after they will not be numerous. In New-England, in the summer of 1809, from the eastern part of Maine to the western part of Massachusetts, they abounded exceedingly. Cats brought them into the house in greater numbers than they could devour; a fox in a certain instance, being suddenly surprised, threw out of his mouth thirteen of them. The next year but here and there one of them was to be found; and for some years after they were not numerous.

Such a multitude of these animals appearing at one time, and they being so few at another time, and so quickly reduced, may teach us to fear God, who for our sins may suddenly raise up such an army of feeble creatures, as shall cut off our hopes, and greatly distress us; also to look to him for relief, seeing he can so readily remove the evils we suffer.

Another kind of field mouse has a long tail; on the back sometimes nearly of the color of the common mouse, and sometimes of a yellowish brown; their belly is white; their eyes are prominent: in shape they exhibit an agreeable symmetry of parts. Their dwelling place is a burrow in the ground, large and commodious, compared with their size; one room of this burrow contains their nest, which is made very soft and warm; the other room contains their provision, which consists of a variety of seeds. In one burrow I once found in Autumn a male and female, and in their store room about four quarts of seeds, some of the buttercup or crowfoot, some of the wild bean, some of the pigeon berry, or sweet brier, but chiefly of the red clover, and all completely cleansed from chaff. Their nest was very clean and soft. This kind I have not often met with.

Another kind of field Mouse I have seen, called *hopping mouse*, somewhat resembling the *Jerboa ;* it is about the size of the common Mouse, but with long hind legs, and is very fleet in running, or skipping from place to place. Its color is reddish brown.

We may next notice the *Shrew-mouse.* It is a very small animal, being but about two and a half inches in length ; it has a long sharp nose, it is sometimes the color of the common mouse, and sometimes of a reddish brown. Its dwelling is in heaps of stones, old walls, rubbish, &c. It feeds on insects, grain, and putrid substances, and has a fœtid smell, so that the cat after having taken it refuses to eat it. They have small eyes, and these are almost hidden in their fur. Their ears are short, and their upper fore teeth have on each side of them a very fine barb, turning backwards.

Another species of Mouse is the Dwarf Mouse of the Cape of Good Hope, scarcely two inches in length, having four black lines running on its back from head to tail ; the tail is naked and black.

In the list in Lev. 11, the Mouse is classed among unclean animals ; but such was the famine in the siege of Jerusalem, that the Jews were constrained to eat them.   In Isai. 66 : 17, we read of those who ate swine's flesh, and the abomination, and the mouse ; of whom the Lord says that they should be consumed together.   Some think that by the abomination is here meant the *weasel,* with which in Lev. the mouse is joined.   The general import of the passage is, that God will no less destroy those Jews, who wilfully disobey his law in small points, than those Pagans, who are guilty of open idolatry.

The Mice that we read of in 1 Sam. 6 : were probably field mice, which were suffered to multiply rapidly, and to make great destruction among the fruits of the fields of the Philistines, while the ark of God was retained among them. This was designed to show that the most sacred things were no defence to those, who profaned them, but on the contrary brought the judgments of God upon them.

In every barn, in every house,
  How many a crumb, how many a grain,
Lost in the rubbish, yields the mouse
  A sweet repast, a welcome gain.

What, tho' the nibbler sometimes makes
  Large depredations on our store?
What e'er from us its cunning takes,
  Its own enjoyment still is more.

The wise Creator's goodness shines
  In all his works, and man may trace
His wisdom in a thousand lines
  Thro' all the animated race.

All share his bounty ; link by link
  Downwards the lengthened chain descends ;
From angel's height to nothing's brink,
  All on his powerful hand depends.

MULE.

In this animal we have a mixed breed, the result of the union of the ass with the mare. The name of the *Mule* first occurs in the bible in Gen. 36 : 24. - - - 'This is that Anah that found the *Mules* in the wilderness.' The Hebrew here is (יְמִם) Jāmĭm, a word found only in this place. Whether Mules are here intended, or not, has been in past ages a subject of much dispute; some think *waters* are intended, because the word bears some similitude to that for waters; this, however, is hardly probable; others think a race of giants is intended, called *Emeans ;* which is somewhat more probable. But the greater part of the Jewish Rabbis suppose that Mules are intended. We next find the name of Mule in 2 Sam. 18 : 9, in which v. it occurs three times; in the Hebrew (פֶּרֶד) Pĕrĕd ; and in the feminine, in 1 Kings 1 : 33. (פִּרְדָּה) Pírdâh; this is the general Hebrew name for Mule in scripture. Hēmĭŏnŏs, Septuagint; Mulus, Latin ; Mulet, French.

The figure is from Bewick.

The Mule in size and shape is between the horse and the ass, but bears the stronger resemblance to the latter. They were used among the Jews, no doubt, long before the time of David; and have been employed in different parts of the world in all ages since. They are but little used in England; a few are used in the northern states of America, in the southern states their use is more common; but they are most used in South America, especially in the mountainous regions, because of their being a very sure footed animal, very rarely stumbling. In some places, where the path passes down a long, steep, smooth declivity, the mule, with his rider mounted, will place himself in convenient position, and slide safely from top to bottom, where man on foot could hardly descend. The Mule is hardy, long-lived, strong, and swift; is patient, but rather ob_stinate.

> It makes me shudder, while I muse and think
> How down the slippery steep the steady Mule
> Glides with his rider, and conveys his trust
> Safe to the valley; nor does less my soul
> Recoil within me, when I see him pass
> Along the ledge, the fearful *ladera*,
> On the steep mountain side, where far above
> Cliff rests on cliff, and far beneath his feet
> Deep after deep descends. O, should he set
> One footstep much awry, or should he lose
> His even balance, down he must descend
> With awful plunge, and with his rider dash
> On ragged rocks beneath.—But God has made
> His creatures for their places; to the Mule has given
> Sureness of foot, and watchfulness of eye,
> To bear his master, where the warlike horse
> Would feel his courage fail.

NIGHT HAWK.

THE original word which is thus rendered in the English bible, is (תַּחְמָס) Tährhmâs ; if the Septuagint has observed the order of the original, it calls it the Lārŏs, or sea-gull ; but there is some reason to doubt whether it has followed the same order in all particulars. Pagnin renders the Hebrew name by the Latin words *Noctua*, *Cymindis*, or Accipiter Nocturnus ; *Nycticorax* ; that is, Owl, Night-Hawk, and Night-Raven. The original name is from a word, which signifies to *seize with violence* from which it is probable that it was some bird of prey; and if properly called a Night-hawk it must have differed widely from what we call a nighthawk in New-England, which does not appear to be a bird of prey ; it is a bird nearly twice the size of the barn swallow, with long, narrow wings, and two bars of white under each of them, and a very large mouth. They usually fly round in an irregular manner in the atmosphere, in summer evenings, uttering a uniform note, which may be nearly expressed by the word *Pe-ag ;* and occasionally pitch down very swiftly towards the ground, with a loud noise, like the utterance of one sudden roar. While moving round in their irregular circles and sweeps, it is probable that they are catching flies and other insects for their necessary food. They lay their eggs, two in number, and speckled, dark brown and white, upon the bare surface of the ground, without any nest. Their young, when newly hatched appear like a bunch of grey moss, differing little in color from the spot of ground where they are deposited, so that they are very likely not to be noticed. This is one of the ways in which God provides for the safety of some of his creatures in their helpless infancy. I have not been able to obtain a subject from which to

make a drawing of this kind of Night-hawk, nor have
I any where met with the figure of one, nor do I think
it the bird intended by Night-hawk in scripture. The
original name is found in Leviticus 11 : 16, and in
Deuteronomy 14 : 15, where it is reckoned among
the unclean birds.

OSPRAY.

THE Hebrew name rendered Ospray, or Osprey, is
found in Leviticus 11 : 13, and in Deuteronomy 14 : 12,
and is (עׇזְנִיָּה) Gnōznĕyyâh. Buxtorf calls it in Latin
Haliaetus, a species of *Sea-Eagle*, and the figure I have
given is that of the Sea-Eagle, or Ospray in the Cabinet,
which answers to the description as nearly as any figure
I have found. The Septuagint has Hālīaiĕtŏs, the
French *Faucon*, a Falcon. It is among the unclean
birds.

The Sea-Eagle, or Ospray, is found in Ireland, in
some parts of Great Britain, and in some other parts of
the world. It feeds principally on fish. It seizes them
when they are near the surface of the water, by dart-

ing suddenly upon them, and piercing them with its talons, which are long, and so hooked, as to form a semicircle. In this way it will draw salmon from the water; and on the coast of Greenland it sometimes draws out young seals. It sometimes feeds on water fowls, and sometimes on land animals. The natural historian, Barlow, saw one of them seize and bear away a cat : but the captive animal made such resistance, that both came to the ground, when Barlow, much gratified with the opportunity, seized the Eagle. He has given a figure of it in the 36th plate of his collection. The body is of a light rusty color, and the extent of the wings from tip to tip is sometimes from 8 to 10 feet.

> With powerful sight, and watchful eye,
> On wing in air, and soaring high
> The *Ospray* spies its finny prey,
> Darts down, and bears its prize away.
>
> The hand that gives the beast his food,
> And feeds the eagles, when they cry,
> Will fill the faithful soul with good,
> And all its real wants supply.
>
> 'Tis God, whose bounteous hands provide
> All needful good for all his friends ;
> Then let our cares, and fears subside,
> While on his grace our hope depends.

OSSIFRAGE.

THIS is one of the list of birds reckoned in the law unclean. The Hebrew name is found in Leviticus 11 : 13, and in Deuteronomy 14 : 12, it is (פֶּרֶס) Pĕrĕs. The Septuagint has Grūps, a Griffin. Buxtorf calls it *Ossifraga*, which signifies a *breaker of bones ;* he says it is a kind of eagle. Pagnin speaks of it as a large bird inhabiting deserts. Its Hebrew name is from a word which signifies to *divide* or to *break in pieces.* The French bible has *Orphraye.*

There is little reason to doubt but that this bird is a

species of eagle, so large and strong, that with its beak
it breaks many of the bones of animals to come at the
marrow. I have not seen any figure of the bird, and
have given none.

> Why does a God of boundless power,
>   And of unmeasur'd skill,
> Permit one creature to devour
>   Another at his will ?
>
> The wolf destroys the harmless lamb,
>   The eagle tears the dove ;
> How shall we vindicate the name
>   Of him, who reigns above ?
>
> The lamb in life enjoys more good,
>   Than all the pain it bears,
> When the fierce beast, that thirsts for blood,
>   The harmless victim tears.
>
> The dove has days and months of peace,
>   Its dying pangs are brief ;
> A moment, and its sufferings cease,
>   In death it finds relief.
>
> The wolf enjoys—the bird of prey
>   Enjoys a sweet repast ;
> More than enough the loss to pay,
>   When all the amount is cast.
>
> Search nature's plan minutely thro',
>   And all its parts compare,
> The more we may of wisdom view.
>   The more of goodness there.

OSTRICH.
[Figure from Mavor.]

THAT this bird is intended in the description given in the book of Job, chapter 39 : 13—18, I think there is no reason to doubt ; but, what is really the Hebrew name of it, is much more difficult to decide. In verse 13, there are three words, each of which has been claimed for the name of the *Ostrich*, by different interpreters, while the others have been rejected.

Mr. Scott, and some others, suppose the first name in the verse generally rendered *Peacocks*, and in Hebrew (רְנָנִים) Renânēm, to be the name of the Ostrich, and the name to which the following description refers ; and they render the verse thus—*The wing of the Ostrich vibrates with exultation ; is it the pinion and feathers of the stork ?*

The English and French translators claim the second name in the verse for the Ostrich, in Hebrew (חֲסִידָה) Hhrässēdâh ; but this name, according to its derivation seems to intend a *bird of kindness*, and is very applicable to the *stork*, and in several other passages, where it occurs, it is rendered stork, and in some of them cannot apply to the Ostrich.

Junius and Tremellius claim the last word in the verse for the name of the Ostrich, in Hebrew (נֹצָ֫ה) Nōtsâh, this word comes from a root, which signifies *to fly*, or to *run very swiftly* ; it is usually rendered *plumage* or *feathers* ; but Buxtorf speaks of some as having rendered it, *the Ostrich*, as if it were the *winged* or *feathered* bird.

I can hardly bring my mind to fix upon the second of the above three words to be the name of the Ostrich, because it is so generally rendered *stork*, and its derivation so well agrees to the stork. Between the first and third of the words my mind wavers. There is so general a concurrence of interpreters in ascribing the first name to the *peacock*, that it seems boldness to dissent from them ; and their want of concurrence in rendering the last word *Ostrich*, makes it doubtful whether we should adopt that rendering.

If peacocks are to be understood by the first name, the literal rendering might be,

The wing of the peacock waves with exultation ;
Is it the wing of the stork, and the plumage ?
Or, Is it the wing of the Ostrich and the plumage ?
Or, Is it the wing of the stork and the Ostrich ?

Taking the first name to be one of the names of the Ostrich, we may render,

The wing of the Ostrich is full of exultation ;
Is it the wing and plumage of the stork ?

The Hebrew name for peacocks in 1 Kings, and 2d Chronicles so widely differs from that rendered peacocks

17

above, that there is on that account the less difficulty in applying that above to the Ostrich.

The Ostrich is a bird inhabiting chiefly the warm regions of Africa and Asia, the deserts of those regions especially. They pertain to one of the largest classes of birds ; and seem to be a connecting link between the larger birds, and large four-footed beasts. From the top of the head to the ground, as they usually stand, they are from seven to eight feet ; from the ground to the top of the back, they are from four to five feet ; when extended in a line, their length from the beak to the end of the tail is about seven feet, the length of the tail one foot. Their head, and the upper part of the neck is white and almost naked, having only a few hairs on them, somewhat like bristles ; some of them are in small clusters of about a dozen hairs from one shaft. The feathers on the lower part of the neck are small ; those on the back and belly are small also, but somewhat larger ; they are commonly a mixture of black and white, and they are more like hairs, or rough threads of cotton, than like feathers. The wings and tail are covered with large feathers, fitted more for ornament, than for other use. Those towards the ends of the wings and tail, are the largest, and are usually white, the next black and white ; the shafts, or stems of these feathers are in the centre of their vanes, or beards, and these vanes are not woven together, as in the feathers of other birds, but are separate from one another, and are long, downy, soft and flexible. The feathers on the wings are used by the bird as fans, to fan itself, and as oars, or sails to assist it in running, but they do not enable them to fly. The sides of the bird under its wings, and the thighs have no feathers on them ; the legs and feet are covered with scales : it has but two toes on each foot ; that on the inside is the longest, being seven inches in length, including the claw, which is about three quarters of an inch ; the outer toe is about four inches long, and has no claw.

The Hebrew word rendered Ostriches in Lam. 4 : 3, is (יַעֲנִים) Yegnānēm ; this word in the singular number, preceded by Băth, or Bĕnōth, is rendered by the English translators of the bible, *owl*, or *owls ;* but it is the opinion of some that it ought always to be rendered, *Ostrich,* or *Ostriches.*

Ostriches generally feed on vegetable food ; they will devour the coarsest plant, and swallow leather, stones, iron, and almost any substances that come in their way. Their appetite is voracious, and their digestion powerful. The female sometimes lays forty or fifty eggs in a litter ; their eggs are large, some of them more than five inches diameter, and weighing more than twelve pounds. With a part of her eggs she feeds her young ; others she leaves by day slightly covered with sand to be warmed by the sun ; and sits on them by night. She is very timid, and a small fright will cause her to forsake her eggs, or young ones, and flee ; and perhaps, she will never return to them, but leave them to perish.

The noise of the Ostrich is loud, hoarse, and disagreeable, resembling sometimes the roaring of a lion, sometimes the bellowing of a bull.

They are hunted chiefly for their feathers, which are much used by ladies for ornamenting their head dresses. When they lift up themselves for the race, the fleetest horses cannot hold way with them. But instead of going off in a straight line, they take a circuitous rout, and the hunters follow round in smaller circles, keeping the Ostrich running by that means with much greater velocity, till he is so exhausted with hunger and fatigue that he can run no longer ; he then becomes a prey to his pursuers.

They are very strong, and will run with a man upon their back, but cannot be guided, but will take their own circuitous course. Several were mounted at Podore, and raced several times round the village, and could be stopped only by baricading their passage.

God calls the notice of Job to the Ostrich, to teach him the wisdom and variety of his works, and his sovereignty in them ; he shows him, that tho' he had made the Ostrich in some degree a dull, stupid, careless creature, and in measure destitute of natural affection, yet he can and does preserve the species in the world. Also, that he can sustain these large and strong birds in life, where most creatures would die for want of sustenance.

Jeremiah in Lam. 4 : 3, says, the daughters of my people is become cruel, as the Ostriches in the wilderness. The distressed situation to which the Jews were reduced, about the time of their captivity was such, as to lead even the pitiful women to treat their young children, as if they had no affection for them. Their sufferings did in a manner overwhelm and drown their natural affection. From the comparison we may gather, that the Ostrich does sometimes treat her young, as if she were without natural affection ; and some writers of natural history have noticed this trait in their habits. In closing I may remark ; how great was that wickedness in God's peculiar people, which led him to bring such evils upon them, that the tender mother could harden herself against her infant.

I shall finish this article with a paraphrase on the passage in Job respecting the Ostrich.

See the tall Ostrich wave her quivering wing,
Proudly exulting. Has the kinder stork

Such wing and plumage ?—Lo, the Ostrich leaves
Her eggs, slight cover'd, in a nest of sand,
Warm'd by the sun-beams ; nor suspects the foot
Of man may crush them ; nor believes the beast,
Wild from the forest, may her hopes destroy;
Hard is her heart against her tender brood,
As if she knew them not ; and, void of care,
She labors oft in vain. Her Maker, God,
Gives her not wisdom, nor in measure large
Stores her with understanding.   But with strength
And speed endow'd she rises to the race,
And leaves the horse-man, with his fleetest steed,
Far in the rear.

OWL.
[Figure from Geo. Edwards.]

—

SEVERAL species of unclean birds are noticed in the
scriptures, which are supposed to be *Owls*. Five species are named in the English bible; the *Owl*, the *little
Owl*, the *great Owl*, of two kinds, and the *screech Owl*.
For these the Hebrew bible has five different appella-
17*

tions, 1. (בַּת־הַיַּעֲנָה) Lev. 11 : 16. Bäth-Hăyyă-gnnâh, rendered in English simply the *Owl*. It may mean literally, the daughter of one that answers, or a kind of Owls, which in their hootings answer one anoth-er, which is the fact with one species at least, and these are somewhat large, and their hootings very loud. The Septuagint has *Glaux*; latin *Ulula*; French *Chat-Huant·* 2. (כּוֹס) Lev. 11 : 17. Kōss; the *little Owl*. Septu-agint Nŭktikŏräx, *Nightraven*. Latin *Bubo*, French *Chouette*. The original is found also in Deut. 14 : 16, and in Psal. 102 : 6, where the Psalmist says, I have been as an Owl in desolate places. Rab. David says of this Owl, that its voice is a *wailing* or *lamenting;* this may correspond with the voice of the little Owl of New-England, the voice of which is very mournful, re-sembling that of a woman, shrieking in distress. 3. (יַנְשׁוּף) Lev. 11 : 17; and Deut. 14 : 16, Jănshôf; and in Isai. 34 : 11, Jănshōf. Buxtorf and Junius and Tremellius have *Noctua*, an *Owl·;* Pagnin has the same, and also *Vespertillio*, a *Bat*. The original comes from a word, signifying *night, twilight, darkness*, the Septua-gint has *Ibis;* French, *Hibou*. 4. (לִילִית) Lēlēth, Isai. 34 : 14. Buxtorf has *Strix*, a *Screech Owl*. Pag-nin has the same. The Septuagint has ŏnŏkĕntaurŏs; a monster, part man and part beast. Different authors have given different interpretations to the name. The French bible has *Orfraye*. The name in the original comes from a word which signifies *night;* and it proba-bly means some bird that flies, and seeks its prey in the night. 5. (קִפּוֹז) Kĭppōz; Isai. 34 : 15. Buxtorf has *Merula*, a *black bird*. Pagnin has *Ericius*, a *Hedge-hog;* the Septuagint has ĕkhinŏs, a *Hedge-hog*. The French bible has *Martinet*, a *Martin*. Some think a very poisonous serpent is intended by the Hebrew name; but the immediate connection applies rather to a bird.

The figures I have given are of the *great horned Owl* of Athens, and of the more common *little Owl*, both copied from the gleanings of George Edwards, and reduced in size; and one of the little brown owl from nature.

The general appearance of the great Owl is that of a yellowish brown, spotted, waved, and streaked with a very dark brown; under the throat are semicircular bands, nearly white, but variagated with small strokes of black : its tail feathers are of light gray, barred with dark gray; its wing feathers are barred with dark brown, nearly black. Its horns are formed of tufts of feathers, which it can raise and depress at pleasure. Its description varies not greatly from that of the eagle owl, nor from that of the great horned owl, noticed by Mavor. The eagle owl is described as very large, almost equaling in size the eagle ; its head and whole body finely varied with lines, spots, and specks, and these black, brown, ash-colored, and rust-colored; its wings are long; its tail short, and barred with dusky bars. It is found in the north of England, and in Scotland; it inhabits inaccessible rocks, and deserted places, and feeds on hares, and various feathered game.

The horned Owl is large in appearance, rather than in real size, by reason of the fullness of its plumage; its horns are composed of six feathers each, varied with yellow and black; these it raises and depresses at pleasure. The breast and belly are of a dull yellow, marked with slender brown oblong spots; the back and wings are varied with deep brown and yellow. It is found in the north of England, and in Wales, and breeds in hollow trees, caverns, &c.

Little Owl.

The little Owl from George Edwards is in general appearance of a reddish brown, varied in its plumage much like the eagle Owl; and much resembling the little owl of New-England, which is near the size of a common parrot, or of a dove, and is frequently found in barns, which it visits in pursuit of mice, and such like small game.

Mavor describes a white Owl, which most of the year inhabits barns, out-houses, &c. and is very useful for clearing them of rats, mice and other vermin. To breed it retires to the woods. It seldom hoots, but snores and hisses, and sometimes screams with great violence.

The figure here inserted is of the little brown Owl, of the State of Maine, drawn from nature, Feb. 3, 1832. Its length was seven inches.

There are a number of other species of Owls, but in general traits they agree with one, or another of those already briefly described.

The whole tribe of Owls are birds of night; their ravages are made in part in the twilight; but especially in moon light they are busily occupied in hunting and seizing their prey. Moon light is to them what fair day light is to us. Their eyes are two tender and sensible to endure well the strength of open day light; it dazzles and blinds them. When day light approaches they generally retire to their hiding places. If they happen to be overtaken by it before they have reached their close retreats, they are the objects of the insults of a variety of those smaller birds, upon which they make war by night, and they appear in an awkward plight in their attempts to defend themselves. The head and face of the owl bears much resemblance to that of the cat; this is especially the case with the horned Owl. Their beak is short, and very hooked; their talons are long, and hooked, like those of the hawk. The hootings of some kinds of them, and especially the sudden screams, and additional mournful notes of others are no very pleasant sounds to those who are travelling alone through the woods by night, as I have found by experience.

Unpleasant as the noise of the Owl is, and unwelcome as their ravages sometimes are upon our poultry, they are not without use in the scale of being. They serve the purpose of thinning off, and keeping within due limits a number of kinds of small animals, and creeping things, which otherwise might so abound, as greatly to annoy us, and bring a famine upon themselves. The pain of the little animals, when destroyed is momentary, and the pleasure of those which are sustained by feeding upon them amounts to a valuable sum of happiness.

In Job 30 : 29, we hear that afflicted man saying, I am a brother to dragons, and a companion to owls. David in Psal. 102 : 6, says, I am like an owl in the desert. Whatever we are to understand by the dragons to which Job here compares himself, they were no doubt a kind of animals, which made a wailing noise, and were probably found alone in most cases, in desolate places; and the owls to which both Job and David compare themselves, we know are a solitary bird, and sometimes their noise is like that of distress. Job and David were among the best of men, but they had their seasons of affliction. The thought of this should be improved by us to lead us to expect, that though we live uprightly, and conscientiously in the world, we are not to expect to escape without afflictions; we should therefore hold ourselves in readiness for them. And further, we should improve it, when we are in affliction, to encourage ourselves, if we feel that we are the friends of God, to hope that we shall at length be redeemed from our afflictions, and in some cases even in this life, for so were Job, David, and many others.—In Micah 1 : 8, God speaks of making a wailing for Samaria, like dragons, and a mourning like owls. This confirms the idea, that the dragons, here alluded to, were animals that at times set up a wailing; and that the owls intended were birds that sometimes made a mournful noise. In the passage before us the mighty God wonderfully condescends, in figure, to speak of himself as a man wailing and mourning for the loss of his family; and from it we may infer the dreadfulness of the destruction that was coming upon Samaria for its wickedness; and at the same time that the blessed God feels a strong compassion for those, whom his justice requires him to destroy.

> Nor earth, nor air, nor brook, nor sea,
> Nor gloomy night, nor shining day,
> Are left alone; from men to worms,
> They're fill'd with life in various forms.
>
> By day the eagle mounts the skies,
> By night the Owl his cunning tries;
> Each in his season finds his food,
> And each enjoys a share of good.
>
> The birds of prey are not in vain;
> The vermin, that would spoil our grain,
> They seize, and keep the pilfering kind
> Within the sphere that heaven design'd.
>
> When saints in anguish mourn and howl,
> As in the dark the lonely Owl;
> Let this console, the night so drear
> Will pass, and days of rest appear.

PALMER-WORM.

—

THE Hebrew name of this reptile is (גָּזָם) Gâzâm,
probably from Gâzăz, to *shear*, from its shearing off in
some sort the leaves of the plants upon which it feeds.
Some have thought a kind of locust is intended ; but
the more ancient interpreters in general call it a worm.
Buxtorf, Pagnin, and Junius and Tremellius render it
in Latin, *Eruca*, which may signify a Palmer-worm, or
canker-worm.   Pagnin speaks of it as a worm feeding
upon pot-herbs, and especially upon cole-wort.   If we
take it for granted that a worm is intended, it may be
impossible at this day to decide of what particular species it was.   The Septuagint has Kămpē, from Kămp-
tō, to *bend*, which gives some color to the supposition,
that it was one of the kind of worms, which progress
by doubling themselves, and then extending themselves.
The French bible has *Hanneton*, a kind of bug.   Of
this reptile I have given no figure.   The name of it is
found in Joel 1 : 4, and 2 : 25 ; and in Amos 4 : 9.   The
first passage is, That which the *Palmer-worm* hath left,
hath the locust eaten, and that which the locust hath
left, the canker-worm hath eaten, and that which the
canker-worm hath left, hath the catterpillar eaten.
From this we may infer that in the days of Joel a very
distressing famine was sent upon the land of Judea ;
probably occasioned in great part by dearth ; but greatly aggravated, and rendered peculiarly distressing by the
destruction made by devouring insects and reptiles.
The description of this famine in the first, and in part
of the second chapter of Joel, is sublime, and very affecting.   It was sent for the wickedness of the inhabitants of the land.   It was designed to impress them
with a sense of the divine displeasure against sin ; and

to stir up the people to seek the favor of God by repentance. Such judgments were more peculiarly needful in those early times, while the word of God was yet incomplete, than they now are, since a future state of rewards and punishments is more clearly revealed.

The second passage is, I will restore to you the years that the locust hath eaten, the canker-worm, and the caterpillar, and the palmer-worm, my great army which I sent among you. This passage implies that the famine was not merely of one year's continuance, but of several years, so that the distress must have been very great; but it contains a precious promise, in case of obedience; a promise of a succession of years, as flourishing and fruitful, as the others had been sterile and empty. The insects and reptiles named in this passage God calls his great army; and if we look with a little attention into the animal kingdom, we shall find that even of insects and reptiles there may be raised up armies astonishingly numerous. Of the class of reptiles, that we commonly call worms, there have been reckoned no less than fifty two kinds, and one of these kinds may contain a number of species.

Some kinds of reptiles have the power of being astonishingly prolific; let the check be taken from a few kinds at once, and the army would be so terrible, that all faces might well *gather blackness* at the view.

In the third passage we read,—Your olive trees increased, and the Palmer worm devoured them; yet have ye not returned unto me, saith the Lord. From this we may gather that the Palmer-worm was a reptile that sometimes at least infested the olive trees.— From the close of the passage we learn, that a people may sometimes proceed to that degree of obstinacy in wickedness, that even severe judgments will not re-

18

claim them. It awaits them then, that destruction must come upon them.

> If we dare to persist in our sin,
>   Our hope to escape must be vain ;
> The justice of God will begin
>   At length to pursue us with pain.
>
> The meanest of reptiles may form
>   An army of millions of foes ;
> O'er all our fair fields they may swarm,
>   And a rod most distressing compose.
>
> But tho' the forbearance of God
>   Should grant us thro' life a reprieve,
> After death we must feel such a rod,
>   That nothing our pain can relieve.
>
> O let us then turn to the Lord,
>   And abandon our devious ways ;
> Submit to be taught by his word
>   And fill up our lives with his praise.

PARTRIDGE.

The name of this bird is not found in the list of the unclean ; its flesh to this day is esteemed a delicacy.

Though the distinction of animals into clean and unclean is designed especially to teach by figure the difference between sin and holiness, and between the friends of God, and his enemies; yet in making this division God was pleased to reckon those in the class of unclean, the flesh of which has generally been esteemed unpalatable, or unwholesome, and in this he displays wisdom and goodness.

We find the *Partridge* mentioned in scripture but twice, and the Hebrew name is (קֹרֵא) Kōrā. The Septuagint in one place has *Nuktikorax, Night-raven;* in the other it has Pĕrdĭx, a Partridge. In three languages the name is almost alike; in Greek and Latin *perdix,* in French *perdrix.* The original signifies, *one that is calling;* it may allude to the drumming of the Cock-Partridge, in which, according to the instinct of the bird, he calls to his mate. Some have argued that the original signifies a *wood-cock;* but for myself I still think the Partridge is intended.

The figure in the cut is of the Hen-Partridge, and this, with the following description, I have given from nature.

The weight was one pound five ounces; length from the end of the beak to the end of the tail one foot two inches; spread of the wings from tip to tip one foot seven inches; length of the thigh three inches; leg two inches; middle toe one and a half inch; outside toes one inch each; heel toe one half inch; length of the tail five inches; full spread of it about ten inches; number of feathers in the tail eighteen; all with a black bar, but the two middle ones; breadth of the bar five eighths of an inch, from bar to end of tail feather three eighths of an inch; which space is light gray, or ash-color, sprinkled with black very delicately. The two middle tail feathers have seven black bars across them of the breadth of one eighth of an inch, in a small measure zig-zag; spaces between them about half an inch. The other tail feathers have ten similar bars; spaces between them one quarter of an inch; these are gray, delicately crinkled over with black. Wings from pinion to tip seven inches; longest wing feather five inches; on the outward edge of it are seven oval spots of yellowish white; fewer on the others, as their length diminishes. These spots when the wing is shut, form bars obliquely across it; between these are bars of dark iron gray; covering feathers of the wing iron gray, sprinkled finely with black; on that side of the stem of the feather, which is towards the back is a crossing bar of black, on the other side, and running parallel with the stem, a stripe of reddish, or dirty yellow. From the shoulder of the wing, when shut, towards the tail, and between the wing and the back, are five or six large feathers; on the upper side of their stem, towards the back of the bird they are chiefly black; on the other side of the stem yellowish white; they cover a space of about four inches in length. The feathers on the back, as far as in sight, are iron gray sprinkled with black; on the middle part of each a black oval spot, of near half an inch in length, in the midst of which is a yellowish white spot of a heart-like shape, the point of it towards the tail. Immediately under the outside feather is another, attached to it, and of down, to protect the bird in winter. The feathers on the belly and lower part of the breast are large, the visible part of the largest more than an inch in length and breadth, and white with a bar of black, or dark slate, three eighths of an inch wide. On the upper part of the breast, towards the throat, the feathers are smaller, becoming gradually of a dark orange, barred with slate color; on each side of the neck, a little above the shoulder of the wing is a tuft of feath- ers barred with iron gray and black, and several black, changeable to green; this tuft is much larger on the male than on the female. On the back of the neck the feathers are orange, barred with black, and tipped with white. On the head is a crown of long narrow feathers, dark orange, barred with black. The tufts on the neck, and this crown the bird erects at pleasure. Each ear is covered with a small tuft of feathers, black and dark orange in stripes. From the part to which the tip of the wing reaches, when folded, a tuft of fea- thers begins, and runs partly under the side of the tail to within two inches of its extremity; they are white, edged with yellow, and barred with quite narrow bars of black, three eighths of an inch distant from each other.

The legs are covered with downy feathers, dirty white, half way to the foot. The beak is short and obtuse, moderately hooked.

The food of the Partridge consists of tender brakes, young clover leaves, Partridge-berries, beech nuts, the buds of trees, and things of like nature. Their flesh is very white, and of a fine grain; and has a little of a spicy taste, with a little of bitterness; is of itself rather dry, but with a little butter is very delicious. Their usual litter of eggs may be reckoned from eight or ten to a dozen, or more; are rather smaller than a pullet's egg, and of a light blue. Their young ones much re- semble the chicks of the barn fowl. When the mother is suddenly surprised, she utters a peculiar note, at which every young one is hidden almost in an instant, so that it is not very easy to find them: the mother

18*

then flutters round with brustled feathers, still drawing her pursuer away from the place of her young, till at a convenient distance, and then takes wing ; but when the danger appears to be over, she returns to the place of her young, and with a peculiar call brings them all quickly round her. I have seen a brood hatched by a hen ; they followed her about like chickens, but in a few days, one after another, they all died.

The Partridge is a bird that will not be readily tamed ; I believe the most ingenious methods to domesticate them would prove fruitless. The easiest way to take them is with snares, hung in the doors of little fences, made across their paths. These snares should be fastened to the end of a pole, so balanced, and fastened to the limb of a small tree, that when the bird is caught, the heavier end of the pole may descend, and raise the bird at the other end into the air ; this prevents their being devoured by owls or foxes ; and when a rabbit is so caught, it prevents his escaping by gnawing off the snare.

The Partridge is diffused over the world in all climates ; varying in some respects with the climate; in Greenland, tho' brown in summer, they are white in winter.

The Partridge in New-England inhabits almost all parts of the forests ; but is more commonly found in the neighborhood of springs and swamps, and in old deserted roads, and in fields that have been cleared, but are grown up again with bushes, leaving some spots still open, and overspread with young white clover.

In 1 Sam. 26 : 20, David says to Saul, the king of Israel is come out to seek a flea, as when one doth hunt a *Partridge* in the mountains. In this he represents himself to Saul as too small, and too unworthy an object, to be so hotly pursued by a king with an army of men.

Saul certainly conducted very foolishly in pursuing his son-in-law in this manner, but he was so filled with jealousy respecting him, that nothing but his death would satisfy him.

In Jeremiah 17: 11, we read : As the Partridge sitteth on eggs, and hatcheth them not ; so he that getteth riches, and not by right, shall leave them in the midst of his days, and at his end shall be a fool. It is said that several Partridges will sometimes lay their eggs in one nest; that then the female that sits upon them cannot well cover them, so that many are spoiled, and are left. This may illustrate the case of a man, who by theft, robbery, or murder, acquires the riches of another, but at length is detected, and is either put to death for his crime, as in the case of murder, or robbery ; or at least is obliged to give up his ill-gotten goods, and to leave them in the midst of his days; and who would not say that such a man is a fool ?

> Dear youth, who deign this book to read,
>   Let wisdom guide your course ;
> Is wealth your object ?   Then take heed
>   You seek it not by force.
>
> Nor let your hand in secret seize
>   Possessions not your own ;
> No, not a *pin*,—'twill God displease,
>   And he will make it known.
>
> Then, when your folly stands display'd,
>   Unveil'd in open view,
> Your guilt with poison'd shafts array'd
>   Will pierce your spirits thro'.
>
> No ! Let your toiling, busy hand,
>   In honest labor plied,
> Bring what you need to your command—
>   Be thus your wants suppli'd.
>
> Let grace withal renew your heart,
>   And on a Savior lean ;
> Then, when the world and you must part,
>   Your mind will be serene.

PEACOCK.

THE name of this bird is found in the English bible three times ; in 1 Kings 10 : 22, 2 Chron. 9 : 21 , and in Job 39 : 13 ; in the two former of these places the Hebrew name is (תֻּכִּיִּים) Tókkĕyyēm, or Tôkĕyyēm. In 1 Kings 10 : the Septuagint has Pĕlekētōn ; in 2 Chron. the name is omitted. Junius and Tremellius have in both places *Pavones, Peacocks*. The French bible has *Paons* meaning the same. Buxtorf, Pagnin, and a number of Hebrew-Rabbis, explain the word of Peacocks. The name in Job rendered Peacocks is in Hebrew (רְנָנִים) Renânēm. The Septuagint has here, The wing of the *delighted ones* exulteth. Buxtorf understands by this name *Peacocks*, and Pagnin the same, but adds that some understand it of the ostrich, from the loud cry of this bird, the name coming from a word which signifies *to exclaim*. The Peacock, as well as the ostrich, has a loud and disagreeable cry. Junius and Tremellius and the French bible have Peacocks ;

but after weighing all circumstances, I think it probable the Hebrew name means *ostriches ;* but the passage
is difficult to translate.

The figure I have taken from a little book, I believe,
anonymous.

The Peacock is a native of the southern part of Asia,
and is found wild, and sometimes in large flocks on the
islands of Ceylon and Java ; in external appearance it is
doubtless the most majestically beautiful bird among the
whole feathered race. Its head is crowned with a crest
of singular form, and delicate texture ; its neck and
breast are of a dark green, changeable to gold color ;
its back is green, glossed with copper color. His tail
is composed of a very long train of feathers, the vanes
of which on the sides of the stem resemble in shape
those of the ostrich feather, being a sort of downy
threads, but towards the extremity of each feather is a
space of two or three inches diameter, in which the
vanes are woven together, as in other fowls, forming a
smooth apartment, in the centre of which is a heart-
shaped spot of dark purple, changeable, which is surrounded with the colors of the rain-bow, in most beautiful arrangement, and very brilliant. Above the longer
feathers are such as are smaller and shorter, lying over
them as shingles on a roof ; and several other courses,
still shortening. When the bird wishes to display himself, he erects these feathers, spreads them fan-like, almost to a circle, opens his wings a little way, and droops
them, till their tips come near the ground, and struts
about, exhibiting the appearance of majesty united with
inimitable beauty. When he turns his broad fan to the
sun, nothing in visible creation surpasses the brilliancy
and richness of the exhibition.

Meantime there is something to balance all this beauty; the bird is very destructive to the fields and garden of the husbandman; he feeds upon various insects and tender plants, but seeds and grains are his most natural food, and he is especially fond of barley, and to supply himself he does much mischief; his voice is a hoarse, unpleasant, and very loud kind of screaming; so that those who are unacquainted with it, are ready to think it the noise of some fearful wild beast. The female is far less beautiful than the male, and indeed exhibits but a moderate share of external charms. She lays for a sitting six or eight eggs, of a grayish white color, and hides them from the male, lest he should destroy them.

When Peacocks were first brought into Greece, they were held of such value, that the price of a male and female was more than the amount in our money, of $130. Many came a long distance to see them, and paid a stated price for the sight.

Solomon, who was a great naturalist, as we learn from the scriptures, had brought to him in his ships from Tarshish, with his gold, silver, and ivory, an assortment also of apes and Peacocks. While they added splendor to the court of his palace, no doubt the description of them added richness to the books, in which *he spake of beasts, and of fowl, and of creeping things, and of fishes.*

It may be here remarked, that the more needful, and valuable qualities of many other fowls secure for them a welcome retreat, where the Peacock with all his stateliness and beauty is not admitted. This should remind those, who feel a temptation to pride themselves in their beauty, or in the splendor of their dress, that many of less comely features, and who are content to appear in humble array, may be called to fill more important stations than they, and occupy in them more usefully. Beauty is certainly not to be despised, if it be found associated with good sense, humility, and active benevolence ; but where beauty is all, that *all* is of but little value.

> Are witless youth of beauty vain,
>   And proud of gaudy dress ?
> The noisy *Peacock*, with his train,
>   May well their state express.
>
> Their rosy bloom awhile may please,
>   Their dress may give delight,
> Their sparkling gems and gold may seize,
>   And charm the unwary sight.
>
> But when they speak, the empty mind
>   Betrays its want of sense ;
> To worthless trifling how confin'd
>   Is all their lips dispense !
>
> Soon beauty fades, and rich array
>   Must many a rival own,
> By many a bird with plumage gay,
>   In all its pomp outshone.
>
> Seek wisdom then ; expend your pains
>   For virtue's nobler store,
> These give a charm, which still remains,
>   When beauty's known no more.

PELICAN.
—

THIS bird is reckoned in the number of those forbidden to the Israelites ; its name is found in the English bible in Lev. 11 : 18, Deut. 14 : 17, and Ps. 102 : 6.

The Hebrew name is (קָאָת) Kââth, found in the above named places, and in Is. 34 : 11, and in Zeph. 2 : 14.   In the two last places the English bible has *Cormorant*.   Bɪxtorf has *Platea*, and *Pelecanus*, both signifying *Pelican*.   He derives it from a word which signifies to *vomit*,   because the pelican swallows shell-fish, and after they are so far concocted, as to be easily opened, vomits them up, and separates the meat from the shell for its food.   Pagnin has *Onocrotalus*, from two Greek words, which signify the braying of an ass, because the bird thrusting his neck into the water, utters a sound, which resembles such braying.   It means the same as the pelican.   Some of the Rabbis have thought the *cuckow* to be intended : but their supposition is not well supported.   The Septuagint has Pĕlekăn, in all the above named places, except Zeph.   Junius and Tremellius have *Platea* in each place, meaning Pelican ; the French bible has *cormorant* in each place.

The figure given is taken from the Cabinet.

There are several kinds of Pelicans ; the more common is about the size of a common goose.   Their general color on the old continent is said to be white ; on the new continent a light gray, or ash-color ; the middle part of the back feathers is blackish, the neck of a yellowish, cast.   Its beak is commonly about fifteen inches in length ; attached to the under part of it is a large bag, or pouch, capable of holding two or three gallons of water.   It is a bird of the aquatic kind, of strong wing, but rather sluggish in its habits.   When impelled by hunger, it takes its flight to the water, and when over a shoal of fish, it darts down with unerring aim, seizes the fish it has its eye upon, places it in its pouch, and rises in air ; it presently darts down again, and continues thus to do, till its expansive receptacle is filled. It then retires to some solitary place, and feeds upon its store, in a half dormant state, till it is exhausted. When hunger again impels, it goes again in quest of food.

The female lays her eggs to the number of five, or six, and hatches them without nest upon the bare ground; she feeds them with masticated flesh from her pouch, till they are able to provide for themselves; but she discovers no energy in defending them, when attacked. The young may be easily tamed, but are useless and expensive domestics, for they are very voracious, and their flesh is not eaten.

It is said by a certain naturalist that he had a Pelican, which at the command of its master, would go off in the morning, and return at night with its pouch filled with prey, a part of which it would unload for its master, and a part retain for its own use. Another speaks of a tame Pelican, the property of the Emperor, Maximillian, that always attended his army, and that lived till 80 years of age.

To gather food, to lounge, to feast and sleep,
Seems near to bound the Pelican's desires;
Useless to him, who would the glutton keep—
So much to fill its appetite requires.

How many a *fowl*, who bears the name of man,
Seeks little else, alike voracious too;
And scarce more useful, spends his narrow span
In doing nought of what he ought to do.

Well, such may feast, and sleep, and dream away
Their precious time; but let the wretches know
Their dreams will end, and then will come a day,
To plunge them headlong in a world of wo.

Let nobler souls their appetites deny,
Restrain their sleep within becoming bounds,
And press their pinions to the blissful sky,
Where glory wheels its everlasting rounds.

19

PIGEON,

—

The name of this bird is found in scripture ten or twelve times; it is reckoned among the clean birds. Its name in Hebrew is (יוֹנָה) Yōnâh; which preceded by Benā, as it is in most cases, signifies *young Pigeons*. In Gen. 15: 9, we have in Hebrew (גּוֹזָל) Gōzâl, rendered *young Pigeon*; the word properly signifies the young of birds, whether pigeons, or other birds. The young Pigeons named in scripture were without doubt the young of the tame Pigeon, or what we often call *young doves*. The common name in Latin is *columba*, in French *pigeon*. I have treated of the tame pigeon under the article *dove*, which see.

As the *wild Pigeon*, in Latin *Columba agrestis*, is a species of the same genus with the tame Pigeon, I here give a figure of it, which I have drawn from nature, with a brief description.

The male, or Cock-Pigeon, may be described as follows ; its length from the crown of the head to the end of the tail thirteen inches, height, as it naturally stands, eight inches. Its head is a shade between purple and ash-color ; its neck changeable from purple to crimson ; the part of the back towards the head ash-color, inclining to purple ; lower down inclining to blue, then to purple again towards the tail. The shoulder of the wing light purple, inclining to slate color ; thence to the large feathers purple, inclining to ash-clor ; quill feathers, and next large feathers, dark slate, with a very narrow edge of white ; upper tail-feathers the same ; under tail-feathers, the half towards the point, white. The throat is white, the breast purple, the belly nearly white, the legs flesh color, the beak and claws black.

The females are somewhat less beautiful in their plumage, than the males ; they build their nests of a few dry twigs interwoven together slightly, upon the small branches of trees, and commonly lay but one or two eggs at a sitting. The young take their food out of the mouths of their parents. When a person comes near them, they put themselves into a frightful attitude, as if to make resolute resistance.

In New-England these wild Pigeons come frequently in large flocks from the south in spring, then disperse themselves thro' the forests, and rear their young, and early in autumn retire in large flocks again ; leaving, however, many thousands behind, which are taken in nets, or otherwise, and furnish a delicacy for the tables of the rich, and of the poor.—They feed on various kinds of berries, and on various kinds of grain ; but the wheat fields, after they are reaped, are their favorite places of resort. They are a bird of a strong wing, and fly about a mile in a minute.

How quick in its motions, how lovely its eye,
How mild and how timid the Pigeon appears ;
How swift in its course, when it rises to fly ;
On its pinions well balanc'd no rival it fears.

The purple, the crimson, the gold and the green,
That gloss its gay plumage, are charms to the sight ;
Its tints sweetly blending in softness are seen,
And give the beholders a thrill of delight.

Its nature so harmless, its love so sincere,
When its mate is once chosen, and yields to the choice,
That her lover will leave her she never needs fear,
To coo to a stranger, and tarnish her joys.

We here have an emblem for those who would join
In dear marriage union, to teach them to live
Most faithfully true, and their skill to combine
To make it their pleasure sweet pleasure to give.

PYGARG.
[Figure from Bewick.]

—

THIS name is found in the English bible in Deut.
14 : 5. In Hebrew it is (דִּישׁן) Dēshōn. In the
Septuagint Pūrgàrgŏs. Junius and Tremellius have
Strepsiceros ; French bible *Chevreuil.* Buxtorf speaks
of the animal as a kind of wild goat, not unlike the

deer. Pagnin merely calls it *Pygargus,* and notes that the Targum has Unicornis. This animal, distinguished in the ceremonial law among the clean beasts, is supposed to be the white Antelope; an animal of the goat-kind, which is seen in large herds on the plains of the Cape of Good Hope. It is not unreasonable to suppose that it inhabits the warmer parts of Palestine.

The height of this animal is about two and a half feet, its length somewhat more than three feet, its tail nine or ten inches, its ears more than six inches; its horns, if straightened, would measure about nine inches; at their base they are three inches thick, and their distance from each other one inch; they widen, till they become about five inches a part, and then bend towards each other till their distance at the tips is but about three and a half inches. Half way up they are encircled with rings, and then are smooth, and end in a sharp point. Their principal color is brown, or light rust-color; the breast, belly, and inside of the limbs are white; the head is white, except a dark brown list, which passes from each corner of the mouth, over the eyes, to the base of the horns. A like list passes on each side, dividing the white on the belly from the rust color above it; the buttocks are white, and a white stripe runs from the tail half way up the back, bounded on each side with a dark brown list. The hair is generally fine and soft, but the dark lists consist of longer hairs.

When they are pursued, it is diverting to see them leap over one another's heads to a considerable height; they are so fleet, that it requires a good horse to overtake them, but sometimes so bold as to allow a hunter, though on foot, to come within gun shot of them. Their flesh is very palatable, is more juicy, and has a

19*

more delicate flavor, than that of other gazelles. At
the Cape of Good-Hope this animal is called by the
Dutch, *Spring-Bok,* by the English, *Springer.* They
migrate in small companies from the interior of Africa
to the neighborhood of the Cape, and continue there
about three months, and then set out for their return in
herds of thousands, pursued by lions, hyaenas, and other beasts of prey, which make great havoc among them.
The lion is such a destructive enemy to them, that the
Hottentots call them the lion's sheep.

——The numerous herd moves on ;
The timorous Pygargs, beautiful in shape,
Of active limb, in color varied, gay ;
In manner sportive, arm'd with curved horns ;
Of charming eye. They gambol o'er the plain ;
Where vernal fields invite their stay, they crop
The tender plants, and leave a waste behind.
But who can blame them ? 'Tis the needful food
Their Maker sends them. All his creatures share
A portion of his bounty ; wide his hand,
His liberal hand he opens, what he spreads
Well pleas'd they gather, and express his praise
In marks not doubtful of exulting joy.

Look ! From his covert, with his shaggy mane,
With leap terrific, and with fiery eyes,
Springs the fierce lion. All the herd alarm'd,
In flight seek safety, but must leave behind
The victim seiz'd. The fierce hyaenas now
Sieze here and there another. Then leaps forth
The cruel tiger, desolation spreads
On every side around him.—All have foes,
And all have sufferings in this world of sin.
The lion, tiger, and hyaena share
Their due proportion of the mass of ill.

Man has *his* foes ; himself the common foe
Of beasts and men, and to the snares expos'd
Of fallen angels. But there comes a day,
When he, who made, will meliorate the state
Of this disordered world, educing still
From evil good, as his great plan matures.

One awful mark of sin's malignant aim,
Deep in the depths beneath the beauteous frame
Of all creation else, where foes of God,
Apostate men and angels must sustain
Just retribution, ever must abide

A needful warning. All beside is heaven,
And bliss and glory, ages without end.

QUAIL.

The name of this bird occurs four times in the bible;
first in Exodus 16 : 13, then in Num. 11 : 31 and 32;
and last in Psal. 105 : 40: In the Hebrew bible it is
found three times in the singular number, (שְׂלָו) Se-
làu; and once in the plural (שַׂלְוִים) Sălvēm. In
the Septuagint ŏrtŭgŏmĕtra. Common Greek ŏrtŭx.
Latin *Coturnix*, French *Caille*.

There is a very general agreement among interpreters
that the *Quail* is the bird intended, and it is reckoned
among clean birds. It is a bird of the gallinaceous
kind, much resembling in appearance and manners the
partridge, but of not more than half the size, being but
little more than seven inches in length, and being a migratory bird.

Mr. Harris in his natural history gives the following
description of the quail. "The feathers of the head
are black, edged with rusty brown; the crown of the
head is divided by a pale yellow line, beginning at the
bill, and extending to the back. Above each eye there
is another line of the same color; the chin and throat
are whitish; the breast is of a pale yellowish red, spot-

ted with black; the scapular feathers," (those on the shoulder of the wing) " and those on the back are marked with a long, pale yellow line in the middle, and with iron colored and black bars on the sides. The coverts of the wings are of a reddish brown, elegantly barred with paler lines, bounded on each side with black. The tail, which consists of twelve short feathers, is barred with black and very pale brownish red; the legs are of a paleish hue."

The Quail builds its nest on the ground, and produces about six or seven young ones at a sitting. It is said that the Athenians abstained from their flesh, but were in the habit of training them to fight for their amusement, as cock-fighting has been a shameful amusement of more modern times. The flesh of the bird, however, is a delicacy, and in more modern times has generally been esteemed so.

Quails are found in great numbers on the coasts of the red sea and on the coasts of some parts of the Mediterranean; they abound in other warm countries. In some places they are taken in nets, into which they are allured by a sound resembling the note of the quail, made with a pipe called a quail-pipe.

We learn from Exodus 16: that when the Israelites came to the wilderness of sin, which is between Elim and Sinai, they began to be short of provisions, and murmured against Moses and Aaron, as if they had brought them into the wilderness to destroy them with hunger. They ought to have remembered how God divided the red sea for them, and to have believed that he was able to provide for them all needful good; and in faith they should have prayed to God for a supply, instead of murmuring. God was angry with them, but for his name's sake he would not destroy them, but sent them flesh and bread in abundance; in the evening Quails, and in the morning manna. The Quails, used temperately, would no doubt have been to them a wholesome and pleasant food; the manna, when baked, was in taste like thin cakes of flour mingled with fresh oil, that is, olive oil, new and good. It would have been grateful food, if they had continued to use it thankfully. The Quails were brought from the sea, the *red sea*, for according to Asaph in Psal. 78 : they were brought by an east wind, and a south wind ; and where the Israelites then encamped there were coasts of the red sea on the west, on the south, and on the east of them.

How long the Quails were continued to them at this time we are not informed ; but probably till through a too free indulgence they grew weary of them, so that they were withheld. But in the course of the second month of the second year after they left Egypt, about the time of our April, the Israelites had become weary of the manna, and longed for flesh again, and Quails were sent them in such abundance, that they were supplied with them for a whole month, at least, though they amounted probably to more than two millions of persons. They were then in Taborah. As a punishment for their murmuring God suffered them, we may believe, to feast themselves with this flesh indiscreetly, and in this way to bring upon themselves the deadly plague, by which a vast multitude of them were destroyed. I may here remark that the Creator of the world has all the laws of nature perfectly under his control, and can dispose of them as he pleases. In some cases, according to the adjustment of his great plan, a people may become wicked in just such time and place, that the laws of nature in their common, (not miraculous) operation, may bring destruction upon them. Such may be the destruction by hurricanes and earthquakes. At other times by a special, or miraculous interposition he may increase, or diminish the power of the operation of the laws of nature, so as either to bestow blessings, or to inflict judgments ; as by withholding rain or by giving it more abundantly, than it would come without such interposition. Thus it was probably in the case of the Quails ; it might have been customary in the common course of events for them to take advantage of south east winds in the spring to migrate from the coasts of the red sea to the west and north west ; but by a miraculous interposition God might send a strong wind from the east, and then from the south, and accumulate the Quails about the camp of Israel ; and by a like interposition he might cause them to be so weary that they could fly no farther, and even scarcely move. At other times he effects his purpose by operating beyond or above the laws of nature ; as was certainly the case, when Jordan was divided, and so when the manna was given.

A lesson which we should learn from this history is, to be cheerfully contented with such things, as God in his providence is pleased to provide for us ; or if we feel the need of a greater supply, to go to him in humble, believing prayer, and ask him to bestow it.

> How unbelieving, and how daring too
>   Were Israel's hosts, when thro' the desert led ;
> Scarce had they pass'd the red sea safely thro',
>   When lo, they murmur—Who shall give us bread ?
>
> God gave them bread ; the manna round them fell ;
>   *So light, so pure, as if 'twere angels food,*
> They see, they wonder ; who its name can tell ;
>   They taste, they feast, and might pronounce it good.
>
> But soon, rebellious, they complain again ;
>   We must have flesh ; our soul remembers still,
> How by the pots, on Egypt's fertile plain,
>   We sat, with bread and flesh and fish at will.

God gave them flesh; he sent the savory Quails;
  In rich profusion round their camp they lie;
But while they feast, his wrath their host assails,
  The plague breaks forth, and they by thousands die.

Learn this, dear youth, the simplest food is sweet,
  Receiv'd with temperance and a thankful heart;
It matters little what we daily eat,
  If God well pleas'd his blessing still impart.

But tho' with Dives in his sumptuous fare
  We sit, and revel, truth divine may tell,
If God's blest presence be not with us there,
  We are but ripening for the woes of hell.

RAM.—[*See Sheep.*]

RAVEN.
[Figure from the Cabinet.]

THE *Raven* is a bird so common and well known, as hardly to need a description.   Its name in scripture is

(עֹרֵב) Gnōrābv; Septuagint Kŏrăx; Latin *Corvus*; French *Corbeau*. The name first occurs in Gen. 8 : 7, where we are informed that Noah sent forth a raven out of the ark, to see if the waters were abated from off the earth; but the raven returned not again; probably he found carcases floating upon the water, upon which he both rested and fed. The Hebrew name above inserted is found eight or ten times in the bible, and is very uniformly interpreted of the Raven, in the Greek, Latin, and French translations; so there is little reason to doubt but the Raven is intended by the original. In Levit. and Deut. it is reckoned among the unclean birds.

The Raven, the rook, and the crow, appear to be distinct species of one general family. The rook and Raven are much alike in size, and other appearance; but the rook may be distinguished by a whiteness round the roots of the beak, occasioned by its often thrusting its beak into the ground after worms, and other insects upon which it principally feeds, and so is rather a defence, than a destroyer of grain. The crow is considerably less than the Raven, and has a straighter beak.

The Raven is of a jet black, glossed on the back with deep blue. Its belly is a dusty black. It is the largest of the crow kind, its length being about two feet and the spread of its wings four feet. It is a native of almost every region, and appears to be but little affected by climate, except that in the extreme north they they are said to be white. The Raven feeds much on carrion, on this account it is useful. It feeds also on frogs and reptiles; sometimes it destroys hares and young poultry. It feeds on various grains; in New-England it is often very mischievous in fields of Indian corn, or maize, pulling it up, and taking the kernel from the root soon after the shoot appears above the ground. Various expedients are used to prevent it. Sometimes yarn, and sometimes cedar bark in narrow strips is drawn over the field, from stake to stake; this frequently keeps them off. A booth, or bough-house, built with bushes by the side, or in the midst of a field, with the image of a person presenting a fowling piece in it, visible through the crevices, has sometimes a good effect; for they are a very shy bird, so that with fire arms it is difficult to get within gun-shot of them. Some soak the corn in warm water mixed with tar before it is planted, some soak it in a solution of Glauber's salts.

The Raven may be easily tamed, but is a voracious, thievish, and troublesome inmate. The female builds her nest on the branches of trees with small sticks, and lines it with slender roots, and lays five or six eggs for a sitting. Their young are generally very noisy in their calls for food; but I believe are not generally neglected, though sometimes, through want of success in obtaining it on the part of their parents, they may suffer with hunger.

In 1 Kings 17: we read that God commanded Elijah, when a famine of three years was about to commence, to hide himself by the brook Cherith, and said to him, I have commanded the Ravens to feed thee there. He did as he was commanded, and the Ravens brought him bread and flesh in the morning, and bread and flesh in the evening. Notwithstanding the conjectures of some writers to the contrary, I doubt not but that Ravens, literally, did bring him bread and flesh, and that the same divine power, which provided manna in the wilderness for Israel, provided bread and flesh in a miraculous manner for these Ravens to convey to him. This providence teaches us an important lesson; it is, to obey God cheerfully in all situations, and to place an

20

implicit trust meanwhile in him, not doubting but that he will order all things to work together for our good.

In Job 38 : 41, God says from the whirlwind, Who provideth for the Raven his food ? When his young ones cry unto God, they wander for lack of meat. When Ravens are numerous, aside from the providence of God, there is something so casual and uncertain in the existence of a supply for them, that probably their Maker suffers them frequently to become very hungry ; on this account they may have an instinct to hasten their young from their nests, that they may early learn to seek a supply for themselves in part, to divide the labor of providing ; these young ones in wandering round may sometimes become so hungry, as to be clamorous for food ; but God will not often leave them to suffer long with pinching hunger ; so it will be, that an individual of the herd or flock of some neighboring husbandman will sicken and die, or be torn of wild beasts, or the offal of some slain beast will be thrown out, and then they will have a feast, and partake of it with a keen relish.

In Psal. 147 : 9, David says of God, who giveth the beast his food, and the young Ravens, which cry. This teaches that God provides generally for all his creatures. Several years ago a young raven, nearly full grown, wandered many days about my fields, having but one leg. It was often vociferous, apparently for food ; its parents appeared to attend upon it with peculiar care ; but for want of a sufficiency of other food, it frequently fed upon green peas, which grew among my potatoes ; even the lame and the feeble are provided for in some way.

In Prov. 30 : 17, Agur says, The eye that mocketh at his father, and despiseth to obey his mother, the Ravens of the valley shall pick it out, and the young eagles shall eat it.   This is a solemn admonition to youth to respect, and cheerfully to obey their parents; otherwise they will be exposed to some peculiar evil at the end of their days, if not before.   I knew in my youth a man of whom it was said that he treated his aged parents unkindly.   He was then rich, reaping the fruits of a large productive farm ; but after a while most of his children became dissipated, and died young.   He fell himself by little and little.   The last I heard of him his estate was gone ; he lived in a hut a long distance from his former home, was miserably poor, and spent no small proportion of what he could earn for ardent spirits.   No doubt but many a disobedient youth, by the very means of having been disobedient, has become poor and pennyless, and has enlisted into some army for bread, and has fallen on the field of battle, where the Ravens and young eagles have plucked out his eyes and devoured his flesh.

In Songs 5 : 11, the Bride, the Church, is represented as saying of her beloved, Christ ; His locks are, bushy, and black as a Raven.   This comparison helps to fix the meaning of the original word, for the Raven in almost every clime is black.   Black hair and bushy locks at the time when Solomon wrote, and in that region, were probably considered a mark of beauty.   The Song of Songs is intended to celebrate the excellencies of Christ, and the graces of the Church by those things among others, which were accounted most pleasant in a shepherdess, and her beloved.

Finally, in Luke 12 : 24, Christ says to his disciples, Consider the Ravens, for they neither sow, nor reap ; which neither have store house, nor barn ; but God feedeth them ; how much better are ye than the fowls ?

As much as to say, If the benevolent Creator is so provident for the less valuable of his creatures, will he neglect to provide for his more valuable creature, *man* ?
We may answer, No.   Let us trust in the Lord, and do
good, so shall we dwell in the land, and verily we shall
be fed.

> The Maker of all has ordain'd a supply
>   The naked to cover, the hungry to feed ;
> He hears the Young Ravens, when loudly they cry,
>   And sends in due season the food which they need.
>
> If the fowls of the air are provided with meat,
>   Tho' they sow not, and reap not, nor lay up in store,
> Why then are we anxious for what we shall eat ?
>   If the fowls are of value, our worth is much more.
>
> The good old Elijah by Ravens was fed,
>   And drank of the brook, where long hidden he lay ;
> But who gave the Ravens the meat and the bread
>   This prophet, so worthy, to nourish and stay ?
>
> 'Twas God who provided ; let's trust in his name,
>   Nor pass our time idly, but fill it with good ;
> We then may dwell safely, nor sink under shame,
>   But share his kind bounty in shelter and food.
>
> Let youth be admonish'd their parents to love,
>   To honor and fear them, and freely obey ;
> Or God will in anger look down from above,
>   And their eyes may soon go to the Ravens a prey.

ROE.
[Figure from Bewick.]

THIS animal, commonly called the *Roe-Buck*, is frequently noticed in scripture. It is reckoned among
clean beasts. The first mention we have of it is in
Deut. 12 : 15. The unclean and the clean may eat
thereof, as of the *Roe-buck* and as of the hart. The
Hebrew name is here (צְבִי) Tsebvē ; it is the same
in most other cases, where we have Roe, or Roe-buck, in
English. In 2 Sam. 2 : 18, we have the Hebrew name
in the mas. plural, with a defect of the letter Vōd. In
2 Chron. 12 : 8, we have it in the mas. plural with
âlĕf inserted before the termination. In Song 2 : 7,
and 3 : 5, we have it in the feminine plural, with âlef
before the termination. In Prov. 5 : 1*,* for *Roe* we
have (יַעֲלָה) Yăgnlâh, which Buxtorf renders *Rupi-
capra, Rock-goat.* The Septuagint has generally Dŏr-
kăs ; Junius and Tremellius *Caprea ;* the French bible
has sometimes *Daim,* and sometimes *Chevreuil,* the former signifying a deer in general terms, the latter a Roe-
buck. Pagnin and Buxtorf have *Caprea,* and *Capriolus,*

20*

either of which may signify the Roe-buck. Some have
supposed that the Gazelle, or Antelope is intended by
the Hebrew, and they remark that the Roe is rarely
found in Palestine, and the region round.   But rare as
they may be in those regions in modern times, they
may have been numerous in the days of Solomon.   So
many interpreters agree in assigning the name of Roe,
that it seems to me probable that the Roe is intended
by the original.

  The Roe is among the smallest of the deer kind ; but
little more than three feet long, and hardly two and a
half feet high.   It is a very good looking animal, very
swift, and very light and graceful in its motions.   Its
horns are round, about nine inches in length, and towards the tops divided into three branches.   Their hair
is generally long ; each hair ash-colored towards the
root, but towards the end barred with black, and the
end itself yellow.   The hairs on the face are black,
tipped with ash-color ; the breast, belly, and legs are
yellowish white, the rump clear white.   They do not
go in herds, but live in families, the male, female, and
their young ones ; and their attachment to each other
appears to be strong.   When the young are able to provide for themselves, they are driven off to form other
families.   The female's time of gestation is about five
and a half months.   She commonly brings forth two
fawns at a birth, sometimes three.   When danger approaches, she hides them, and suffers herself to be pursued.   When they range in their native wildness,
their flesh is pleasant, especially when they are about
eighteen months old.   When kept in park, it is rather
insipid, for they refuse to be domesticated.   The Roe,
when hunted, runs in circles, repeatedly coming into
the same track, and then leaps aside from it into some

thicket, and lies still, while the hounds pass by, and miss him. They shed their horns in autumn and renew them in winter; the first year they have no antlers. They are found in various parts of Europe and Asia, and in some parts of America. Formerly they were found in Wales, and in the North of England, but of late have disappeared from the island, except in Scotland.

In the time of King Solomon they were among the luxuries of his table. Their elegance of form and gracefulness of motion has given them a place in the song of songs, to set forth in figure the moral beauty of the Church of Christ, and the glory of Christ himself. From their very great swiftness, they are named to illustrate the swiftness of some of David's soldiers. But they are so liable to be hunted, either for their flesh, or for amusement, that Babylon, when God in his wrath was about to bring the forces of Cyrus against it, is in Isai. 13 : 14, compared to a chased Roe, it should find no place of safety, no rest.

> The Roes of the mountains, how graceful and fleet,
> Of shape well proportion'd, and light with their feet ;
> With their eyes they look pleasant, to gain our esteem,
> But we hunt, and destroy them, and pitiless seem.
>
> The Roe's a fine emblem of family peace ;
> His love for its partner is ne'er known to cease ;
> He 'bides with her daily, as friend with his friend,
> Nor quits her in danger, but seeks to defend.
>
> Let *us* then observe them, and learn the true art
> Of peace in our dwelling, and how to impart
> Pure joy to our inmates, who seek in our shade
> A rest from the dangers and ills that invade.

SATYR.
[Figure from Bewick.]

—

THE English name, Satyr, we find in the bible but twice; first in Isai. 13 : 21. And *Satyrs* shall dance there. Next in Isai. 34 : 14. The *Satyr* shall cry to his fellow. The Hebrew name in the mas. sing. is (שָׂעִיר) Segnēr; this Hebrew name with its plural is found in several other places in the Hebrew bible. Sometimes it is rendered, *he-goats*, sometimes *devils*, sometimes *rough* or *hairy*. The Hebrew name is from a root, or primitive word, which signifies to be *horribly afraid*. Probably in the first place, some ape, baboon, or hairy orang-outang was seen standing, or walking erect, by some person or persons not acquainted with such animals, and these persons were much frighted, and gave it a name signifying great fear, or horror. The name might afterwards be given to he-goats because of their hairy, shaggy appearance, and antique motions. When the idea of evil spirits was contemplated on some occasion, the imagination might form some hideous shape to represent them, as a form made up in part of man, and in part of beast; and persons afterwards might suppose that evil spirits would sometimes appear in such fearful shapes; so the name might be appropriated to devils, or daemons; and devils at length might come to be worshipped under the form of he-goats, apes, or orang-outangs. I think it probable that what are called Satyrs in Isaiah, were literally orang-outangs, or some other species of the ape kind; though it is possible that wild goats are intended. I have, however, given the figure of the orang-outang, which is sometimes called the Satyr.

Answering to the Hebrew name, the Septuagint has Daimōn, *Dæmon*, or devil; and Mātaiŏs, a vain thing. Junius and Tremellius have *kops*, *a horrible bird;* and *Dæmon*, *Devil.* French bible *Lutin*, a *Fairy*, or *Ghost*, and *Diable*, a *Devil.*

The historian, *Pliny*, speaks of certain animals found on some of the mountains of India, sometimes running upon all four, and sometimes walking erect, and being exceedingly swift, so as not to be easily taken, except when old or sick. These animals might give the ancients the idea of their *Fauni*, or gods of the woods.

The orang-outang, a figure of which I have given, is the largest of the ape-kind, being sometimes six feet in height, and of strength sufficient to overcome a man. Their bodies are covered with dark hair, thick on their backs, but thin on their breasts, and forward parts. They resemble man in shape, more than any other animal, and being destitute of human reason, this resemblance seems to render them the more disgusting to the sight. This animal is more mild in his disposition than

the baboon, and less frivolous, than the monkey. His
natural food is nuts and fruits ; but, taken young, he
may be tamed, and will feed on a great variety of food,
and may be taught to sit at a table, and take tea with a
good measure of dexterity.

In their wild state they will assemble in companies,
and assault and kill negroes ; and will also drive away
elephants from the places of their abode. They are
found in Madagascar, Africa, Borneo, and some parts of
the East-Indies.

Long before the event took place, God by the prophet, Isaiah, threatened the overthrow, and utter ruin
of Babylon, and that the place of the city should become the place of the resort of a great variety of fearful
and disgusting wild beasts, birds, and creeping things ;
and among them Satyrs are reckoned, whatever they
were. The prediction has been fulfilled ; the place
has been a desolation already more than two thousand
years.

> Sin—what an evil, what a bitter thing !
> What desolations thro' the earth are found,
> The fruit of man's transgression. Sin will bring
> Wo where it reigns, and make distress abound.
>
> What mighty empires thro' the lapse of time
> Have risen to splendor ; we can say, They've been ;
> They had their birth, their infancy and prime,
> They fell to ruin, overthrown by sin.
>
> Must sin and ruin hold perpetual sway,
> And blight the beauty of this world below ?
> Sweep all that's lovely from the earth away,
> And scatter scenes of desolation ? No !
>
> The Lord of worlds, from whose creating hand
> Sprang at a word the universe that is,
> Will in due season give the strong command,
> And wo and ruin will give place to bliss.
>
> War then will cease, the arts of peace abound ;
> Earth-quakes and storms in quiet silence lie ,
> Life-giving influence will o'er spread the ground,
> And love look smiling from a placid sky.

SCORPION.

—

The name of this reptile is found repeatedly in the bible, both in the Old and New Testament. Its name in Hebrew is (עַקְרָב) Gnăkrâbv; in Greek Skŏrpĭŏs; Latin *Scorpio*, and *Scorpius*; French *Scorpion*. The figure is from the cabinet.

The Scorpion in general terms may be called a reptile; but is reckoned by naturalists in the class of insects. The few that are found in cold regions are very minute, hardly worth noticing; but in hot countries they are formidable, being some of them from two to four inches in length, and some of them of the size of a small lobster. Those of this large size are found in Africa, particularly on the gold coast, and on the island of Java. Those of the common size are numerous in Italy, Spain, and the southern parts of France; also in the deserts of Arabia, and probably in other warm climates. There are some of them yellow, some black, and some brown. They have eight legs on which they creep, and some say four, and others say eight eyes. Their body is divided, or marked with six narrow, transverse bands, of a light color. From near the head of the scorpion proceed two arms, with large claws at the ends of them, very much resembling those of the lobster, and bearing much the same proportion to the size of its body. Its tail, which is largest near the end, is divided by several articulations ; the extremity of the tail is a hooked point, armed with a very poisonous sting, the venom of which, in the case of the largest, is generally fatal to those who are stung with it. They harbor in stony places, among old ruins, and behind the furniture of houses ; so that in some hot countries they are among the greatest pests with which the people are afflicted. In such countries persons are liable to be stung by them when moving furniture, which has been for some time undisturbed, and when working among old ruins. The pain of their sting is very distressing, even when it does not prove fatal.

In Deut. 8 : 15, Moses admonishes the Israelites never to forget the Lord their God, who led them thro' that great and terrible wilderness, wherein were fiery serpents, and *Scorpions*, and drought. Upon this passage I may observe—1. It should teach us to acknowledge God, as the kind Being, who has preserved us thro' all the difficulties and dangers from which we have come forth in safety.—2. It should teach us to put our trust in God, and go forward in duty, notwithstanding all the formidable evils that lie in our way.—3. It admonishes us never to forget God, but to keep him always in our grateful remembrance.—4. The wilderness in which were the Scorpions alluded to above, lay to the north-east of the eastern branch of the Red sea, and to the south-east of the Dead sea. It was a portion of the great deserts of Arabia.

In 1 Kings 12 : 11, Rehoboam says to the people of Israel, I will chastise you with Scorpions. By Scorpions is here probably meant a kind of scourges, armed with thorns, the points of which to the persons scourged were, for the moment, somewhat like the stings of Scorpions. The idea which Rehoboam intended to convey was, that he would rule the people with much more rigor, than his father. But the event may teach us, that it is much better policy for rulers to govern with mildness, than with severity. Those however, who will be refractory under a mild government ought to be treated with severity.

In Ezekiel 2 : 6, God exhorts the prophet not to be afraid, though he dwelt among Scorpions. By Scorpions we are here to understand wicked men, who are disposed to turn their hatred and malice especially against those, who are most faithful in the service of God. But by what God says to Ezekiel, we should be taught to admonish the wicked faithfully, though it may expose us to persecution.

In Luke 10 : 19, the blessed Savior says to his disciples, Behold I give unto you power to tread on serpents and Scorpions. By serpents and scorpions we may understand the subtle and mortal enemies of the gospel ; and the promise of Christ amounts to this, that ultimately his faithful followers shall triumph over all their enemies ; in many cases they shall be wonderfully delivered from them in this life ; but in the coming world their victory will be complete, though here they may seem to be vanquished.

Luke 11 : 12. If he ask an egg, will he offer him a Scorpion ? Will any earthly parent so treat the request of his child ? In ordinary cases he will not. And will our heavenly Father give his children evil for good, in answer to their humble requests ? Far from it. If he withhold the particular thing, which they desire, it will be because he sees that it is not on the whole good for them. But he will bestow something better instead of it. But their requests should be made with sincerity and submission.

In Rev. 9 : 3, we read of locusts coming out of the smoke which ascended from the bottomless pit; and that power was given to them, as the *Scorpions* of the earth have power. These locusts were probably Saracens, or Arabians, followers of Mahomet, who for five months, that is, five times thirty prophetic days, equal to one hundred and fifty years, made rapid conquests, and dreadful ravages around them, and then became a settled people, after which their power began to decline. The power of the Scorpion is the poison of its sting ; the worst mischief which the Saracens, or early Mahometans did, was to infuse into the minds of thousands, and of tens of thousands, the poison of their destructive sentiments,—Let us hence learn to beware of error in religion; it may be more fatal to destroy the soul, than the poison of the Scorpion to destroy the body.

How painful and deadly the Scorpion's sting
To the man, or the beast, who receives its deep wound ;
Its poison—how sharp is the smart it will bring ;
What a pest are these reptiles, where much they abound.

But errors and falsehoods in matters divine
Are poisons more fatal, than reptiles contain ;
To a death ever during the soul they consign ;
A death, which in essence is keen, living pain.

Then learn, my dear readers, to seek for the truth,
In things of religion, much more than for gold ;
This truth will prepare you to flourish in youth,
When suns are decaying, and time waxes old.

SERPENT.—[*See appendix.*]

SHEEP.

THIS animal is found in all parts of the world. It is of different species in different climes and countries, and of different varieties in the same country. It appears from scripture that they were a domestic animal from the creation, even Abel was a keeper of sheep. They were kept in large flocks in ancient times in Judea, and in the countries round about. The name of sheep occurs in some form more than a hundred times in the bible. For the gratification of the curious, who have not leisure to investigate, I give the name in its different forms in several languages in the following table.

The figures given by the cuts are copied from the Cabinet.

	Hebrew.	Greek.	Latin.	French.
1	צֹאן Tsōn :	*Probata.*	Pecus,Oves.	Troupeau.
2	אַיְל ăyĭl ;	*Krios.*	Aries.	Belier.
3	רָחֵל Râ-hrhāl ;	*Probaton.*	Ovisfemina.	Brebis.
4	כֶּבֶשׂ Kĕbvĕs ; כֶּשֶׂב Kĕsĕbv ;	*Ars,arnos.* *Amnos,arnion.*	Agnus.	Agneau.
5	כִּבְשָׂה Kĭbvsâh ; כִּשְׂבָּה Kĭsbvâh ;	*Amne.*	Agna.	Jeunebrebis.
	שֶׂה Sāh ;	a lamb, or kid, male or female.		

1 flock, sheep. 2 Ram. 3 Ewe. 4 He-lamb. 5 Ewe-lamb.

EWE.

THE Sheep kind is distinguished by having hollow horns, bent backwards, some of them in a bow, some of them in a sort of spiral wreath, and all encompassed more or less with wavy rings : also by having eight cutting teeth in the lower jaw, and none in the upper.

Among the different sorts we may reckon the common sheep, the Guinea or African Sheep, and the Cretan, or Wallachian Sheep. Among the varieties, the broad-tailed sheep ; its tail sometimes a foot broad, and so long, that the shepherds have occasion to put under it a little board with wheels to keep it from the ground ; it is found in Persia, Syria, and in the north of Africa. The many horned sheep, having from three to eight horns, their wool long, and resembling hair ; found in

Iceland, and other cold, northern regions. The fat-rumped sheep ; the male light brown, mixed with white, the female black and white, their wool long and thick ; instead of a tail they have a large protuberance of fat, covering the rump, which is esteemed a dainty, and eaten with the lean of the mutton.—The Guinea sheep is large, strong, and swift, with coarse wool, short horns, and pendulous ears.—The Cretan or Wallachian sheep, has curious spiral horns, growing upright, and winding much in the form of a cork-screw ; they have long shaggy wool ; and are said to be the *strepsiceros* of the ancients.—The Spanish or Merino sheep are remarkable for the fineness of their wool, the thickness of their fleeces, and for retaining their wool longer than the common sheep.

Some sheep are kept for the fine flavor of their flesh ; some for the fineness of their wool, which is manufactured into broadcloth ; some for the length and strength of the pile, suitable for worsted ; some for the largeness of their size.—Great improvements have been made in England by crossing, or mixing the breeds of sheep. Similar improvements are making in the United States.

We may now say of the Sheep in general terms, that next to the cow, it is the most valuable animal, which the benevolent Creator has been pleased to form for the use of man. It prepares the best of manure ; its entrails, bones, and horns are brought into the manufacture of many useful articles ; its flesh is agreeable and wholesome food ; its skin is valuable for parchment, book-binding, and many other uses. In some countries its milk is esteemed for making excellent cheese. And what shall we say of its wool ? For the colder climates it is of almost indispensible necessity for clothing our persons, and for furnishing our beds.

21*

Such is the mildness and gentleness, and patience of the sheep, that it has been in almost all ages the emblem of these virtues in man.

In the spring, when the fields are spread with their green flowery carpet, what can be more delightful, than to see a dozen, or a score of lambs, with their snowy fleeces, chasing one another round in circles, leaping up and down the rocks, and putting themselves into all manner of antick postures, manifesting the height of animal enjoyment! They afford much diversion for children, and give them much delight.

The sheep has its enemies. Among the most destructive of these is the wolf; though sometimes the ram, with his hard forehead, will make a severe attack upon the dog, yet sheep in general are but poorly able to defend themselves against their many invaders. They depend upon man; to him in some sense they look up for protection; and seeing how much comfort he derives from them, he seems to be under obligation to make them as safe and comfortable as may be, the little time it is consistent for them to live.

When Abraham was on his way to Mount Moriah, at the commandment of God, to offer his son, Isaac, in sacrifice, what an affecting question it was that Isaac proposed; Behold the fire, and the wood, but where is the *lamb* for a burnt offering?——It was an interesting and prophetic answer, which Abraham returned: My son, God will provide himself a lamb for a burnt offering.—The harmlessness, innocency and gentleness of the lamb has caused that it should be the most common sacrifice under the typical dispensation, and that it should be especially the emblem of the Son of God, who gave himself to be a sacrifice for our sins. *Behold the lamb of God that taketh away the sin of the world!*

In more than twenty places in the New Testament the Son of God is called a Lamb. There is no one thing in the universe, that has come to our knowledge, more astonishing, than the condescension of the divine Word to be a sacrifice for sin; and no one thing calls more imperiously for our sincere and lively gratitude.

See the young Lambs, so brisk and gay,
  With fleeces clean and white,
Sport o'er the meads in harmless play—
  How pleasant is the sight !

What mildness in their look appears ;
  What innocence and peace ;
Their sport the vernal season cheers,
  And makes dull sorrow cease.

But oft the lamb, when more mature,
  Must fall beneath the knife,
A greater blessing to secure,
  To save the shepherd's life.

Thus once the Lamb of God was slain,
  His life he freely gave,
From sin, and guilt, and endless pain,
  The sons of men to save.

What endless thanks we mortals owe
  For this display of grace ;
Shall we reject the favor ? No !
  To day the gift embrace.

SNAIL.

—

THIS reptile is twice named in the English bible. 1.
in Lev. 11 : 30, where the Hebrew name is (חֹמֶט)
Hrhōmĕt; Buxtorf, *Limax, Testudo*; *Snail, Tortois.*
He notes that some others call it a *Lizard.* Pagnin
agrees with Buxtorf, except that he seems rather to decide for lizard; he calls it also a *land cockle;* the Septuagint has *Saura*, a *Lizard;* Junius and Tremellius
have *Chamœleon;* French bible, *Limace*, a Snail. If
we call it lizard, we have in this passage lizard twice
in immediate succession; I incline rather to the idea of
Snail or *Tortois.*

We have the name, 2. in Psalm 58 : 8, or 9, in Hebrew (שַׁבְּלוּל) Shäbbelôl; Buxtorf and Pagnin both
have *Limax*, the *Snail;* Septuagint Kĕrŏs, *Wax;* Junius and Tremellius, *Limax;* French bible *Limacon, Snail.*
The name is from a root, or primitive word, which signifies a *way* or *path;* the Snail, as he moves, leaves a
path after him of the slime, which proceeds from his
body. In this latter place I hardly doubt but that the
Snail is intended.

The Snail more common in New England is of two
kinds, one without a shell, in shape somewhat resembling the half of a bean, but more pointed at each end,
and its back more raised; it is nearly of a light choco-
late color, except its belly, which is flesh color. It

has no legs, but progresses, very slowly, by means of a muscular motion of the parts of the belly ; and it leaves, as it moves, a portion of slime behind it, which in dry weather appears to waste it away, so that for removing it generally chooses wet weather. The other kind has a shell of a spiral form, beginning from a centre, and enlarging, as it winds, till it comes generally to a size somewhat larger than a walnut, and is much of the same color; at the large end of the spiral is an open mouth, at which the Snail, when about to move, protrudes the forward parts of its body, and thrusts forth from its head something like a pair of horns; it then progresses, but almost as slowly as the shadow of the sun-dial; whence the proverb, *As slow as a Snail.*

In Leviticus the Snail is named among the unclean reptiles. In Psalms it is brought forward as a term of comparison, to show how the sacred penman desired that the wicked, and especially wicked rulers or judges might melt away, and become extinct, as if they had not been. It is certainly desirable that the wicked should disappear from the community, either by renouncing their wickedness, and ceasing to be the wicked, which is most desirable ; or by being taken away out of life, which is more desirable, than that they should continue to destroy the peace of society. The apparent melting of the Snail, as he moves, is a fit emblem of the desirable wasting away of the wicked from a nation.

> Slow, as the dull, scarce moving, lazy Snail
>   Gains on his journey, so the slothful dream
> In every worthy plan ; their efforts fail,
>   For mere cold wishes all their efforts seem.
>
> Slow moves the Snail, and on his path behind
>   Leaves filthy slime to mark his useless course ;
> So, could we trace the sluggard's worthless mind,
>   There we should find of filth a fruitful source.

But as the Snail, progressing, wastes away,
    So may the wicked from the earth subside,
Till heaven can look, and see a brighter day,
    And truth and justice thro' the world preside.

SPARROW.

The name is found in the English bible in Psalm 84 :
3, and 102 : 7, in the old testament; and in Matt. 10 :
29, and Luke 12 : 6, in the new.   In the two places in
the old testament the Hebrew name is (צִפּוֹר) Tsĭp-
pōr; Buxtorf renders it *Avis, Avicula*, a *bird*, a *little bird;*
but he notes that it may in some cases be rendered,
Passer, that is, *Sparrow*.   Pagnin agrees in substance
with Buxtorf, but is somewhat more particular.   The
Hebrew name frequently occurs in the bible, and is
sometimes rendered *fowl*; generally, *bird;* rarely *Sparrow*.   The Hebrew word was probably a general name
for birds, especially small birds, but sometimes meaning
some one species.   The Septuagint in the two places
in Psalm has Strŏŭthĭŏn, *Sparrow;* and the same Greek
word is used in the passages above named in the new
testament.   It may signify a little Sparrow, and also a
small bird.

The figures of the Sparrow I have taken from the
Cabinet, which gives the following account of them.

" The Sparrow builds its slovenly nest under the eaves of houses, and in holes of walls ; but, very often, it is said, it takes possession of the nest of the martin. Mr. Pennant has repeated a story to show that this insult, to the expelled martin, does not pass unrevenged ; for he assembles his companions, and having, by their assistance, plastered up the hole with dirt, flies away, twittering in triumph, leaving the miserable invader to perish in the possession of his robbery. Sparrows are a perpetual tax on rural industry ; and no precaution can prevent them from sharing in the mess allotted to the pigeons and the poultry. But though they are most familiar birds, they are so crafty, that they are not easily taken in a snare. In autumn they collect in large flocks, and are often shot by dozens in the barn yard, and on the neighboring trees and hedges. Sparrows have no song ; and, in the country, we are reconciled to their disagreeable cherrup, as we are in town to the incessant noise of the street. This species is common in Europe, and is met with in most parts of Asia and Africa. The body is variegated with brown, gray, and black ; the chin of the male is black. The female lays five or six eggs of a reddish white, spotted with brown, and has commonly three broods in a season."

This description appears to agree in some respects with a bird in New-England of about half the size of the robin, which sometimes comes in large flocks a little before harvest time, and feeds on several kinds of grain, especially oats, of which it makes great havoc a little before they are ripe.

The Sparrow, not timid, but cautious and sprightly,
    Desires near our dwellings to fix its abode ;
Not gay in its plumage, but still not unsightly,
    It sports on the hedge, and enlivens the road.

It throngs oft the barn-yard, it visits our tillage,
    It picks up the hay seed and grain from the ground ;

Sometimes on the house-top, alone, in the village
  Bemoaning the loss of its young it is found.

It builds in old ruins, but shows little art in
  The style of its nest, and a hole in the wall
May serve for its dwelling, but oft the poor martin
  It robs of its lodging, and plunders its all.

But not unavenged the martin endures it;
  He comes with his fellows and closes the door,
With clay, twigs, and stubble he firmly secures it,
  And leaves the poor Sparrow his fault to deplore.

So may the vile thief, who our dwellings would plunder,
  Be caught in his mischief, and shut up in gaol,
Where bars are so strong, that to break them asunder
  His arts and his efforts forever must fail.

But Sparrows are harmless, compar'd with transgressors
  Among—shall I say it?—the proud human race;
The thieves and the robbers, the cruel oppressors,
  The lewd and profane, that our image disgrace.

The Sparrow, so little, so common, so many,
  That when in the market they're offer'd for sale,
E'n five can be purchas'd for less than a penny,
  Not one without leave of our Maker shall fail.

If God so provides for the birds, nor denies them
  A pittance to nourish, to comfort and cheer;
And hears the young Sparrows, and amply supplies them,
  His friends and his children he surely will hear.

Then trust, my dear youth, in his merciful kindness,
  But trust as his children, and live as his friends;
He'll feed you, and clothe you, and heal you of blindness,
  And make for your sorrows an ample amends.

Spiders. J.F.

Hazle-nut Spider.

SPIDER.

—

THE name of this insect is found in the English bible three times. 1. In Job 8 : 14, literally, The house of a *Spider* his trust. 2. Isai. 59 : 5; the web of a *Spider* they will weave. In these passages the Hebrew for Spider is (עַכָּבִישׁ) Gnăkâbvēs; Septuagint Arä-khnē. Junius and Tremellius, *Arancus,* French, Araig-nèe; all meaning *Spider ;* Buxtorf and Pagnin agree in the same definition. The name in the third place is found in Prov. 30 : 28, The *Spider* with hands will take hold. Here the Hebrew is (שְׂמָמִית) Semâmēth ; Junius and Tremellius and French bible render it Spider, as in the other places. Pagnin rather favors the idea that the ape is intended; but names the Spider, the newt, which resembles a lizard, and one or two other animals. Buxtorf rather decides for the Spider, but speaks of the newt, as not improbable ; but attrib-

22

utes the notion of the ape to the latter Hebrew Doctors. The first name intends the Spider without dispute. The second is more doubtful; the hesitation is between spider and newt; but I cannot conceive of any thing peculiarly wise in the manners of the newt; but Agur is speaking of four things very wise, and the operations of the Spider exhibit great sagacity; I conclude therefore for the Spider.

The figures given I have drawn from the life. The different species of Spiders are somewhat numerous; they vary much in size, shape and habits. Some of them at their full growth appear to be not much larger than the head of a great pin; others, even in New-England, have the abdomen as large as a common hazle-nut, and in some of the tropical climates they are so large as to be frightful, and their bite dangerous. The Spider of Martinico is said to have the abdomen as large as a hen's egg, and covered with hair.

Some Spiders have long legs, and run very nimbly; others have short legs, and when disturbed, gather up their feet, and feign themselves dead. The color of the different species is various; the more common house Spider is nearly gray; but some of them are almost black, with ornamental white upon the back. The field Spiders differ one from another very much in their colors. The largest of which I have given a figure, I call Hazle-nut Spider, its general color much resembles that of a hazle-nut, but it is ornamented with numerous crinkling lines of a darker color; its legs are barred with alternate light and dark. The other large one represented, is jet black, ornamented on the back with bright yellow. Time would fail to describe all their colors. They differ in shape; some have the corselet almost as long as the abdomen; others are al-

most all abdomen ; some have the abdomen round, others oval. Their food varies ; most of them feed on
flies, but some of the larger kinds feed on grass-hoppers,
and the filaments of their net are nearly as strong as the
thread of the silk-worm. Their webs, or nets differ.
House Spiders, in general form their webs of innumerable filaments, 'running in every direction ; and they are
attached to the corners of rooms and windows, and at
the inner side of the web they have a hole formed, like
a little tunnel nose, where they lie concealed, till their
prey is entangled, and then dart upon it. One kind of
the field Spiders spread their nets horizontally, from
four to eight inches broad, upon the tops of the stubble
of grass, which in a dewy morning may be seen for
many rods round, sometimes nearly one in every square
yard. The filaments of these nets run in all directions,
and are closely woven ; these also have their hiding
holes. Another kind hang their nets perpendicularly,
in the form of a wheel, the spokes of which are crossed with a spiral thread from the circumference to the
centre. Spiders have different modes of depositing
their eggs ; some deposit them under the eaves, window stools, and loose shingles of houses, and in such
like places, enclosing them in close woven cods, on the
outsides of which are other coverings. Some enclose
them in round, white cods, resembling a pea, and, when
they travel, they carry it with them, attached to their
tail. These when hatched attach themselves by dozens to the back of their parent, and are conveyed by
her from place to place at pleasure.

Spider.

The large black and yellow Spider, of which I have given a figure, was drawn from life, August 12, 1826, while on the center of her wheel-net.   Soon afterwards I found, suspended by the side of her net, a cod in the shape of a pear, of the size of a lady's thimble, and of a reddish brown color; I took it away, and found the covering nearly as strong as common silk stuff; on opening it I found in the centre a little round cod, of the size of a large pea, encompassed on every side with a silky substance, like a lock of fine wool and containing the eggs.   I visited the Spider again some days after, and found another cod, like the former suspended nearly in the same place; this I left remaining; and I could not but admire the wonderful instinct, which the benevolent Creator has given to all his creatures to preserve their kind.

On the 20th of August 1825, I was amused with seeing a wheel-net Spider, within the space of about an hour demolish his old net, and construct a new one. The old one was decayed, and partly broken; to remove it he began at the centre, and leaving a new thread behind him, as he went, he progressed towards the circumference, gathering up several of the old filaments with his hands, and so disposing of them, that I could see them no more. Having come to the circumference in one direction, he returned to the centre, and progressed in another direction, till the old wheel was all removed, and then part of the radii, or spokes, of the new wheel were placed; he then fixed the remaining radii, that were needed, and finished his net with a spiral thread from the circumference of the wheel to the centre, fastening it to every spoke, where it crossed it. The revolutions of the spiral were about one fifth of an inch distant from each other, and the diameter of the wheel about eight inches. When his work was done, he placed himself at rest upon the centre of it watching for the flies that might be entangled.

The Spider spins its thread from a glutinous substance in its abdomen, through a number of little orifices, spining at once more, or fewer threads, which at a little distance from the Spider unite in one, making a thread more fine, or coarse, as occasion requires. It has also the power of shooting out this thread to some distance from itself, that the wind may take it and draw it away to some remote, elevated object, to which it adheres, as soon as it touches it; the Spider can then run upon it to this object. I was once passing a meadow recently overflowed; by the side of it was a wall, and the wind was breezing in the direction from the wall to the meadow; on this wall were thousands of Spiders, with their heads towards the wind, and with their threads protruded from them, and floating in the air to the distance of some rods, being seen by glistening in the sun-beams. At another time I saw a Spider nearly as large as a common window fly, sailing over a common at the height of a number of feet, with some

22*

yards of his thread extending from him in several directions.—-Who taught them thus to fly? and who teaches them at other times to turn their heads to the wind, that the breeze may draw their thread from them to the branches of some neighboring tree? It is God, who gives them this wisdom; they are exceedingly wise. The Atheist may say—All this happens by chance. I say, no, it is the work of God.

In Job 8 : 13, 14, we read, The hypocrite's hope shall perish; whose hope shall be cut off, and whose trust shall be a Spider's web. What is more tender, and what more easily broken, than the Spider's thread? What a lively figure is here given us of the vanity and worthlessness of the hypocrite's hope! As a very gentle touch of the finger snaps the filaments of a spider's web; so the hour of death will give to the winds every hope of future happiness, which is not built through faith and repentance upon Jesus Christ. Even those, who flatter themselves that there is a probation state after death, in which they may yet become prepared for happiness, will find their expectation fail them, when they come into the world of spirits.

In Isaiah 59 : 5, we read of the wicked, that they hatch cockatrice-eggs, and weave the Spider's web; the cockatrice-eggs probably mean in this passage destructive errors, and the hatching of them the broaching of these errors. The weaving of the Spider's web intends the framing of those false refuges, under which the wicked think to hide themselves; or those thin coverings, with which they hope to veil their wickedness, so that they may escape the just punishment due to them; but God sees through their veils, and marks their iniquities, and the hail shall sweep away their refuges of lies.

Who gives to the Spider its wisdom and skill,
  Or instinct of wonderful power,
To spread its net fitly to catch and to kill
  The insect it means to devour ?

'Tis God ; his creation displays on its face
  The marks of benevolence pure ;
To each class he has form'd the descent of its race
  Thro' ages he gives to secure.

The Spider, as if with intelligent hand,
  Takes hold of the threads of her net ;
And the king this intruder in vain would command
  His royal rich palace to quit.

When the hypocrite spins a fair hope in his mind,
  That his days will be ended in peace,
Grim death his vain fancies will give to the wind,
  And cause his fond visions to cease.

The men of injustice, oppression, and fraud,
  Oft weave, like the spider, a veil.
To hide their transgressions and follies from God,
  But at last their thin cover will fail.

From the Spider learn wisdom, dear youth for the ends,
  For which your Creator has made you ;
Of God and the Savior be always the friends,
  And your consciences will not upbraid you.

S T O R K .

[Figure from Goldsmith.]

—

THE name is found in the English bible five times,
and the original in the Hebrew bible six times. In
Lev. 11 : 19, and Deut. 14 : 18, it is reckoned among
the unclean birds. The name in Hebrew is (חֲסִידָה)
Hrhässēdâh ; from a word which signifies *kindness.*
Buxtorf renders it *Ciconia, stork ;* Pagnin the same,
except in Job 39 : 16 ; where he supposes it to mean
the ostrich. Septuagint Erōdiŏs, heron. Junius and
Tremellius *ciconia ;* French bible, *cigogne,* both meaning *stork.*

The stork is a bird of passage ; it is found in the
neighborhood of marshy places in almost all parts of
Europe, where they make their appearance about the
middle of March, and continue through the summer,
and then retire to warmer climates. When about to
retire, they assemble in large flocks, and take their
flight together in the night, leaving none behind. They

sometimes visit the isle of Great Britain, but do not breed upon it. They are rather larger than the common heron, and in external appearance much resemble the crane, but differ in color and in manners. The crane is ash color and black, the stork white, and dark brown, or black ; the head, neck, breast and tail are white ; the feathers between the tail and back, and the outside feathers of the wings are black. The beak and legs are long, and of a reddish color. The crane has a loud, shrill voice ; the stork is silent, except that it makes a peculiar snapping with its beak. The crane feeds on vegetables and grain ; the stork on frogs, fish, birds, and serpents. The crane lays but two eggs, the stork commonly four, and builds her nest on the tops of houses, on old ruins, and on trees. The crane shuns the abodes of men ; the stork is familiar among them.

Storks are said to nourish their aged parents, and to bear them, when weary, upon their backs ; and as their very name in Hebrew signifies *kindness*, it is supposed to have been given them on account of this filial affection. The English name, stork, is supposed to have come through the Saxon from the Greek Storgē, which signifies natural affection.

In Psal. 104 : 17, we read, As for the Stork, the fir trees are her house. Though Storks build their nests very frequently upon the highest parts of old ruins, and upon the tops of houses, yet several ancient writers speak of them as building upon trees.

In Jer. 8 : 7 we read, Yea the Stork in the heaven knoweth her appointed times, and the turtle and the crane, and the swallow observe the time of their coming ; but my people know not the judgment of the Lord. It appears from this that the Stork was migratory in Palestine ; and the regularity with which this, and some other birds observed the time of their coming, and of their departure, God is pleased to notice, as a reproof of his people, who, though endued with rational pow- ers, were ignorant of the import of his dealings with them. They would not see, and believe, that the dis- tresses and afflictions, which he sent upon them were a chastisement for their sins; nor would they, even when solemnly warned of their danger, break off from those evil courses, on account of which they were threatened.   A similar unbelief, and indifference to the judgments of God, or at least a disowning of them to be intended for corrections, appears in modern times; it appears in our own favored land.

In Zech. 5 : 9, we read of two women, with wings like a Stork, bearing an ephah through the air from Je- rusalem to Shinar. These women were probably an emblem of those judgments of God, which should at length scatter many of the wicked Jews into the land of Shinar, and other regions far east from Judea, and fix them there in a state of hopeless captivity. This should warn all to fear and serve God ; for if we con- tinue to indulge in sin, though the judgments of God may seem for the present to delay, they will come at length, as on the wings of the wind, and will overtake us, before we are aware of it.

> Children and youth, your parents fear,
>   And as their age comes on,
> Let love in all your deeds appear,
>   To cheer their setting sun.
>
> Grudge not the help their age requires,
>   But let your hands bestow
> The needful good their soul desires,
>   And stay the tears of wo.
>
> Consider well the feeble days,
>   While infancy endures,
> And how the hand parental stays
>   The child, as strength matures.

What anxious cares the parent's breast
  Full many a day invade ;
How oft depriv'd of needful rest,
  When thoughtless youth have stray'd.

What hourly toil to form the mind,
  And well incline the soul ;
With due restraint the passions bind,
  And wild desires control ;

Consider this ; and as you hope
  That your declining day
Will find in filial love a prop,
  Your faultering steps to stay ;

So learn your parents to requite
  For all the kindness shown,
And your own sun, serene and bright,
  May then in peace go down.

SWALLOW.
[Figure from the Cabinet.]

THE name of this bird is found in the English bible
four times ; in Psalm 84 : 3, and Prov. 26 : 2, where the
Hebrew is (דְרוֹר) Dheror ; Buxtorf and Pagnin both
render it *Hirundo, Swallow ;* and note that it is so called, because it is indulged with the liberty of building
its nest in the habitations of men, for its name in Hebrew signifies *liberty.* They quote several Jewish Rabbis in support of this definition. Septuagint, Trūgŏn,
the *Turtle ;* and Strŏûthŏs, the *Sparrow.* Junius and
Tremellius have *Hirundo ;* French bible, *Hirondelle.*

Several other interpreters suppose the ring-dove to be intended, but in my own mind the evidence preponderates in favor of the Swallow. The ring-dove builds its nest on trees, and will not be domesticated, but it would well correspond with the habits of the Swallow to build on the deserted altars of the Lord.

The name of Swallow is found also in Isai. 38 : 14, and Jer. 8 : 7, where the Hebrew is (* * *) Gnâgôr; for which Pagnin, Buxtorf, and Junius and Tremellius have *Hirundo, Swallow;* some render it the mag-pie, some the crane. I think it probable that one of the kinds of Swallows is intended; but with respect to this, and some other birds, the particular species common in Pal_estine may vary from the particular species under the same names, that are more common with us.

The Swallows of New-England are of four or five species; the most common, I believe, is what we call the *Barn Swallow*, which builds its nest with mud, and a few spires of grass mingled with it, and lines it with feathers, that are shed from the poultry. Its nests are attached to the ribs, or to the rafters, on the insides of the roofs of barns and out houses.

They lay from four to five eggs for a sitting; they feed their young with flies, and other winged insects, taken in the air, and they are careful that each young one shall have its portion in succession, as I have seen by watching them. The male and female both spend much of the day flying round in mazy circles, collecting food for themselves, and for their young. Their note is rather lively and merry than melodious, and seems more like social conversation, than a song. When their nest is disturbed they cry, *tweet, tweet*, with a sharp voice, and dart swiftly near to the head of the invader. They appear in spring, and retire in autumn, but whether this species of Swallow is generally migratory I am not able to say; but that in many instances it spends the winter enveloped in mud, and at the bottoms of ponds, in the neighborhood of their summer abode, the evidence is such, that I cannot doubt it.

I may next notice the *Eave-Swallow.* This species build their nests under the eaves of barns and houses, making them chiefly of mud, in the form of little ovens, with a hole on one side, like the oven's mouth, through which to enter. Sometimes the whole space under the eaves of one side of a barn forty or fifty feet long, will be occupied with these nests, side by side, as I have repeatedly seen.

Another species is the *Ground-Swallow,* which much resembles in appearance the Eave-Swallow; for their nests they make a hole in a sand bank, most commonly on the shores of rivers, or of the sea, where the earth is so washed away as to leave steep banks; and, like the king-fisher, they place their nest at the further end of the hole.

Another species of the Swallow kind is the *martin,* larger than any of those commonly called Swallows, and usually depending upon the hospitality of man to build for it a house, in which to place its nest. Several years ago a pair came and perched on an out house, near which I was at work, and seemed as if by wishful looks to invite me to provide for them. Within a few days I constructed for them a convenient house, well painted; I had scarcely set it up, before they took possession of it; and it has been occupied every summer since. The male is black, glossed on the back with dark purple; the female on the back is dark slate color; on the belly nearly white. They are a garrulous bird,

23

and have several different notes to express their different passions.

Chimney Swallow.

The last species I shall notice is the *Chimney Swallow*. These are all over nearly black, but not of so deep a black as the crow. They build their nests in the flues of chimnies, that in Summer are not used, and sometimes in barns, and in hollow trees, as I have myself seen. These nests are made of small twigs, glued together with a gum, very much resembling that, which oozes from the cherry tree, without any mixture of mud. The nest is thin, and projects horizontally about three or four inches from the place to which it is attached. Their only note is a peculiar twitter, which they utter somewhat rapidly as they fly. Their tails are not forked, but the shaft of each feather extends beyond the vanes nearly half an inch like a black pin; by means of these little spears they help to support themselves,

when adhering to the side of a board, or chimney flue
These, as it appears from the testimony of persons who
have witnessed it, have been found early in the Spring,
clustered by hundreds, if not by thousands, in the
trunks of hollow trees, where they appear to have pas-
sed the winter, as bees in their hives. In a town in
the western part of New-Hampshire a respectable person, with whom I had some acquaintance about the
year 1791, related that early in Spring he met with a
large hollow tree in the forest, which he struck with
his ax, and a vast multitude of these Swallows issued
from the stump of a hollow limb towards the top of the
tree, in a continual stream for some length of time.
Since that time I have met with similar accounts from
other sources. How wonderful is that providence of
God, which furnishes a habitation for every kind of
creature, and which adapts every creature to the habitation designed for it !

The figure I have given of the Chimney Swallow, I
drew from the life, July, 1794. From the crown of its
head to the end of its tail it was four and a half inches, and to the end of its long narrow wings five and a
half inches. In the day time they are much upon the
wing, in pursuit of flying insects, and their flight is usually higher than that of the barn swallow.

The inspired penman of the 84th Psalm, whoever he
were, appears to have been, at the time he wrote it, in
a state of exile from Jerusalem, and much afflicted with
the thought that he was deprived of the privilege of
worshipping, on God's holy days, in his holy temple.
He seems to have almost envied the sparrows and swallows, which occasionally found places about the temple and altars of God to build their nests. The pious
feelings of the Psalmist are strongly marked in the as-
pirations of this Psalm ; and the like feelings ought to

pervade the bosoms of all, who profess to be the friends of God.

In Prov. 26 : 2, Solomon says, As the bird by wandering, and the Swallow by flying; so the curse causeless shall not come. The Swallow comes not without wings, and the curse of God falls not upon men without a just reason. In the day of adversity, then, let every one consider why he suffers; wherein have I transgressed? Is this the curse of an incensed God, a justly provoked Sovereign? Or is it the correction of a faithful father and friend?

In Isai. 38 : Hezekiah says, As a crane, or a Swallow, so did I chatter. To whatever birds the afflicted king here alludes, no doubt but the expression of his grief bore some resemblance to the note of those birds. I may here remark that the wise Creator has given not only to man, but also to many of the irrational creatures the power of expressing distress by peculiar exclamations, and tones and modulations of voice, which are readily understood by others. The utterance of the note of sorrow has a momentary effect in relieving distress; but the instinct for this utterance was probably given for a still more important purpose; even to excite the sympathies of those who hear it, to move them, either to endeavor to afford relief, or to shun impending danger; and also to excite an interest among creatures, which may on the whole, promote the cause of happiness.

In Jer. 8 : the Swallow is mentioned with other birds as observing the time of its coming. This passage, in addition to other uses, should remind us, as rational creatures, to observe the times and seasons, which God requires us to observe, with fidelity; and to be always in season for the discharge of the duties devolving upon us.

The twittering Swallow takes his flight,
    And round and round he flies
From morning's dawn, till sable night
    Ascends the eastern skies.

Of daily food the needful share
    With toil and skill he gains;
Such relish sweet attends his fare,
    As well rewards his pains.

'Tis *action* gives to life its joys;
    The sluggard is not blest;
The man who well his time employs,
    At night can sweetly rest.

'Tis action—not of every kind,
    But such as God inspires—
Which raises man, and forms his mind
    To join the heavenly choirs.

Let hands, and mind, and heart unite
    In labor, thought, and love,
As God approves, 'twill give delight
    Like that in realms above.

SWAN.

Figure from the Cabinet.

THIS celebrated bird is noticed among the unclean in
Lev. 11 : 18, and Deut. 14 : 16 ; the name in Hebrew
23*

is (תִּנְשֶׁמֶת) Tĭnshĕmĕth; Buxtorf has *Monedula*, the *Jack-daw*, and several other definitions, none of which correspond with the company with which the bird is associated in the original text. Pagnin has first *Cygnus*, the *Swan*, and then several other definitions. The Septuagint has Pŏrfūrīōn, an aquatic bird with purple feet and beak; unless it has varied the order of the names, which I some suspect it has; for at the end of verse 18, of Lev. 11 : it has Kūknŏs, the proper name for *Swan*. Junius and Tremellius have *Monedula;* the French bible, *Cigne, Swan*.

The Swan is an aquatic bird of which there are several species, as the wild, the tame, and the black Swan. The wild Swan inhabits cold northern regions; it is found in the forests and about the lakes in Lapland, where in summer it rears its young, and comes not into the warmer climates, unless compelled by severity of cold. It is smaller than the tame Swan ; it is of an ash color down the back, and on the tip of its wings ; the rest of its plumage is white. Its eyes are bare and yellow, its legs dusky. In New Holland the black Swan, (rara avis) rare bird as it is in Europe, is very common.

The tame Swan, much celebrated by the ancient poets, is in Great Britain the largest bird they have. Its plumage the first year is ash color; after they enter upon the second year it is white. Its flesh in modern times has been but little esteemed, though in times more early it was considered as a very important part of a great feast. Its legs are short, and on land its gait is not very graceful; but on its more congenial element, on the pool, or on the stream, no other bird can vie with it in elegance and majesty. The curve of its neck, the fullness of its breast, and the ease and gracefulness of its motions, as it sails forward, or wheels round upon the smooth surface of the lake, are such as to excite admiration.

The Swan enlivens the artificial pools of the man of fortune. It is a bird of peaceable deportment, but fierce, when irritated; its strength is such, that it will sometimes throw down, and trample upon a youth of fourteen or fifteen years of age, and break a man's leg with a stroke of its wing. No bird, but the eagle, dares to attack it, and he sometimes loses his life in the conflict. It builds its nest of withered grass near the water's edge, and lays seven or eight eggs, and its time of incubation is nearly two months. While the wild Swan has a loud, shrill voice, which may be heard at a great distance, the tame is silent, except that it sometimes hisses. It is supposed to live a hundred years, when nothing peculiar happens to shorten its life.

See, with his long, smooth, slender, graceful neck,
Now rais'd upright, now bending in a curve,
Now turn'd a spiral, while he looks behind him;
With snowy plumage, and with swelling breast,
And conscious grandeur, on the silvery pool
The Swan sublimely sails. To right and left
He wheels with graceful ease. The ducks and ducklings play
Round him, and at respectful distance eye
His majesty of motion. Thus on Ocean's wave
Is borne the lofty ship; with towering masts,
And snowy sails, in majesty it rides,
And breasts the foaming billows. At command
It feels the helm; its rapid course repress'd,
It wheels, and sails again. Around it sport
The little barges, with their narrow wings,
Due distance keeping.
         Like the Swan, dear youth,
Among the ducklings, would you thus appear
Among the baser throng? Respect yourselves;
Adorn your minds from wisdom's treasur'd stores;
Your busy musings turn to noble themes;
Let your whole hearts be warm in virtue's cause,
And venerate religion; fear the Lord,
And trust and love the Savior.—Be it then
That scorners shall reproach you, triflers vent
Their spleen and envy; you may sail unharm'd
Across life's ocean to the port of peace,
While others dash, and founder.

Wild Boar. J. F.

SWINE.

—

THIS is a general name for that class of animals commonly called *hogs ;* the male is designated by the name of *boar*, the female by that of *sow*, the young ones are called *Pigs*. They were forbidden to the Jews, as unclean. The name Swine occurs somewhat frequently in both testaments. In Hebrew it is (חֲזִיר) Hrhăzēr; in Greek, Hūs, Sūs, and Khŏĭrŏs ; in Latin, Sus, and Porcus ; in French, Pourceau.

Swine may be considered as holding an intermediate rank between those animals that feed on flesh, and those that feed on grass ; like the latter they are cloven footed, and feed chiefly on grass and vegetables ; like the former they feed readily on animal substances, and do not chew the cud. They are diffused over almost all parts of the earth, except what lies within the polar circles. The common parent of them is supposed to be the *wild boar ;* this animal is smaller than most of the varieties of the common hog, and his color is uniformly of a dark gray ; his ears are short and black, his hair long, and about

the neck and shoulders rather bushy. His snout is longer than that of the common hog; and he is armed
with two tusks in each jaw; those in the upper jaw
turn backwards, and then upwards ; those in the lower
jaw turn upwards and then backwards, and are sometimes eight or ten inches long; and frequently give
mortal wounds to the enemies that attack him; they
serve him also for tearing up roots, which are no small
part of his chosen food. The wild boar in his full
strength will turn out of his way for no single enemy,
not even for man. He is hunted by being pursued with
heavy dogs, till wearied down, and is then slain by the
spears of the hunters. His flesh is esteemed as agreeable food.

Common Boar.

The domestic hog is of several varieties ; their general color is a yellowish white ; but they are sometimes
black, sometimes about half black ; sometimes white,
spotted with black ; and sometimes reddish brown,
spotted with black. They vary in size ; some are large
and quite long, and tall in proportion to their bigness,
and require much food to fatten them. Others are
large, and their length moderate, compared with their
size ; their ears are broad and pendulous ; these require
less food than the long breed, are gentle in their disposition, but extremely filthy in their habits. Another

variety, which forty years ago was much the most numerous in New England, is smaller than the last mentioned, in shape well proportioned, with upright ears,
somewhat fierce in their disposition, but not so filthy
about their nests, as some other breeds. Another species is the Chinese breed ; small, short-legged, and re-
quiring but little food, they are almost always fat, if not
kept very penuriously. Their flesh is peculiarly well
flavored, and the grain of it fine. Other breeds have
been obtained by mixing some of the foregoing, and in
some cases considerable improvement has been made by
such mixtures.

In most parts of the world swine's flesh, which we
call pork, appears to be wholesome food, especially for
laboring people; and it is found very useful. The food of
the swine consists, much of it, of the offal, and wash, produced in the family, which otherwise would be thrown
away ; and their flesh will take up no more salt, than
is needful to preserve it ; to be sure, therefore, to keep
it sweet, put in more than is barely needful into the
tub, and what it does not need, will remain for the next
year. The figures given are reduced from Bewick ;
that of the sow was taken originally from one of the
mixture of the large British with the Chinese breed ;
she had at the time a litter of nineteen pigs to support.

Sow.

As a reason of the divine prohibition of swine's flesh to the Jews, besides that of teaching them to distinguish between sin and holiness, sinners and saints, it is not improbable that their filthy habits, their wallowing in the mire, &c. was taken into the account. It has also been said, that their flesh in and about Palestine is apt to promote the plague, and that this was a natural reason for the prohibition; but if there were no such reasons, God's will should satisfy us.

The herd of two thousand swine, of which we read in Matt. 8 : Mark 5 : and Luke 8 : were probably kept by Israelites to sell to their Gentile neighbors, which was not consistent with a due respect for that law of God, by which their flesh was forbidden to themselves, this might give the blessed Savior an occasion to permit the devils he had cast out, to enter into them, and destroy them. Those who explain this event by the supposition of a disease, merely, sent upon these Swine, do but little honor to the truth of the divine word.

The apostle Peter, in 2 Epis. 2 : very fitly compares apostates from christianity, or professors, who after a fair outward walk, maintained for a season, turn back again to their old sinful practices; to a washed *sow*, returning to her wallowing in the mire; this he speaks of as a true proverb; it is certainly very applicable to the case; and it may teach us that sin in the sight of God is a most loathsome thing, and that those, who live in the allowed practice of it, are no better in his sight than filthy Swine.

The holy Savior gives command,
The devils hear, nor can withstand;
They fear his word; the man possess'd
In haste they leave; they cannot rest.

The dæmons fear a threatening doom,
And tremble, lest the day be come
To send them down from earth to hell,
In hopeless torments there to dwell.

Near by upon a sloping green
A numerous herd of Swine is seen,
Fed by the Gadarenes with pains,
To fill their coffers with the gains.

As one the devils all implore
A short reprieve; they ask the power
The Swine to enter; leave is given,
And down the steep the herd is driven.

They plunge, and perish in the lake,
Their keepers fear—the place forsake,
Their owners see their hopes are lost,
And pray that Christ would leave their coast.

At their request the Lord withdrew,
And with him went his blessing too;
Thro' unbelief they lost a friend,
The kindest, best, that heaven could send.

Dear youth, be warn'd, your spirits train
For virtuous deeds; from vice refrain,
Nor roll, like Swine, in all the mire
Of filthy lust, and loose desire.

If thus ye do, and leave the path
Of heavenly truth, the Lord in wrath
May say, 'My grace shall strive no more,
'I give you up to Satan's power.'

TORTOIS.
[Figure from Mavor.]

—

THE name is found in the bible but once. It is in Lev. 11 : 29, where the creeping thing intended by it is reckoned among the unclean. The name in Hebrew is (צָב) Tsâbv ; Buxtorf has *Bufo*, and *Testudo* ; the *Toad*, and the *Tortois*. It is from a root, which signifies literally to *swell*; figuratively, *to be arched*. The toad swels and the Tortois has an arched roof over him. No one would probably think of eating the toad ; some however do eat the tortois ; but it seems probable that it would be prohibited to the Israelites. Pagnin has *Crocodilus*, the *Crocodile;* the Septuagint has Krŏkŏdeĭlos ; Junius and Tremellius, *Testudo ;* French bible, *Tortne*. The same word, Tsâbv, is used in scripture for the arched covering of a wagon, to which a Tortois bears no very distant resemblance ; and I think has as good a claim to the name above, as any other animal.

The Tortois is of several kinds, as the Sea-Tortois, the fresh water Tortois, and the land Tortois. The Sea-Tortois is usually called *Turtle*, and is larger than the fresh water Tortois, or the land Tortois, their weight being from two hundred to eight hundred lbs. They have a shell somewhat resembling that of the

24

land Tortois, but their feet are between paws and fins, formed for swimming, rather than for walking; and the fore paws are longer than those behind. Bruce has given a drawing of one taken from the Red Sea, the length of the shell of which was three feet seven inches. They abound among the Isles of the West Indies, where their flesh is much esteemed. They are found of good size in the Mediterranean, and are fat, but their flesh is coarse, and is not thought to be whole-some.

The fresh water Tortois is found in large and small ponds, and in still brooks, and varies in size from those that are not larger than a man's fist, to those that weigh one hundred lbs. or more. The shells of the large ones are shaped nearly like the shells of the land Tortois, and their color is of a greenish gray, or much like that of an oyster shell. These are esteemed for their flesh. Some at least of the small fresh water Tortoises have the shell under their belly much broader and longer than that of the land Tortois of the same size, and checked with red, black, yellow, &c. It is in shape a parallellogram, with the corners rounded off, and the length about twice the breadth. The shell of its back is dark brown, and in shape like that of the land Tortois.

The land Tortois of common size in New England is from the nose to the end of the tail from ten to twelve inches long, and its breadth from about five to seven inches. Its shell is in substance between bone and horn; it consists of a number of irregular, figured squares, united firmly together; when taken off, and turned upside down, it resembles in shape an oblong bason. The under shell is attached on each side to the upper, and is small and flat, shaped to accommodate the legs. Its head much resembles that of a serpent, and from the point of its nose a sharp hook bends downward, with which it will hold the end of a stick, thrust into its mouth, so firmly, as to suffer itself to be dragged about with it. The paws of the Tortois bear some resemblance to those of the common toad, and its toes have sharp claws at the ends of them. When molested they draw up their head and feet completely into their shell, and turn their tail under the edge of it, so that a dog may tumble them about, till he is weary, without hurting them; but if they have an opportunity to seize their antagonist with their hook, their bite is sharp, and their hold not easily broken.

The Tortois lays her eggs in the sand, to be hatched by the sun. It is said that some land Tortoises have been found five feet in length, and one and a half feet across the back. They are extremely tenacious of life, and will live some days after the head is severed from the body. When a youth I once endeavored to sever the shell from a fresh water Tortois, after his head had been off some time, and every muscle seemed to be so alive, that my feelings were not a little wounded. I have heard of a large Sea-Turtle, upon the back of which a large man and woman stood upright, and it raised itself upon its legs, after its head had been off, I think, three days. They are very long lived; there is an instance recorded of a land Tortois, kept in the garden of Lambeth Palace, England, which was known to have lived one hundred and twenty years.

Who gave to the Tortois her covering?
She carries her house, as a shepherd his tent;
It is her shield of defence, when assailed;
It is her shelter from the rain and the cold;
Would she lodge for the night? Her inn is at hand.
Is she yet young and small? Her house is also small;
Is she large and strong? Her house has grown with her growth.
Her room is ample, but none of it waste,

And it never decays till she needs it no more.
Who gave the Tortois her house, so complete?
It is God, the Creator, who gave it.
He furnishes all for their state.
The strong may rejoice in their strength;
The weak he protects and defends;
For *all* his rich goodness provides;
O let us then trust in his care,
And he never, no, never, will fail us.

Rhinoceros. J. F.

UNICORN.

[Figure from Bruce.]

—

THIS name is found in the bible nine or ten times;
we meet with it first in Num. 23 : 22, where Balaam
says of Israel, *He hath as it were the strength of a Unicorn.* From this we may infer that it was some very
strong animal; the name in Hebrew is (רְאֵם) Reām;
and by contraction (רֵים) Rām. Buxtorf *Monoceros,*
and *Unicornis;* both words signify a beast with one
horn, the former from the Greek, the latter from the
latin. Pagnin has in addition to Buxtorf, the name
Rhinoceros; signifying, *horn on the nose.* The Septua-

gint has uniformly Monŏkerŏs, except in one passage. Junius and Tremellius, *Unicornis*, French *Licorne*.

I have no doubt but that the Rhinoceros is the animal intended ; it is a land animal, and the· largest known, next to the Elephant. His length is from ten to fourteen feet ; his height from five to seven. His general shape is much like that of a hog ; his eyes are small, his ears erect, his snout long ; his upper lip hangs over his mouth, and ends in a point ; he can contract and protrude it at pleasure, and it serves him as a hand to gather his food to his mouth. On his nose are generally two horns, one behind the other, the forward one is from twelve or fourteen inches, to three feet in length ; is round, solid, hard, and at the point bends a little backward. These horns are his weapons of defence, and serve him also for splitting into laths the small trees on which he feeds, which are usually trees of a soft texture, somewhat resembling the stump of the cabbage, and are common in the regions where the Rhinoceros resides, and are his chosen food. He is covered with a thick, tough, unyielding skin, which falls over in wrinkles, or folds about the neck, shoulders, and thighs, to facilitate the motions of the animal. His legs are clumsy, rather crooked, and terminate in feet, divided forward into three parts, each of which has a hoof on it. At the end of his tail are a few strong, thick hairs, of some length, and he has a few hairs also on the ears, but no where else. His general color is like that of common mud, when beginning to dry. The figure given is from Bruce's travels.

Another variety of the Rhinoceros has but one horn on the nose, and may be consistently called Monoceros, or Unicorn ; the figure of such a one was drawn in London in 1752, by George Edwards. It was a female, not

24*

full grown.   Her height to the top of the shoulder was five feet eight inches.

The rhinoceros is frequent in Africa, and is some-times, but more rarely, found in Arabia, and some other parts of Asia. In modern times the kind with a single horn is quite uncommon. In some seasons they are greatly afflicted with flies, and to defend themselves they roll in mud till they become encrusted with it, which affords them a temporary relief. They rarely meddle with smaller animals, or with man, unless pro-voked ; but they are the enemy of the elephant, and with him they have severe encounters, in which some-times one, and sometimes the other is slain.   Their flesh in taste is much like pork, but coarse, and not very palatable ; but there are many in the partially savage state, who feed upon it. The hunters some-times take him at unawares, when rolling in the mire, and give him deadly wounds with their spears, at other times men on horse back pursue him, and when abreast of him, the one behind slipps off, and with a sword cuts his hamstrings, and escapes, while the wounded beast endeavors to pursue the other, who rides forward. The natives of Africa use the forward horn in making handles for their daggers. In manners the rhinoceros is stupid and untractable, generally peaceable, but some-times the subject of paroxisms of fury. One that was sent by Emanuel, king of Portugal, to the Pope, in 1513, became thus infuriated, and destroyed the vessel that was transporting it. Another more lately, on its way from Paris to Italy, was drowned in a similar man-ner. The female produces but one young one at a time, which, during the first month, is about the size of a large dog. The chosen place of resort of the rhinocer-os is moist, marshy ground, in the neighborhood of rivers.

In Job 39 : God calls the notice of Job to this great beast, and asks, *Will the Unicorn be willing to serve thee, or to abide by thy crib ?   Canst thou bind the Unicorn in his furrow ? Will he harrow the valley after thee?* By this God would convince Job that it was in vain to contend with his Maker, seeing some of God's creatures around him were too strong for him to manage.

David in Psalm 22 : personating the Messiah, says, *thou hast heard me from the horns of the Unicorns.* It is probable that the Unicorn, when provoked by some beast like the tiger, would thrust his horn into him and throw him into the air.   The situation of Christ on the cross was not very dissimilar to that of the poor beast on the horn of the Unicorn ; and on the cross the Father heard him.

In Psalm 92 : he says—*My horn shalt thou exalt, like the horn of the Unicorn.* He had just said that his enemies, the workers of iniquity, should be scattered. As the horn of a beast is the index of his power, so the idea of David might be this, 'As the Unicorn puts forward his horn, and scatters the beasts that come in his way, and then lifts it up ; so God will enable me to scatter my enemies, and cause my power to be exalted over them.'

Who shall contend with Him, whose powerful word
Gave being to the world, himself the Lord
Of all creation ?   Who will dare withstand
The operation of his mighty hand ?

He spread the sky, and earth's foundations laid,
Pour'd forth the ocean, and the creatures made,
Gave birth to angels, and to man his form,
Rides on the winds, or stills the threatening storm.

Those beasts of earth, so bulky and so high
They seem like mountains in a mortal's eye,
To him are emmets on their sandy hill,
Crush'd by his finger whensoe'er he will.

Man, stand in awe ; be still, and hold thy peace ;
Dare thou no more, but let thy cavils cease ;
Lest thy Creator, with one angry frown,
Look, and in hell thou sink forever down.

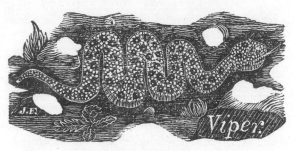

VIPER.

—

THIS is a small, venomous serpent, the name of which
first occurs in Job 20 : 16 ; The *Viper's* tongue shall
slay him.   It is found again in Isai. 30 : 6, 59 : 5.   In
the new testament it is found in Matt. 3 : 7, 12 : 34,
23 : 33, Luke 3 : 7, and Acts 28 : 3.   The name in Hebrew is (אֶפְעֶה) ĕfgnāh ; Buxtorf has *Vipera*, the *Viper ;* Pagnin the same, and also *Regulus*, the *Basilisk*, or
Cockatrice ; the Septuagint has ŏfĭs, ăspĭs, Băsalĭskŏs ;
Serpent, Asp, Basalisk.   Junius and Tremellius, *Vipera ;*
French, Vipere ; in the new testament the Greek is
Ekhĭdnā.

The figure given is from Bruce's Travels, and represents the *Cerastes*, or horned Viper ; this is a venomous
serpent, abounding in the desert parts of Syria Arabia,

and Africa. It is about thirteen or fourteen inches in length, and five sixths of an inch thick. It is of a reddish brown, spotted with black; it eats but very little. Bruce kept two of them two years in a glass vessel, without giving them any thing to eat. They cast their skin on the last days of April. The natives where this snake is found, are by some means or other, so defended from his bite, as to handle him familiarly, without any apprehension of danger.

The Cerastes has sixteen small, immovable teeth, and in the upper jaw two canine teeth, hollow, and crooked inward; near one fourth of the bottom is strongly fixed in the upper jaw, and folds back, like a clasp knife, the point inclining inwards; the greatest part of the tooth is covered with a green, soft membrane; immediately under this is a slit along the back of the tooth, which ends near the middle of it; through this aperture from a bag at the bottom of the tooth it is supposed to shed its poison.

On the Island of Great Britain, and on the islands in the neighborhood of Scotland, a poisonous serpent is found, called a Viper, about two feet in length, its ground color a dirty yellow, marked on the whole length of the back with a series of diamond-like spots of black, the points of which touch each other: the sides are marked with triangular spots, the belly is all black. It is slow in its motions; it brings forth its young alive; these, when in danger, retreat into their mother's throat. It feeds on toads, frogs, young birds, &c. It can sustain long abstinence; one has been kept in a box without food six months, without losing its vivacity. The more common remedy for its bite is a free use of salad oil, applied to the wound and taken inwardly.

Zophar, in the book of Job, says of the wicked, The Viper's tongue shall slay him. The Viper's tongue is here put for the Viper's poison; and there may be allusion to that more deadly poison, which flows from the tongues of scorners and infidels.

In Isai. 30 : 6, the Jews are represented as carrying their treasure into a land from which the Viper, &c. comes, to hire help against their enemies; but it is declared to them that it would be unavailing. We may gather from the connection that Egypt is intended, and that the Viper was a native of Egypt; and that the Jews might hope as well for help from lions and Vipers, as from the Egyptians.

Christ, in the new testament, and also his forerunner, John, compares the Scribes and Pharisees to a generation of Vipers, on account of their hypocrisy, and the destructive doctrines which they taught, which were as fatal to the souls of men, as the poison of the Viper to their bodies.

When Paul, on the island of Melita, shook a Viper from his hand, and received no harm, the promise of Christ concerning the signs, that should attend his apostles, was in his case fulfilled.

The Viper's tooth inflicts a wound,
　Which often ends in death ;
The scorner, still more dangerous found,
　Kills with his very breath.

The Viper's venom kills us here,
　The scorner kills forever ;
Then let us turn away our ear,
　And hearken to him never.

The Viper bites in self defence,
　The scorner seeks occasion
His deadly mischief to dispense,
　And scatter desolation.

Dear youth, the scorner's path avoid,
　And let your way be plain,
Lest, by his poisonous tongue destroy'd,
　You mourn at last in vain.

VULTURE.

Figure from the Cabinet.

—

THE name in the English bible is found in Lev. 11 :
14, and in Deut. 14 : 13, where the flesh of it is forbidden to the Israelites. It is found also in Job 28 : 7, and
in Isai. 34 : 15. In Lev. the Hebrew is (דָּאָה) Dââh ;
and in Deut. and Isai. (דַּיָּה) Dăyyâh ; and in Job
(אַיָּה) ăyyâh. For the first, Buxtorf has *Milvus*, the
Kite ; Pagnin, *Vultur*, the *Vulture ;* Septuagint, Gūps,
the *Vulture ;* Junius and Tremellius, *Milvus ;* French
bible *Vautour*. The Vulture is probably the bird intended.

For the next word Buxtorf, Pagnin, and Junius and
Tremellius have *Milvus ;* French bible *Autour*, the
Goss-Hawk.

For the last word Buxtorf has *Cornix*, the *Crow ;*
Pagnin has *Pica*, the Mag-pie ; Septuagint, *Gups*, Juni-
us and Tremellius, *Cornix ;* French bible *Milan*, the
Kite.

From so many different opinions of interpreters we
may learn, that there is in modern times much uncer-

tainty, what, in many cases, the animals were, of which we have names in scripture. I think it probable the names above mentioned intend some kinds of swift-flying, keen-sighted birds of prey, among which might be the Vulture, and some of its kindred species.

The figure given is of the King Vulture, from the Cabinet.

This bird is a native of South America; it is larger than a turkey; the skin at the base of the beak stretches out on each side lik e an indented comb, and is of an orange color. From a small tuft of black down behind the head, a wrinkled piece of skin, brownish, and shaded with blue and red extends beneath the throat. The iris of the eye is of the color of pearl, and the skin surrounding the eye is of a scarlet color. The skin on the top of the head, and upper part of the neck, is flesh color; on the back of the neck, scarlet; on the fore part of the neck, dusky red. A collar of long, downy feathers, of ash color, surrounds the lower part of the neck, and covers the breast; within this color, as a tortois in his shell, it can so hide its neck, that it shall hardly be perceived that it has one. The rest of the body is ash color, beautifully marked with black and white. These vultures are very useful in South America, for eating up the carcases of beasts, that are slain for their skins, which being left on the ground, would otherwise taint the air. They also destroy many of the eggs of the Alligator, and prevent a dangerous multiplication of that formidable animal.

Vultures of different species are numerous in all quarters of the globe, but especially in warm climates. In Hindostan they follow the companies of pilgrims, and devour those who die by the way, and are left unburied.

Vultures are generally placed by naturalists at the

head of rapacious birds; they may be distinguished from those of the eagle kind, which they most resemble, by the nakedness of their heads and necks. Besides devouring carrion, they feed on mice, lizards, and other small animals. The Condor of South America is reckoned in the class of Vultures. This is an enormous bird; according to some writers, the expansion of its wings is eighteen feet, and the length of one of its largest feathers nearly two and a half feet.

Job, in Chap. 28: says, there is a path which no fowl knoweth; the Vulture's eye hath not seen it. He is speaking of some of the wonderful works of God; and here perhaps he alludes to those subterraneous passages, which have sometimes been explored a little way by man, but into which no fowls of the air enter. Some of these are among the wonders of the world; they teach us that God works upon a great scale, as well as a small.

In Isai. 34: the judgments of God are threatened against Idumea for its enmity against his people; speaking of its desolation, God says, There shall the Vultures be gathered together, every one with her mate. Vultures were very numerous in Arabia and Egypt; and it is natural to suppose, that they would resort to the ruins of towns and cities, to feed upon the vermin, that multiply in such places. When we contemplate such ruins, we may well exclaim, how great is the evil of sin!

Death stalks resistless o'er the embattled plain,
Vultures and eagles follow in his train;
The hands, unseen, that mow the warriors down,
With plenteous food the wild-bird's table crown.

The birds rapacious, and the beasts of prey
Their laws of instinct in their spheres obey;
Keen is their smell, with willing haste they fly,
And cleans the fields, where putrid masses lie.

25

Death comes by sin; but many a Vulture lives
On that which death to feed its hunger gives;
And Vultures, feasting, from the earth remove
A source of death, which would more fatal prove

The wise Creator centres in his plan
Such traits of skill, as may astonish man;
But while we wonder at his skill and power,
And taste his goodness, let our souls adore.

WEASEL.

[Figure from Bewick.]

—

THE name of this little active animal is found in the bible but once; it is in Lev. 11:29, where it is reckoned among creeping things to be accounted unclean. Its name in Hebrew is (חֹלֶד) Hrhōled, Buxtorf and Pagnin both have *Mustela, Weasel;* Septuagint, Gālē; Junius and Tremellius, *Mustella;* French bible *Belette;* all signifying *Weasel.* Respecting this name we have among interpreters an unusual agreement. The name corresponds with a word in Hebrew signifying earth, the dust of which is reddish; and with a word used by the Rabbis for *rust,* which is usually reddish. The more common of Weasels in New England are of a rusty red; some, however, are mouse colored, and some, that are commonly called Weasels, are milk white, except their ears, and a little space round them, and the end of their tails, which is black. I have seen one that was killed, after having taken the blood of several hens; its body was of such snowy whiteness, even to the roots of the fur, that, whether it were Weasel, or Stoat, I can hardly believe that it ever changed its color. The flue of the hare, that is white in winter, is still brown next to the skin.

The Samaritan Weasel is on the back of a brownish black, striped and spotted with dirty yellow; its head, feet, and the under side of its body are quite black; its ears are round, edged with long, white hairs, its mouth is surrounded with white; the head is crossed beyond the eyes with a white band, which goes down to the throat; from the back part of the head a band of yellow passes obliquely towards the shoulders, and beyond this, towards the back, is another; the tail is dusky, and towards the end becomes quite black.

White Weasel from nature.

The Weasel is long, and slender of its size; its common length is from six to seven inches, exclusive of its tail, which is about two and a half inches. It motions are exceedingly quick, and it leaps as it runs. It will look at you from a hole in a wall near your feet; strike at it, and in a moment you may see it looking at you from another hole. Rats and mice, or the blood of them,

seem to be its most common food ; when these fail it
seizes little birds and poultry, draining them of their
blood, and leaving them. It is said, however, to eat
their flesh after it becomes putrid. The farmer, when
troubled with rats and mice, is often pleased to see this
visiter ; but for the service it does him, he often must
repay it with some of his hens, chickens, ducks and
eggs, and rabbits too, if he have any.

The Weasel when irritated, or wounded, emits an
odor that is extremely fœtid. They are not easily
tamed, but in some instances have been tamed, so as to
be completely familiar. It generally sleeps by day, and
makes its ravages by night. Its bite is keen, and aim-
ed at some vein in the throat of its prey, so as to be
generally fatal. The Cabinet mentions an eagle that
seized a Weasel, and mounted into the air with it, but
the Weasel had so much of his liberty, that he seized
the throat of the eagle, and soon brought him to the
ground, and then escaped.

> Active, slender, sleek and cunning,
>   See the Weasel chase his prey,
> See him seize the mouse, while running,
>   See him bear his prize away.
>
> Rats, and moles, and other vermin
>   Seek their holes to hide in vain,
> Tho' his fur be white as ermine,
>   Soon their blood the white may stain.
>
> 'Tis ordain'd that every creature
>   Here on earth shall have its foe ;
> Could *we* plan the system better?
>   We may safely answer, No.
>
> Man himself of skill and labor
>   To defend himself has need ;
> But that man should in his neighbor
>   Find a foe, is base indeed.
>
> Roll, ye planets, bring the season,
>   When—the earth renew'd by grace—
> Virtue, faith, and heaven born reason
>   Shall of folly take the place.

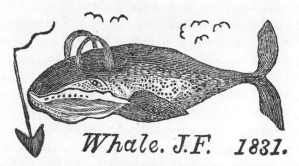

Whale. J.F. 1831.

WHALE.

This name occurs in the English bible four times. 1. In Gen. 1 : 21, And God created great whales. 2. Job 7 : 12, Am I a sea, or a whale ? 3. Eze. 32 : 2, Thou art as a whale in the seas. 4. Matt. 12 : 40, As Jonas was three days and three nights in the whale's belly, &c. The Hebrew is (תַּנִּין and תַּנִּים) Tănnēn, and Tănnēm, in the singular, and (תַּנִּינִם) Tănnēnēm, in the plural. Buxtorf has *Draco, Dragon; Balæna* and *Cetus, Whale;* and *Serpens,* Serpent. Pagnin defines it, *Serpent,* or *Dragon,* and a great fish, like a dragon, such as the Whales are. The Septuagint in Gen. 1 : 21, has Kĕtŏs, *Whale;* in all the other places Drākŏn, Dragon. The Greek in the new testament is Kētŏs. Junius and Tremellius, in Genesis and in Matthew, have *Cetus,* and in Job, *Cete,* the *Whale;* in Ezekiel they have *Balæna;* the French bible *Baleine, Whale,* in all the above named places.

In Job 41 : 1, God calls the notice of Job to an animal of great strength and courage, by the name of *Leviathan;* the Hebrew name is (לִוְיָתָן) Lĭvyâthân; it is found in Job 3 : 8, where it is rendered *mourning;* it is found in Psalm 74 : 14, Thou breakest the heads of Leviathan. Also in Psalm 104 : 26, That Leviathan

25*

thou hast formed to sport therein; and Isai. 27 : 1, I will visit upon Leviathan, the oblong serpent, and upon Leviathan the crooked serpent. Buxtorf has *Balœna*, Pagnin, *Draco*, and *Cetus marinus.* As the description in the book of Job agrees better with the Crocodile, than with any other known animal ; and as the prophet Isaiah probably has in view the king of Egypt, when he speaks of God's punishing *Leviathan*, and as the Crocodile was common about the Nile, and in other neighboring regions, and so a fit emblem of a tyrannical prince of Egypt; I think it most likely that by Leviathan we are to understand the Crocodile, for a description of which see the article, *Dragon.*

As for the word Tănnēn, and its variations, I suspect that it sometimes intends the Crocodile, and sometimes some very large fish found in the Mediterranean, which might be called, *Whale,* and yet much differ from what is called Whale upon the coast of North America ; and that by such fish the prophet Jonah was swallowed, when cast into the sea, as he was on his way to Tarshish, or *Tarsus.* Also by Tănnēnēm, in the plural, and Tănnēm, the contraction of it, I suspect we are in some cases to understand, in general terms, huge, formidable creatures in the water, and fearful, poisonous serpents on the land. The serpents into which the rod of Moses, and the rods of the Egyptian Magicians were transformed, are called, Tănnēnēm, but doubtless were neither Whales nor crocodiles.

If by Tănnēnēm in Gen. 1 : 21, we are to understand in general, *huge monsters of the deep*, which I suspect is the fact, we may reckon the Whale among them ; I shall therefore give a description of those two kinds of the Whale which are the most common.

The figures are from Mavor.

1. *The Common Whale.* These are found in the northern seas about North America, and in the Indian seas; in the former they are usually from sixty to ninety feet in length. In the latter they are sometimes seen one hundred and fifty feet in length. Its head in proportion to its body is very large, but its throat is but about four inches wide, and its eyes not larger than those of an ox. In the middle of its head are two orifices, thro which it spouts water to a great height. To its upper jaw adheres what is called whale-bone, which consists of thin plates, parallel to each other, and some of them four yards in length, ending in a sort of brush, like the brush of a broom. This whale-bone is used in manufacturing umbrellas, and for various other purposes, being very elastic. Its food is said to be small snails, and a kind of a sea-blubber. It carries its tail horizontally. The female commonly brings forth two young ones at a birth, which she suckles, carries on her back by the help of her fins, and defends with great affection and resolution. The belly of the common Whale is white, its back sometimes red, sometimes white, sometimes mixed, but usually black. The enemies of the Whale are the *whale-louse*, a small testaceous animal, which adheres closely to the skin of the Whale, and feeds upon his fat; the *sword-fish*, an enemy still more dreadful, which leaps upon the Whale, and cuts his flesh with a kind of sword, which projects about three feet from the nose, or upper jaw of the fish; and the *killer*, another enemy more fatal to the Whale than the sword-fish; armed with strong, sharp teeth, they tear his flesh on all sides, till, wearied out, he yields to them, when they seize and devour his tongue.

The Whale is taken chiefly for his fat, or blubber, which is melted into oil. Many vessels are employed in this kind of fishery; but the taking of them is attended with some danger; when two are together, as soon as the first is harpooned, the other frequently rises, and with his tail dashes the boat in pieces, sometimes killing some that are in it. For the safety of those that survive, a second boat is usually near at hand to receive them.

2. *The Cachalot.*

This is a species of Whale much differing in several respects from the common Whale. Its size is less, rarely being more than sixty feet in length; its head is very long and large, being more than one third of its whole bulk. The upper jaw is one third longer than the lower, and of enormous thickness. The under jaw is slender, and contains about twenty three teeth on each side, answerable to which there are cavities in the upper jaw. The teeth are like ivory; the eyes are very small, and placed far back in the head. It has a wide throat, and its stomach is found filled with a multitude of fishes of various kinds, some eight or nine feet long, and in different states of digestion. Near its snout it has an orifice for spouting water; its tail is comparatively small and forked. There are several varieties of this kind; the principal are the blunt-headed, the round-headed, and the high-finned. They are taken for the spermaceti and the ambergris, which they contain; the former, signifying the seed of the Whale, but improperly so called, is really their brain; when they are taken the head is severed from the body with a large cleaver, called sometimes a spade; the nose is then turned downwards, and from the cavity, which presents itself, the spermaceti is dipped out with buckets. The ambergris is found in lumps in a bag in their belly. These were once highly valued by the apothecary and the perfumer, but in times more modern their value has decreased; and as the whole of the oil of the Cachalot can be converted into spermaceti by boiling, it is now used principally for candles.

The taking of this kind of Whale is more difficult, than the taking of the common Whale; it fights with its nose and mouth; it will sometimes drop its lower jaw, which alone is moveable, and will run its upper jaw over a boat, and then bringing up its under jaw will crush it in a moment.

> Compare the little eel that in the cruet sports,
> A mere white atom, slender, scarcely seen,
> With those huge monsters, which on ocean's wave
> Lie like a ridge of mountains, or leap up
> High o'er the surface, and with frightful plunge
> Raise up a tempest, with a solemn roar,
> Like cataracts descending; O how vast
> The intervening space! What numerous grades,
> Step after step descending, wisely fill
> The wide extended chasm. Downward still,
> With microscopic eye, and fancy's power,
> The chain we may pursue; and where it ends
> No mortal knows. The cruet's sportive eel,
> The vinegar its ocean, there may play
> In those domains a huge leviathan,
> Compar'd with ranks below it. All this world,
> This universe of being, has its worth;
> Each link above to links beneath is bound,
> And each beneath by those above is held,
> And all existence is a mighty scale
> From man to nothing downward, and from man
> In grades ascending to the one supreme.

WILD BOAR.—[*See Swine.*

WILD BULL AND WILD OX.

[Figure from Bewick.]

—

In Deut. 14 : 5, we read, in the account of clean animals, the Pygarg, and the *Wild Ox*, and the Chamois.
The Hebrew here is (תְאוֹ) Teō; Junius and Tremellius have *Bubalus*, a kind of Wild Ox. Pagnin and
Buxtorf have the same, and explain it by *Bos Sylvestris*,
the Wild Ox. The French bible has *Dœuf Sauvage*,
meaning the same. The Septuagint has ŏrūgā, a kind
of wild goat. The Bubalus is supposed by some to be
the *Buffalo*.

In Isai. 51 : 20, we read, Thy sons have fainted;
they lie at the head of all the streets, as a *Wild Bull* in
a net. The name in Hebrew is (תּוֹא) Tō; and all
the authorities above quoted render it as Teō is rendered, except the Septuagint, which has, the herb, *beet*,
half cooked.

I suspect the word in both cases intends some kind
of Wild Bull, which was sometimes taken, by being
entangled in a strong net; and which, after struggling
for a while in vain to escape, would lie, as if dead, as I
have seen the Hare, when taken, feign itself dead, that
it might be let go, and then escape.

Wretched indeed was the state of Jerusalem, when the young men of the city were so faint, by reason of famine, that their strength failed them in the streets, so that they fell down, as if their feet were entangled in a net, and then lay, as if dead! This evil was predicted for a warning before it came; but the people refused to take warning, and in the time of the Babylonish captivity they realized in full measure what God thus threatened. The unrestrained indulgence of sin plunged them into these miseries. May you, my dear youth, take warning by their sufferings; for if you in like manner indulge in sin, you may bring down like sufferings upon yourselves, and upon the place of your abode.

> See the *Wild Ox*, ensnar'd, and on the ground,
>   In sullen stillness lying;
> So at the head of all the streets are found
>   The sons of Zion dying.
>
> The warning voice of God did not avail
>   To turn them from their sinning;
> Now pinch'd with famine they are weak and pale,
>   And fainting, drooping, pining.
>
> Such is the fruit of long indulged sin,
>   A fruit, O how distressing!
> Be warn'd, O sinners, turn to God, and win,
>   Instead of this, a blessing.

WOLF.
[Figure from Bewick.]

—

HERE we have an animal too well known, and too often mentioned in the bible, to leave much room to doubt what animal is intended by the scripture name, which in Hebrew is (זְאֵב) Zeābv; in Greek, Lūkŏs; Latin, *Lupus*; French, *Loup*.

The Wolf is a native of each of the four quarters of the world; he is reckoned in the class of canine animals, or those of the dog kind.   He is larger than the dog, but resembles him very much in shape, and in his internal structure, and has been known in some cases to intermix with the dog, and to produce an intermediate race.   In the shape of his head he differs from the dog, his snout is sharper, and the general appearance of his head more like that of a fox, than of a dog.   His eyes are placed more obliquely, than those of the dog; his ears are erect, and pointed, like those of the fox. He is very strong about the chest; his tail is bushy, and bends inwards between the legs.   His color is usually a pale yellowish brown; but in very cold, northern regions some are found white, and some black.   His howl

somewhat resembles that of a dog, but is louder, and
more terrifying. He is fierce, rapacious, cruel, blood-
thirsty, but withal cunning, and cautious. Of the
sheep he is the most destructive enemy; of the fold
the most mischievous pillager. In one night they will
seize a number of the flock by the neck, draw much of
their blood, and leave them half dead; upon one or
two they will then satiate their hunger. Such was
once their treatment of my honored father's flock.
When pressed with hunger they will attack large animals and even men. I once saw an account of a man
in the western part of New England, who, returning
from work in a forest at night, was attacked by a drove
of them. He placed his back, as it appeared, against a
tree, and with his ax killed six or seven of them; but
was then overpowered, and killed by the others. He
was found soon after with the dead wolves by him.
When much pinched with abstinence, it is said that
the horse only, among domestic animals, is able to
withstand them; the salutation of his heels is too solid for them to relish it. Their track is much like that
of the dog, but where the print is plain may be easily
distinguished from it; the ball of the foot is very nearly an equilateral triangle, a little rounded at the points,
and between the ball and the toes the space is longer,
than in the case of the dog; this I have particularly
noticed in very fair, new made tracks. The female's
time of gestation is about fifteen months, and she usually produces from five to seven at a litter. These,
taken very young, may be tamed, so as to be quite gentle, till about eighteen months old, when they begin to
show their savage nature, and need to be chained.
Their sense of smelling is very powerful, so that they

26

sometimes perceive the scent of carrion at a league's distance.

They were once numerous on the British Isles, but have been so closely hunted, that for many years they have disappeared; the last known to be found on the Isle of Great Britain was killed in Scotland in 1680; the last killed in Ireland was in 1710. The modes of taking them are various; they are sometimes taken in large steel traps; sometimes they are caught in pits over which a dead sheep is hung, and the pit slightly covered with brush; sometimes a piece of tainted meat is dragged round through the woods, and then hung up a little above their reach, and just at night the hunters with their muskets creep towards the place, and have the opportunity sometimes to dispatch several at once, while they are jumping to reach the bait.

They sometimes follow armies, and devour the slain, that are left on the field of battle; and sometimes when pressed with hunger will rob graves of their dead; happy, if there were no other monsters to do the same.

In Gen. 49 : 27, Jacob in blessing his sons a little before his death, says, Benjamin shall ravin as a *wolf*. From this we infer that the Wolf of those regions was a rapacious animal; and Jacob's blessing, which was doubtless prophetic, intimates that the tribe of Benjamin should be a warlike tribe, and take much spoil from his enemies. The deliverer of Israel from Eglon, king of Moab, was Ehud, a Benjamite. The account of the contest between Benjamin and the other tribes of Israel in Judges 20, in which twenty six thousand of Benjamin were victorious two successive days, over four hundred thousand of Israel, shows that Benjamin was a fierce and warlike tribe.

In Isai. 11 : 6, and 65 : 25, the prophet foretells a time when the lamb should dwell with the Wolf; the spiritual meaning is, that the earth would be blessed with a period, when all, who before were the enemies of the lambs of Christ's flock, and like Wolves to them, would either be taken out of the way, or be subdued in their spirits, and become the friends of Christ, and the friends of truth.

In Jer. 5 : 6, God threatens the Jews for their wickedness, that a lion out of the forests should slay them, and that a Wolf of the evening should spoil them. The evening and the night is the usual time for the Wolf to seck his prey, and to make his ravages. I doubt not but that in some instances wild beasts were sent upon the Jews literally, so as to slay some of them, and make destruction among their flocks; but by these wild beasts might be intended the merciless Assyrians and Chaldeans, who were soon to be sent upon them, and to make dreadful havoc among them.

In Eze. 22 : 27, God says by the prophet, Her princes in the midst thereof are like Wolves, ravening the prey, to shed blood, and to destroy souls, and to get dishonest gain. When a nation becomes wicked, it is usual with God to punish it with wicked rulers; avaricious and blood-thirsty men work their way into office, and then for gain make a prey of such as are too feeble to defend themselves. O my young friends, follow virtue in all its branches, and form the habit of it in youth ; you may then administer to the happiness of the nation in the midst of which it shall be your lot to dwell.

In Habakkuk 1 : 8, the horses of the Chaldeans are said to be more fierce than the evening Wolves; this confirms the idea that Wolves in those regions were

very fierce, and made their ravages in the evening. It
is probable that by a figure of speech in this passage
the fierceness of the Chaldeans themselves is attributed
to their horses. God in due time will bring fierce enemies upon wicked nations.

In Zeph. 3 : 3, the princes of Judah are compared to
evening Wolves.

In Matt. 7 : 17, false prophets are compared to ravening Wolves. They pretend to prophecy; their object
is filthy lucre. In Matt. 10 : 16, and Luke 10 : 3,
Christ says to his apostles, I send you as sheep into the
midst of Wolves. Were ever poor sheep destroyed by
beasts of prey with such cruelty, as christians have
been destroyed by the enemies of God?

In Acts 20 : 29, the apostle Paul admonishes the el-
ders of Ephesus, that after his departure grievous
Wolves would enter in, not sparing the flock. It is a
dreadful scourge to a people to have such settled among
them for teachers, as care not for their souls, but whose
leading object it is, to enrich themselves with their
spoils. To avoid this let those who have faithful teachers, profit under them, while they have them.

ISAIAH 11 : 1—9.

Behold, a branch from Jesse's root shall spring ;
  On him the Spirit of the Lord shall rest ;
A spirit, such as in its train shall bring
  Wisdom and Virtue for his mind and breast.

Just and impartial shall his judgment be ;
  With keen discernment he shall know the heart,
From cruel wrong the needy he will free,
  And to the meek a just award impart.

His rod of truth shall smite a sinful world,
  And by the power of his almighty breath
The sons of malice, from their stations hurl'd,
  Shall feel his vengeance, and shall sink in death.

Justice his loins shall as a girdle brace,
  And faithfulness and truth shall well maintain

His steps, while marching to display his grace,
   And cleanse the earth from its polluting stain.

Then shall the *Wolf*, from savage state reclaim'd,
   Dwell with the lamb, and in one peaceful nest
The kid, the leopard, and the lion, fam'd
   For bloody carnage, with the calf shall rest.

A child shall lead them, and the cow and bear
   Shall feed together, and their young repose
In peace; the lion with the ox shall share
   The tender grass, which on earth's bosom grows.

The sucking child around the hole shall sport,
   Where dwells the asp; the weaned child shall lay
His hand on dens, where Basalisks resort,
   Thoughtless of danger, and without dismay.

My holy mountain then shall all be free
   From those that hurt, and would the righteous kill;
And as the waters overspread the sea,
   So all the earth the name of God shall fill.

So speaks Jehovah, let us then believe
   The faithful word, and with a cheerful hand
Those holy truths, which we ourselves receive,
   Spread far and wide, thro' every heathen land.

26*

APPENDIX.

For this part of the work I have reserved several articles respecting animals not named in the English bible, but supposed by some authors to be intended by several of the names in the Hebrew bible. Also, a brief notice of some of those animals, which are mentioned by their generic names, or names of the whole kind, but not by their specific, or individual names.

Then some short account of several varieties of the human species.

And lastly, some general concluding remarks.

SECTION I.

1. HYÆNA.

In Jeremiah 12 : 9, the Hebrew words, rendered in the English bible, *speckled bird*, are rendered in the Septuagint, spēlaiŏn hūainēs, the den of a Hyæna. I doubt the correctness of this rendering; but as some authors favor it, I here give the figure of the Hyæna from Bruce, with a brief description.

This animal is about the size of a wolf, and bears some resemblance to the wolf in shape. His proper name among the Arabians is *Dubbah*. The one from which Bruce took his figure was slain at Teawa, in Africa, between Lat 13° and 14° N. and Long. 34° and 35° E. of Greenwich ; not far from Sennar, in Nubia.

His length from the nose to the rump was five feet, nine inches; his height from the bottom of the forefoot three feet seven inches; the length of his tail one foot nine inches. He weighed about one hundred and twelve pounds. His color on the back and tail was reddish brown ; his body in general yellowish brown. His legs were marked with numerous black bands, which began at the lower joint of the hind foot, and continued thence to the top of the thigh ; then turned broad and circular, and reached across the whole side. Over his shoulders were two semicircular bands, and a black streak down his throat. His nose was black at the point, and dark several inches above.

The Hyæna resides in caverns of mountains, in clefts of rocks, and in holes, which it digs in the ground. It is very ferocious, and cannot be tamed. It lives by depredations, like the wolf, but is stronger, and more daring. In the dark its eyes shine, and it appears to see well in the night. When destitute of other provisions, it opens graves, and devours putrid human bodies.

Its voice in its beginning resembles the moaning of a human voice, and at the end it is like a violent effort to vomit.

They inhabit Persia, Syria, and Turkey in Asia, and various parts of Africa. They are very courageous, and will defend themselves with great obstinacy against much larger animals. They will sometimes attack the Ounce, and when they do, they usually conquer.

There is another kind of Hyæna which is spotted, and very common about the Cape of Good Hope, where it is called a *Tiger-wolf.* It lives by depredation, but is less courageous than the striped Hyæna.

The ravenous *Hyæna* prowls round for his prey,
  Where the folds of the shepherds are spread o'er the plain;
When a lamb, or a kid from its dam goes astray,
  'Tis seiz'd by this ruffian, and borne to his den.

There lurks an arch prowler around all our domes;
  So cunning, so fierce, so rapacious and cruel,
He fain would allure us away from our homes,
  For the fire, which torments him, to make us the fuel.

This prowler's no less than that foe of mankind,
  Who walks to and fro thro' the earth's wide domains,
To see what poor souls to ensnare he can find,
  To drag them to ruin, fast bound in his chains.

Then watch, my dear readers, the drift of his wiles,
  Nor yield for a moment to tamper with sin;
Lest, before you're aware, you be caught in his toils,
  And he shout o'er your fall with a horrible din.

2. WOODCOCK.

THIS bird is supposed by some, as Bochart and Le Clere, to be intended by the Hebrew name, Kōrā, which is rendered *Partridge* in 1 Sam. 26 : 20, and in Jere. 17 : 11. (See Partridge, article 64.) Though I am satisfied myself that the Partridge is intended, yet on account of the difference of opinion among the learned, I will here give a short description of the *Woodcock.*

The length of this bird, including the beak, is about fourteen inches; the beak about three inches, and convenient for searching after their food, which consists of worms, and other insects, in soft and muddy ground. Its back is curiously barred with reddish brown, black, and gray. Its breast dusky white, barred cross-wise with lines nearly black. Their flesh is very tender and delicate, and they are much sought after by the fowler. In summer they reside in the mountainous regions of Norway and Sweden; they are also found in Switzerland, Prussia, England and Scotland, and in the New England States in America, and probably in many other parts. Their winters they spend in more southern regions. Their nests are carelessly constructed of twigs and withered grass, and they lay for a sitting, four or five eggs, about the size of those of the Pigeon, of a brownish gray, marbled with darker spots. Their young ones, like chickens, run about as soon as they leave the shell.

In the evening they are frequently seen flying, with a twittering noise, in an ascending spiral, into the air; and then descending near to the spot, from which they rose; they then utter, at considerable intervals, a note in sound somewhat resembling the word, *Pank ;* they then rise again as before.

I have killed several while hunting for the Partridge; but in New England they are not very numerous.

> The Woodcock mounts up in a spiral, and sings ;
> So rises the soul of the saints ;
> But soon like the Woodcock, with faultering wings,
> Descends, and is weary and faint.

> The time is at hand, when the saint shall ascend,
> No more to this earth to come down ;
> But to sing, and be joyful in bliss without end,
> Adorn'd with white robes and a crown.

FISH, FISHES.

THIS is a general name of a kind of aquatic animals, of which there are very many different species. Tho' the word *Fishes*, plural form, often occurs, the word *Fish*, like *sheep*, has a plural as well as a singular meaning. The name frequently occurs in scripture, and relates probably to such as were taken in the Nile, on the Eastern shores of the Mediterranean, and in the Lake of Tiberias, and especially the latter, upon which the disciples of Christ appear to have been frequently occupied in taking fish.

The name for *fish* in Hebrew is (דָּג) Dâgh, from which comes *Dagon*, an idol of the Philistines, which above the navel had the form of a man ; but below, the form of a fish. The word for *fish* in Greek is ïkhthūs ; in Latin, *Piscis ;* French, *Poisson*. What peculiar species of fish were taken in and about Palestine I have not the means at hand to inform myself.

Among the most useful fish, that are taken on the coasts of North America, we may reckon the *Cod* and *Haddock*. Vast quantities of these are taken and cured, and afford a valuable article of commerce, being in a state to be kept good for several years, and to be conveniently transported.

Not knowing the specific names of the fish caught in Palestine, I shall give a sketch of the two species above named, the *Cod* and the *Haddock*, with figures representing them taken from the Cabinet.

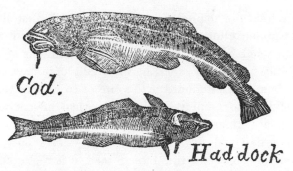

Cod.

Haddock

1. *Cod.*

Those usually taken of this fish in modern times are from two to three feet in length, and weigh from five or six to fifteen or twenty pounds. Many are taken smaller than of five pounds, and some larger than twenty. In 1755, one was taken in the neighborhood of Scarborough, England, measuring in length five feet eight inches, and in girth round the shoulders five feet—it weighed seventy-eight pounds; but this might be considered as a giant among the race.

The color of the *Cod* on the back and sides is nearly that of ashes, with small yellowish spots; its belly is white; some, however, are found a little differing in color from this; the *Rock Cod,* so called, has a reddish hue about the head and neck. They are a full-breasted fish, large forward and thick in proportion to their length, compared with many other fishes. Their tail is not forked, and a small beard issues from the extremity of the lower jaw.

These fish are said to be found in the greatest perfection between the latitudes of 50° and 66° N. but they are taken in great quantities between the latitudes of 40° and 45° N. but not farther south than 35° N. They deposit their spawn most numerously in the seas of Greenland and Iceland, that their young may be se-

cure from the depredations of those fishes that abound
in warmer climates. From one Cod of middling size
Leuenhock counted more than nine millions of eggs.
So it is said, but it seems hardly credible; to have counted them himself alone, at the rate of two every second,
would have employed him more than seventy-seven
days, at sixteen hours to the day ! However, this fish
being destined by a kind providence to supply with
food very many of the human race, it is rendered very
prolific, that the species may not be exhausted. The
young, when somewhat advanced, come in vast shoals
to the banks of Newfoundland, and to other parts of
the coasts of the Atlantic, to seek food where it is more
plentiful. It subsists on small fishes, worms, crabs,
and various testaceous animals.

Before the American revolution fifteen thousand
British seamen were employed in the cod fishery; and
their principal place of resort for this occupation was
the banks of Newfoundland. These banks appear to
be the flat tops of submarine mountains, extending in
length about five hundred miles, and in breadth about
three hundred. They lie east of Nova Scotia, between
the latitudes of 40º and 50º N. The Cod not only
abounds on the north-eastern coasts of North America,
but also on the coasts of Norway; and is found in most
of the British seas, and in the Baltic.

The best part of the fishing season is between February and June; the fish being then in their greatest
state of perfection, and most easily cured. In times
past the greater part of the cargoes of fish have been
disposed of in Roman Catholic countries, in the seasons
of Lent, when their superstition forbids them to eat other
flesh; of late, as this superstition has declined, there
has been a decrease of this trade in those countries;

but other markets have been opened, and the trade continues profitable.

How kind is our God, and how great the supply
  He provides for our wants, and how good!
The beasts of the field, and the fowls of the sky,
  And the *fish* of the sea is our food.

The *Cod* and the *Haddock*, in shoals without number,
  The ocean itself, tho' so vast, might encumber;
But the hook and the line, to secure the rich prey,
  Are drawing them yearly by millions away.

The rich and the poor of all regions are fed
  With this wholesome provision in measure;
The seas of the north are the wide spreading bed,
  Where reposes this bountiful treasure.

For this we our Maker will praise and adore;
  The earth with his goodness and mercy is crown'd;
The land and the sky, and the sea with its shore,
  With the marks of his wisdom and kindness abound.

2. *Haddock.*

This fish is often taken in the same waters where cod is found, and when we are fishing for the cod. Its back and sides are of a dark ash color; its belly whitish. It is more slender in proportion to its size than the cod, and from the top of the head to the nose it is gently tapering; between the head and the first fin on the back there is a prickly roughness; down the middle of its sides runs a black line from its head to its tail, which is forked. On each side, back of its gills, there is a dark spot, as if it were the mark of a thumb. Its scales are much larger, than those of the Cod. Its general weight is from two to three pounds, some have been caught weighing ten or twelve pounds. The *Haddock* is generally considered as a delicacy, when fresh, but not so good for salting and drying, as the cod. They are said to be in their greatest perfection in November : but out of season from January till May. They annually visit the British coasts in vast numbers. Shoals of them are sometimes found, extending one hundred miles in length, and of great breadth. Beyond these shoals there is abundance of dog-fish, by which they appear to be driven together. Their food in summer is principally herring : in winter a kind of worm, called by the fishermen, *Haddock's meat.*

Tradition tells us that it was a fish of this kind, from the mouth of which St. Peter took the tribute money for himself and for his divine Master; but it is a tradition not at all to be depended upon. The miracle, however, should be always remembered; and it may teach us, that if we put our trust in God, we shall find him ready to provide for us in our exegencies, if not in a miraculous, yet often in an unexpected, and sometimes in an extraordinary way.

A *fish* brought the tribute for Peter to pay
  For himself and his Master divine.
This *fish* must the word of its Maker obey,
  And yield to the hook and the line.

If in straits while our calling we faithfully ply,
  If God be our hope, and our friend,
We need not distrust him our wants to supply,
  He will help us, and save to the end.

2. SERPENTS.

The Hebrew word for Serpent is (בַּחָשׁ) Năhrhăsh, from a word signifying to *soothsay* or *presage ;* alluding perhaps to the cunning of the Serpent. This reptile is vulgarly called the *Snake* The idea that some Serpents have the power of charming birds seems to have too much evidence in its favor to be hastily rejected. I once, with another person, came upon a large black snake with his head near to a night hawk ; the bird immediately flew, but the snake continued stretched out at full length, till I and my companion furnished ourselves with clubs, and gave him a blow, and then killed him. His length was five feet three inches. We thought it probable he was holding the bird in charm ; but I am not confident of it.

The Greek word for Serpent is ŏfĭs ; the Latin *Serpens,* from *Serpo,* to creep. The notion of Dr. Adam Clark, that the animal employed in the seduction of Eve was the *monkey,* is too simple to require a serious refutation ; nothing in the original indicates such a thing.

The Serpents of New England are the Rattle-Snake; the common Black-Snake ; the long, white ringed Black-Snake ; the Striped-Snake ; the Green-Snake ; the small dark brown, red-bellied Snake, with a yellow ring round his neck ; the small, light brown, red-bellied Snake ; the House-Adder ; and the Water-Adder. The three former of these I have never seen east of the Penobscot, but they were frequent in Massachusetts. Of the two first I shall give a brief sketch.

1. *The Rattle-Snake.*

This is a venomous Serpent, and rather thicker in proportion to its length, than the others, except the adder. They are said to be sometimes six feet in length, and then to be of the thickness of a man's leg. Its back is dark brown, variegated with a succession of spots still darker. Its tail is furnished with shells of a horny substance, not joined together, strictly speaking, but so locked one into another in succession, as not to be readily separated. It is supposed that a new shell is added every year; with these it makes a loud rattling, when disposed. Its upper jaw is armed with two teeth, which are commonly covered with its upper lip; and at the roots of these teeth its poison is deposited; with these it inflicts a wound that is often fatal, but which with seasonable attention is sometimes healed. I knew a man in my youth, who was bitten by a Rattle-Snake a little below the knee, when mowing in a meadow. He killed the Snake, and then bound his garter tight round his leg a little above the bite. It was some hours before a physician could be obtained; his leg swelled exceedingly; he was in great pain; he drank milk in which the herb, Rattle-Snake weed, was boiled; this relieved him a little. The physician lanced the flesh round the bite, and a greenish liquid issued; he applied some kind of salts, and attended upon the man a short time, and he recovered; but the flesh for about two inches in length, and one in breadth, putrified, and came out, leaving a permanent sore of this size, after the wound was healed. I have heard of others, who have recovered; but the poison is very virulent, and is said to be frequently fatal.

The Rattle-Snake, when about to bite, will coil itself, and jump almost with the quickness of lightning, so that the animal, that shall be at the moment within the reach of its length, can rarely, if ever escape. But in their progressive motion they are slow; and seem to be furnished with their venom by a wise providence for self defence. The leaves of the white ash are said to be a mortal poison to them; and about the time when these leaves begin to fall, they retire to their dens.

Rum is a fatal poison to them. The soldiers on our frontiers towards Canada, in our revolutionary war, would sometimes meet with them, and set the breech of their guns upon their necks, when the snake would raise its head with open mouth, into which from the canteen they would turn a few drops of rum, and the snake would soon expire in agony. O that rum drinkers among men would consider that when they swallow this liquor, they are taking that which is likely to be a deadly poison to their souls, as well as the ruin of the health of their bodies!

> Dear youth, beware, or Satan's wiles
>   Will end in your undoing;
> This cunning Serpent oft beguiles
>   The thoughtless soul to ruin.
>
> 'Tis thro' the mind, in truth's fair form,
>   His venom he instills;
> This proves to many a soul the charm,
>   Which in the issue kills.

27*

2. *Black-Snake.*

[Figure from Nature.]

—

I am not able to say how extensively this reptile abounds in the United States; Williams, in his History of Vermont, mentions them as found in that State, but not as very numerous. Fifty years ago they were rarely to be met with in Massachusetts, west of the Connecticut river; but in the central parts of that State, they were somewhat common. They were usually from three to five feet in length; sometimes six feet or more; I speak of the common Black-Snake. All, except their belly was of a glossy, jet black; their belly of a bluish white, blending into the black on their sides. They ran with great swiftness, with head elevated from six to twelve inches, according to the size of the Snake. I once met a large one in a wood, having no weapon in my hand; he turned, and threatened me, and vibrated his tail repeatedly among the dry leaves like a humming-bird's wings. As soon as I had found a club, and approached him, he fled with too much speed to suffer me to get a stroke at him. In the neighborhood of my abode a heifer was once found, apparently killed by one of these Snakes. By the indentation left upon her it appeared that he wound himself once round her body, and made a wound in her neck, from which he drew some part of her blood. A Black Snake of unusual size and length was several times seen in the near vicinity of the place, but immediately retreated to a large collection of stones, so that he could not be killed.

The egg of the Black-Snake is about the size of the robbin's egg. I once found in one of them, which was more than five feet long, twenty six eggs of this size, but their shells were soft. I once took about twenty from a large water adder, in each of which was a young adder, to appearance perfectly formed, but very small.

About fifty years ago one of my friends related an adventure of an acquaintance of his with a white-ringed Black-Snake, near the central part of Massachusetts. He was felling a piece of wood, and being about to return to his house, stuck his ax into a stump. He had not proceeded far before one of these Snakes accosted him, and in a moment was round his legs, and threw him down. He then began to ascend towards the man's waist, not by moving round him, but by rolling himself over, as one might roll over a rope round a tub, to raise it towards the top. The man grasped the neck of the Snake with one hand, and with the other drew himself towards his ax. Presently the Snake began to whip with his tail the hand with which his neck was held, and whipped the skin off. The man succeeded at length to confine head and tail with one hand, and with the help of the other gained his ax; but by this time he found himself severely girded by the Snake, and saw at a distance another coming towards him with head elevated, and with full speed. He gave a blow with his ax across the Snake, over his leg, which just divided the Snake in two, without injuring his leg. The Snake uttered a sort of shriek, and the other turning about, made off, as fast he approached. In this manner, through a kind providence, the man escaped.

A young man in Dedham, Massachusetts, between forty and fifty years ago, killed one of this kind of Snake about twelve feet in length. Their haunt is especially in land that has been once cleared, and then left to grow up with briers and bushes.

I may here add that *Serpent* is a general name given to a race of animals, between which and man there is almost a universal enmity. There are but few persons, whose nerves are so braced, but that, coming upon a Serpent suddenly, they will start with unpleasant feelings; and a degree of terror and disgust will generally be excited, while we look upon the Serpent, though it be one that is known not to be poisonous. However any may be disposed to reject the idea, I have but little doubt, but that these feelings towards Serpents is the result of a divine constitution, the object of which is to keep in remembrance the instrument, used by the prince of the devils, in tempting our first parents to eat of the forbidden fruit. The great, and ever abiding enmity is between the spiritual seed of the woman, and the devil himself; but there want not the traces of a corresponding enmity betwen man and the literal Serpent.

The common Serpent, in size and thickness compares nearly with a whip stick; but from this their size varies to the little brown snake of but a few inches long, on one hand; and to the *Boa-Constrictor*, (ox-binder,) on the other, which in length sometimes exceeds thirty feet.

The Serpent is a reptile generally living on land; is long and slender, compared with its thickness; without legs or feet, covered with a skin much resembling very small scales on the back, and on the belly resembling larger scales, reaching transversely from side to side. It commonly progresses forward with a waving motion; but sometimes the larger Serpents will go forward with great rapidity, almost in a straight line, and with elevated head; perhaps they assist themselves by their scales on their bellies; but their speed is really wonderful.

Common Serpents annually shed their skins. By some means they succeed in turning back the skin of the upper and under jaw, and fastening it to grass, stubble, and the like; they then progress forward, crawling out of it, while it is inverted over them, as a stocking over the leg, as we draw it off, when it happens to be wet. The skin soon after the snake has left it, is soft as the finest silk stuff, wholly inside out, and nearly transparent; the skin to the very eyes, with the concave side towards us, will be seen, attached to the head.

The poison of venomous Serpents is repeatedly mentioned in Scripture, to set forth that native depravity of which man is the subject, especially when the fruit of it is come to an aggravated measure of wickedness. Most desirable it is that we be divested of this poison by the renewing and sanctifying influence of the Holy Spirit. The prince of the devils is repeatedly called a Serpent in Scripture, in allusion to the animal that he abused as an instrument in tempting to eat the forbidden fruit.

SECTION 3.

HAVING closed the history of the lower orders of animals, named in scripture, I come now to that of Man.

In *Man* we behold the noblest of the works of God in this lower world. Man in his original state was but a little lower than the angels, and crowned with glory and honor. He was constituted the lord of the earth, and all the other creatures were subject to his dominion. Had he retained his integrity, the earth would have remained a Paradise, and its rational inhabitants would have bloomed in immortal youth, and in uninterrupted happiness. Man was made Male and Female, that he might propagate his kind, and that the social affections might be exercised in the highest degree of perfection. Man, by means of a rational mind, was constituted the connecting link between the merely animal, and the purely spiritual world. Man by his fall has lost his primeval dignity, and subjected himself to changes, which otherwise would never have happened to him.

By means of the fall Man has become universally a depraved creature; his heart is polluted, his appetites disordered; the vigor of his mind is impaired, his moral dignity is gone. The very first person, that sprang from our fallen first parents, imbrued his hands in a brother's blood. Between sixteen and seventeen centuries from the creation God suffered the inhabitants of the earth to continue to multiply without interruption; and as they multiplied, wickedness increased, till the earth became full of violence, so that God saw it needful to sweep it with a besom of destruction. He brought a flood over the earth, by which all its inhabitants, but the family of Noah were destroyed. By the three sons of Noah the earth soon began to be repeopled again; but a various fortune awaited the descendants of these three. Noah, the father of the New World, having planted a vineyard, drank of the wine of it, probably without being aware of its strength, and became in measure intoxicated. While in this state he became uncovered in his tent, so as to expose himself in an indecent situation. Ham, the father of Canaan, probably with his son with him, saw him in this situation, and instead of immediately covering him, it appears that they made light of it. But Shem and Japheth in a very modest manner covered their aged father. For this a blessing was pronounced upon them, thro' the prophetic inspiration of Noah, after the wine had left him; and a curse upon Canaan, or the posterity of Ham. The curse denounced against Canaan fell more immediately upon *his* descendants; but implicated all the sons of Ham. The children of Ham extensively were destined to be for long ages subjected to bondage.

The sons of Ham were Cush, Misraim, Phut, and Canaan. The descendants of Cush inhabited the coasts of the Red Sea, on both sides of it, but especially on the African side. They were called Ethiopians, because they were a black people; for the word *Ethiops*, means a black countenance. The descendants of Misraim dwelt in Egypt, the name of which in Hebrew is *Misraim.* They were a dark people, and with the Ethiopians, and with the descendants of Phut, as some think, populated that part of the Globe called *Africa.* From these are the Negroes. The posterity of Canaan first settled in that part of Asia, which lies on the east of the Mediterranean; and west of Jordan and the Dead Sea; they also extended themselves south-east into Arabia. These felt the fulfillment of the ancient curse in being wasted and destroyed in vast multitudes at the command of God, for their wickedness, by the Israelites. As for the Africans, it is well known that at this day they are generally a dark or black people; and that millions of them have been for ages enslaved, and continue to be enslaved still. The Negroes of Africa, in particular, form a quite marked variety of the human species. The following figure from Mavor represents one of them.

1. *The Negro.*

This appellation is from the Latin word *Niger*, which means *black*. The countenance of the Negro is, in a popular way of speaking, black, but not strictly so; it is rather black, with a mixture of red, yellow, and white, in which the black greatly predominates. His nose is flat, his lips thick, his jaws protruded forward rather more than those of other varieties. Their skin is very smooth, their eyes generally hazel, or light brown, their teeth white, their hair black and curled, or frizzled. They are of about a middling stature, and generally not so strong and nervous, as the European. The land of their nativity is more properly that part of Africa, which lies between the Tropics; but they are found in multitudes in the West Indies, in the South part of North America, and in parts of South America, and scattered here and there in other places, to which they have been carried captives from their native land for slaves, and where they have much increased by propagation. Their mental powers have no doubt generally shared in the debilitating influence of the climate, where they have been long the inhabitants; but I believe they have suffered more from that oppression, which they have extensively experienced from other nations, more powerful and domineering than from climate. Whether the color and features of the Negro are wholly the effect of climate, as some suppose; or whether there were a mark of distinction put upon the race of Ham by a special providence of God, to be a memorial of the divine displeasure against immodesty; are, in my mind, questions not easy to be resolved. If it be admitted that their complexion, and wooly hair, are altogether the effect of climate, I must believe that it was through a superintending providence of God, that they received their lot in a part of the world so much calculated to fit them to be servants, in fulfilment of the ancient prediction.—But whenever we look upon an African, let us not say within ourselves, This man was made for a slave, and it is right that we should enslave him; but rather let us say; If the iniquity of Ham, in his immodest conduct, have been so long visited upon his posterity; let us cultivate modesty, and due respect for our superiors, with the most scrupulous attention.

We are no more justified in enslaving the Africans, because God by Noah denounced a curse upon Canaan, than Saul was in slaying the priests at Nob, though it was a fulfillment of the threatening of God against the house of Eli. How much more noble it would be to labor to christianize and civilize the Africans, and to be the means of their abandoning all those evil man-

ners, which now bring them into servitude. Let them
become generally virtuous and pious, and they will
not find the childrens' teeth to be set on edge, because
the fathers have eaten sour grapes.

Haste the time, the happy day,
  When Afric's Sons shall all obey
The glorious gospel's friendly voice.
  Their cruel bondage then will cease,
  And tribe with tribe will dwell in peace ;
And Afric's mourning realms rejoice.

Ye Colonizing Bands, proceed,
  'Till all the slaves shall taste the mead
Of freedom fair, and bright, and pure ;
  Ye Heralds of salvation too,
  Do what the gospel bids you do,
And fix their freedom on a base secure.

2. *The Laplander.*

[Figure enlarged from Mavor.]

The Esquimaux Indians, the Greenlanders, the Ice-
landers, the Laplanders, the Nova Zemblians, the Samoid Tartars, and the Kamtschadales, most of whom
are within the Arctic circle, are considered by some as
forming a distinct variety of the human race. For a
general description of them we may say, they are of a
rather low stature, their heads large, their faces broad,
their noses flat, their cheek bones high, their lips thick,

their eyes brown, the color of their skin a dark yellowish brown, their hair black and straight. Their women
are chaste, and both men and women strong of their size,
but prone to indolence. They are generally of a peaceable and hospitable disposition, but violent, when provoked. Though this may serve as a general description of this variety, the several divisions of it differ
somewhat one from another; the Laplanders, and some
of the others have thin beards; but the Esquimaux
have thick beards, and foul teeth; and the Samoid Tartars are represented as subject to great nervous excita-
bility; a sudden noise sometimes throws them into
convulsions.

The garments of the inhabitants of these cold northern regions are made of the skins of beasts, dressed
with the hair on; and much of their food consists of
flesh, dried without salt, and eaten raw. They live in
huts and caves; have plain, common sense; but in respect to science their minds appear to be stunted, somewhat like the productions of their land, by the rigor of
their climate. The wealth of the Laplander consists
principally in his herds of Rein Deer, which serve to
convey him from place to place on the sledge, and to
furnish him in part with milk, which is sometimes
made into cheese.

The religious ideas of these nations are few, and obscure; but they are susceptible of instruction in the
doctrines and duties of Christianity, and of feeling its
obligations and comforts, as appears from the effects of
the labors of the persevering Moravians among some of
them.

3. *The Tartar.*

This variety of the human race is supposed to include the Chinese and the Japanese, who, from the contour of their features, and their color appear to be of Tartar descent.

[Figure from Mavor.]

The Tartars inhabit the middle regions of Asia, from the Caspian Sea on the west to the Gulph of Corea on the east. They are generally of a middle stature, strong and healthy. Their general complexion is a greenish brown; their forehead is broad, and at an early age becomes wrinkled; their eyes are small and wide apart; their eye-brows thick; their noses are short and flat; the lower part of their face is narrow, tapering to the chin, which has but little beard on it; their cheek bones are high; their hair black; the men generally shave this off, except a lock on the top of the head, which they suffer to grow long, and usually wear it braided. The more common Tartar dress is a jacket

and a sort of pantaloons reaching to the feet, made of
deer skin with the hair outwards. Their complexion
from various circumstances differs in different parts, and
so their general visage ; for though the Circassian Tartars have something in their looks approaching beauty,
the Kalmucs are said to be very ugly in their appearance. They are very fond of horses, and very dex-
trous in managing them; and are not often seen travelling on foot. Their favorite food is horse flesh. They
are very expert in shooting with the bow and arrow.
They are generally a roving people, removing in large
companies from place to place to find pasture for their
cattle and horses, the care of which occupies most
of their time, as they do little at cultivating the ground.
They are generally cheerful and hospitable to strangers.
Their religious ideas are vague and various, according
to the religions of the nations, upon which they border : but most of them are worshippers of the Grand
Lama of Thibet.

Though the Chinese and Japanese differ much in their
habits and manners from the great body of the Tartars,
and are much more attentive to the arts and sciences ;
yet from resemblance of color and features, and some
other circumstances, they are supposed to have descended from the Tartars, and with them to constitute one of
the varieties of the race of man. They are almost all
Pagans ; but measures are now in train to introduce
pure Christianity not only among the Tartars, but also
into the great empire of China ; and though the isles
of Japan, by reason of the proud, overbearing conduct
of the Papists, once among them, are now the bitter
enemies of Christianity, the time is doubtless coming,
when, by seeing Christianity on their borders in its
pure, unadulterated form, they will consent to embrace it.

28*

4. *Native Americans.*

These are called *Indians ;* also *Aboriginals,* because of the difficulty of tracing their origin.

Some of the peculiar characteristics of this class are, that their color much resembles that of copper, whence they are frequently called red men ; their faces are rather broad, their noses a little flattened, their cheek bones high, and their eyes rather small. They have but very little beard ; their hair is black and straight. They are of a roving disposition, not willing to be long confined to one place. Much of their food is obtained by the chase ; they are good marks-men, and active in running. In size they differ but little from Europeans, or Anglo-Americans in general. They occupy their time in hunting, raising indian corn, making baskets, brooms, &c. and bowls and boxes of the bark of the grey birch, ornamented with the quills of the hedge-hog. They wear a shirt without wristbands or collar; over this a close waistcoat, and over this a loose coat, coming down below the knees, and girded round them with a girdle, to which is attached a case with a long knife, a tobacco pouch, and a purse made of the skin of some small animal. For their legs they have cloth leggins, reaching from the upper part of the thigh to the ancles, and sewed in such manner, as to leave a broad list on the outside of the leg. For their feet they have *moccasins*, made of skin, drawn together on the top of the foot. On their heads they often wear a cloth cap, painted at the top, and having a flap behind, falling over the shoulders. Such has been the usual dress of the natives of the north east part of the United States, since they have been able to furnish themselves with cloth from Europeans; and since that time the have laid aside the bow and arrow, and have adopted fire arms, in their stead. Their houses are usually made of poles, meeting near together at the top, but leaving a hole for the passage of smoke, and for letting in light. On the outside of these polls they spread the bark of the grey birch, and over that the boughs of ever-green trees. In the centre of this hut is their fire; around it they sit and lie on the boughs of trees, over which are sometimes spread the skins of beasts. Their hut is in some parts called a wigwâm; in others a *camp*. In one side of it is a small opening, where they enter, which has a screen before it. In front of this door they have a porch, where they lay their wood in winter. Those, who live in the neighborhood of the Anglo-Americans, gradually adopt their manners and dress.

They have generally some notion of a future state, and of a great Spirit above, who rules the world. Where the Roman Catholics have had access to them, many of them have become bigoted to their religion; where they have not, they are to a good measure accessible by Protestants, and somewhat readily receive instruction in pure christianity. Their youth are found to possess a good measure of genius for the pursuit of science. They are generally chaste, hospitable, and honest. They long remember a kindness done them, but do not soon forget an injury. Their prevailing vice is the intemperate use of ardent spirits, for which they have a peculiar fondness; when once they have tasted them. Many of their white neighbors, destitute of humane principle, take advantage of this propensity, and ruin multitudes of them by furnishing them with this deleterious drug. Pious missionaries have done much to meliorate their condition; and were it not for wicked, avaricious whites in their neighborhood, they might in the course of a few years become christianized, civilized, and respectable among Christian nations

5. *Southern Asiatics.*

[Figure from Mavor.]

In this class we may include the Jews, the Arabians,
the Syrians, the Armenians, the Persians, the Gentoos,
or Hindoos, the Siamese, the Burmans, and the Ma-
lays; with a large portion of the inhabitants of the
isles on the south of Asia.   Generally speaking these
nations are descended from Shem, one of the sons of
Noah; but are mingled no doubt in many cases with
the posterity of Ham and Japheth.   Though they may
be classed in one great variety, they differ very considerably among themselves.   At this we need not wonder, when we consider the extent of territory over
which they are spread; their lying so open to the commerce of all maritime nations, and the wars and revolutions in ages past among them.

For a general description it may be said, that in stature, and in the form of their faces they do not greatly
differ from Europeans.   They are rather more slender,

and in color they vary from a pale greenish brown, or olive, to black. They have long, straight, black hair; the men have thick beards and suffer them to grow long.

In some parts they shave their heads, except a lock on the crown, and they wear Turbans. These in Persia are sometimes made of a sheep skin, dressed with the wool on it. The women wear stiff caps, with something like horns to them, resembling those of a Jewish mitre. They are generally well formed; their women are, many of them, delicate, and in some parts exhibit in the countenance a measure of beauty; but in other parts their appearance is quite forbidding. They usually sit cross-legged, either on mats, or on the naked ground.

They extensively believe the doctrine of the transmigration of souls; and that at death their spirit passes into the body of some beast, bird, or reptile; on this account some of them will eat nothing that ever had animal life. The more common food of the Hindoos is rice and vegtables, cooked with ginger and other hot spices. Many in the eastern part of India, prefer dog's flesh to any other. A common dish among the Persians is mutton and fowls, boiled together, till it becomes almost a soup. They eat also such kinds of fish as have fins and scales. Most of the food of the Arabians consists of the milk and flesh of the Camel.

The Southern Asiatics in general have neither chair nor table in their houses, nor knife, nor fork at their meals. The Arabians and Persians are chiefly Mohamedans; in writing, like many other orientals, they begin at the right hand, and proceed towards the left. In Persia the number of Scribes is almost incredible, as they allow of no printing in the kingdom. The Hindoos, Burmans, and Siamese are generally pagans, and

the number of their idol gods is very great. Among
them are a few Mohamedans, a few Jews, and a
few that bear the name of Christians, but have little
more than the name. Of late, however, the means are
using to introduce among them Christianity in its purity; and we have reason to believe that ere long God
will show, that he has not forgotten the blessing long
ago pronounced upon Shem, and will bring his long
wandering posterity into the tents of godliness, and
cause the descendants of Japheth to mingle with them
in sharing the blessing; and that his anger against Ham
will not remain forever, but that *his* posterity will also
be remembered in mercy.

6. *Europeans.*
[Figure from Life.]

In this variety may be included the Russians, and
some of their northern neighbors; the Prussians and

Germans, and their neighbors; the Turks, Greeks, and Italians; the French and Spaniards, and their neighbors; the inhabitants of the Isles of Great Britain and Ireland; the Spaniards and Portuguese of S. America; and the Anglo-Americans of N. America.

They are generally robust, athletic, and disposed for active labor. In stature they range from five to six feet. They are well shapen; have most commonly long, silken brown hair, of different shades from light to dark; some have black hair, some red, some sandy, some flaxen. In their features they exhibit, for the most part, an agreeable symmetry; some of them are enchantingly beautiful. This beauty is the result, however, not of the regularity of features alone; but springs in part from their color; the fair, ruddy, white temples, with their blue veins; the rosy cheeks, and ruby lips; all animated with sparkling eyes, some blue, some black, some hazel, or light brown—add greatly to the agreeable proportion and disposition of features to complete the beauty of the countenance. Regularity of features is a prevailing characteristic of this variety of the human race, but there is a considerable diversity in color; in some of the more southern parts of Europe, Spain, and Portugal, for instance, even the ladies are of a swarthy, yellowish, and olive complexion.

As respects universality of genius, strength of mind for deep investigation, patience in labor, and boldness of enterprise, the Europeans doubtless excel all the other varieties of mankind; no others to an equal measure surround themselves with the comforts of life; no others are in general so cleanly in their modes of living. But, what is more important than all the rest, no others to a nearly equal degree enjoy the blessings of Christianity—the privileges for becoming acquainted with the way to future happiness. In the mean time it must be confessed that vast multitudes neglect, and abuse these privileges to the aggravation of that future condemnation, which they bring upon themselves by so doing.

We should not, however, be discouraged by the knowledge of this; we begin to see harbingers of a reform, and of better days; and the sure word of prophecy respecting this should animate every true Christian Philanthropist, to do his utmost to hasten this reform.

29

CONCLUSION.

IN the preceding pages, for the use of the rising generation, I have given a short sketch of those living creatures, that are mentioned in the Holy Scriptures; in doing this I have desired to promote their progress in useful knowledge; and especially to lead them into a more intimate acquaintance with the works of God, and through his works to a knowledge of some part of his character. The works of God are so numerous, and so various, that we have no reason at all to wonder, if some appearances seem to us, short sighted creatures, to contradict what the general language of his works indicates; even that God is a Being of unspeakable benevolence. To endeavor to clear the subject of this difficulty, in some small measure, is what I have principally in view in the following reflections.

1. We see that the smaller tribes of living creatures are often destroyed by hundreds, and by thousands by the instrumentality of man. When thus destroyed they suffer. The mass of their suffering is not inconsiderable. Why is this suffering found in the world, if the Creator of it be of infinite benevolence? In answer to this I shall say, that it must be admitted that the greatest sum of happiness in the world cannot be produced without involving a measure of suffering. Creatures, to enjoy, must *feel*; they must have sensibilities. In their destruction these sensibilities will occasion a measure of suffering. But, to avoid this, shall they all be sustained always in life? they would at length

in such case, overcharge all habitable space, and greatly incommode one another, and also other creatures ; in
this there would be unavoidable suffering. In such
case also, the husbandman must not clear a field, and
burn the brush of it ; for in so doing he must burn up
thousands, perhaps millions of reptiles and insects.
But, without clearing and cultivating the ground, man
cannot subsist. The only remaining alternative to a-
void this is, not to give being to these little animals ;
but then the world is deprived of a vast amount of enjoyment. It seems reasonable then to admit, that, if
the amount of enjoyment resulting from the subsistence
of these minute creatures may be more than a balance
for the suffering that must result from their dissolution,
it is benevolence to give them being. The sum of happiness without doubt is increased by their being. Generally their pain in dying can be but momentary ; their
enjoyment is for hours, days, and months, and in the
case of some, for years. Their lively motions often in-
dicate to the nice observer a high degree of enjoyment,
considering their smallness. Who can tell but that,
in every individual instance, the enjoyment is more
than the suffering ? If it be, is it not benevolence towards the individuals to give them being ? But without
doubt the sum of enjoyment among them all is far greater than the suffering : and then there is great benevolence in giving them being.

2. We see that vast numbers of insects and reptiles
are devoured one of another ; not often by their own
species ; but in many cases very many individuals of one
species are the food of another species ; how many flies
and other insects are the prey of the spider ? How is
this consistent with the goodness of God ? I answer ;
as there must be a dissolution, as well as a generation of

insects, that they may not overwhelm the earth; and as it is probable that the suffering of an animal, that does not anticipate its death, may be even less when suddenly destroyed, than when removed by a lingering natural death; and seeing that many more species, and even individuals may subsist, and experience enjoyment, by reason of the feeding of some upon others, it appears to be very wise and benevolent in God to ordain that one class in many cases should feed upon other classes.

3. We see much the same economy in the case of the larger animals, as among the smaller, the insects and reptiles. Each species has its enemies; the wolf is the enemy of the lamb; the Lion is the enemy of larger beasts; the Elephant and Rhinoceros are often mutual enemies. There are carnivorous beasts and fowls of the air, as well as granivorous and herbivorous. Animals of the milder classes often suffer fear and death from the more savage. Why is it thus? I answer, the same reasoning will apply generally in the case of these, as in the case of the smaller tribes. They must have checks upon their natural prolificness, or they would so multiply as to pine away and die with hunger. Though such as are the prey of others do suffer in measure through fear, this fear is a needful principle, implanted in them to lead them to provide for their safety, and does secure so many of them, that generally no more are taken, than is needful to supply with food those that subsist upon flesh. If it be asked, why might not all the animals have been made to subsist upon vegetable food, and their powers of multiplying have been circumscribed within such limits, that they would not have superabounded? I reply, that in such case there would not have been vegetable food to supply near so great a

number of animals, as subsist under the present economy; and the lingering old age, and infirmity, and natural death of these animals would probably involve much
more suffering, than their usual, much more sudden,
though violent death, with all its fears.—The procrea-
tion and rearing up of the young animals, appears to
be to their parents a source of much enjoyment, and
this goes to the general sum of happiness.

To illustrate the subject, I will suppose that by
means of the several kinds of carnivorous animals, three
animals subsist where otherwise but two could have
subsisted. I will suppose that each of these animals
enjoys as much as either would have done, if there had
been but two; in this case the enjoyment is as three
to two. I will next suppose the comparative enjoyment of animals to be, on an average, nine degrees, for
one degree of suffering; this gives eight degrees of
positive enjoyment for each animal. If there are three
animals for two, there are eight degrees of enjoyment
gained in twenty-four. Let us suppose the suffering
under this economy diminished one third, which I think
probable, then in the case of three animals the degrees
of suffering will be but two, and the degrees of positive
enjoyment by means of rapacious animals twenty-five,
instead of sixteen.

Is it not then real evidence of benevolence in God,
that there are rapacious animals? Surely we have reason to praise God for very great benevolence displayed
in the creation of the irrational creatures. Let us set
the average absolute enjoyment of each animal, after
all suffering is balanced, at about eight degrees; multiply this by the number of animals; O, how great is the
sum of positive happiness!

4. While multitudes of the fish of the sea feed upon
29*

others that are smaller, they themselves in turn afford us a wholesome and pleasant repast; and thousands of mankind are sustained by means of them. Multitudes of beasts of the field feed on grass, herbs, and other vegetable substances; they enjoy their food; but in turn they are food for us. Very many fowls of the air feed on grain, grass, herbs, seeds and insects : They, themselves, at length are among the delicacies of our tables. Very many others, too small to be food for us, gather up a vast multitude of seeds, which otherwise would be lost, and devour a vast multitude of insects, that would otherwise greatly afflict us by their numbers; and in the mean while, morning and evening they delight us with their songs. In the neighborhood of the streams, the devout Psalmist reminds us, the fowls of heaven have their habitation, that sing among the branches. The little birds are at length a prey to the rapacious birds; but it prevents a slow, lingering natural death, to which otherwise they must be subjected. The rapacious birds, as well as the others, delight us with the varied elegance of their forms, and the variety and beauty of their plumage. The leaves and fruit of the trees, the grass, the herbs of the field, yea, every green thing, is fed upon by tribes of insects, almost innumerable. In these there is life and enjoyment, where otherwise there would be but insensible vegetation. Many of these insects delight us with the exquisiteness of the workmanship of their Creator. The flowers of the field while they charm our eyes with the variety and delicacy of their tints, and regale us with their perfumes, yield a nectareous juice, which sustains a vast number of insects of the winged race; one kind of these, the bee, treasures up stores of it, which man is permitted to take, and use for his own comfort and gratification. I might enlarge, for the theme is inexhaustible; but I should swell my little work to a size too cumbrous and expensive for its object.

5. When we come to take a survey of man, as he is brought to view in scripture, in a fallen state, and when we contemplate the past, and present effects of the fall, as they extensively appear in the case of the greater part of the rational tenants of the earth, we have certainly a somewhat gloomy picture before us. Much of the history of the world is a history of warfare, of fighting, of slaughtered multitudes, fallen by the hands of brethren, even by the hands of those of the same flesh and blood with themselves. It is a history of intrigues, of deception, of oppression, pillage, murder, lasciviousness, and crimes too numerous to specify. God is forgotten; the lowest of his creatures are worshipped; famine, pestilence, and misery in a multitude of forms, visit, in turn, every part of the inhabited earth. How can this be consistent with the supposed benevolence of the Creator? Why is it thus? To this I answer, could we see the universe, as God sees it, I doubt not but all the misery of the fallen world would appear to be but a small dark spot, to set off by contrast an immensity of moral beauty; and as a slight measure of suffering to heighten an immensity of enjoyment.

The more immediate cause of suffering is sin; sin is the voluntary departure of moral agents from the path marked out for their feet by infinite wisdom. God has determined its existence, without doubt, for some vastly important purpose, of which we at present can understand but a little. With reverence and humility, however, we may ask, If sin had not been suffered, how could the beauty of holiness have ever appeared in so conspicuous a light as it now does? How could the attributes of God have ever been displayed, and understood to the measure that they now are, and yet may be ? How could his hatred of sin have been so clearly manifested ? How could his love of holiness have appeared in a light so glorious ? How could his justice have been so plainly seen ? How could his sovereignty have so strikingly appeared ? How could the boundlessness of his love have been made known to a universe of intelligent creatures, as it now is in the work of redemption by Jesus Christ ? How could the evil of sin have been proved, as it has been by the sufferings of the Son of God, to atone for it ? A vast portion of the happiness of intelligent minds arises from an immense variety of motives of action, brought into the world by the wise Governor of the universe. Without motive to stimulate, the mind falls into a dormant state, in which its enjoyment, if it can be said to possess any, is but a sort of negative affection. In suffering sin to be, an astonishing variety and multitude of motives, by which intelligent minds are actuated, is brought into being by the blessed God, which otherwise could not have been.

To illustrate this in the case of an individual, we will say, a true christian. Sometimes he is stirred up to action by the desire of securing to himself the greatest measure of lawful, refined sensual happiness ; sometimes to secure the same for others. Sometimes he is moved to exercise to obtain the greatest consistent measure of spiritual happiness ; sometimes to assist others in obtaining it. Sometimes he is moved by salutary fear ; he is actuated to shun temporal danger, and to escape spiritual danger ; sometimes his concern is that others may escape. Sometimes he is moved by a sense of the duty of gratitude to God, and to the Lord Jesus Christ, for the work of redemption ; he is stirred up to the delightful exercise of thanksgiving. Sometimes the circumstances connected with the work of redemption move him to meditate deeply upon the character of God, as displayed in part by this work; in this meditation he sees wisdom in God, goodness in God, justice in God, mercy in God, truth in God, and a glorious assemblage of moral beauty, which humbles, astonishes, and delights him to a measure of rapture, of extacy. Then he is moved with a desire to lead others to similar meditations, that they may have similar delight. Angels in the mean time look with wonder upon the displays of the divine character, made in the great plan for the salvation of sinners; they have a world of motives to lead them to pry into the mysterious subject; they also have happiness in ministering to the heirs of salvation.

The fallen angels and the finally impenitent of the human race are indeed to be forever miserable; but in this they receive in just measure the due reward of their deeds; and amidst all their suffering they choose to continue in rebellion against their rightful Sovereign. As moral agents are actuated by moral motives; so the perpetual suffering of these for their sin, affords a perpetual evidence that God will maintain the integrity of his law, and a perpetual and immensely strong motive to unnumbered millions of holy, intelligent creatures to preserve their allegiance to the King of kings. To principalities and powers in heavenly places will be made known by the church the manifold wisdom of God.

This may illustrate in some small measure, the subject of the multiplication of interesting motives of action, suited to enlarge the happiness of holy immortal minds, by means of the being of sin, and the manner in which a God of infinite wisdom is disposing of it.

To return to the state of this lower world, I may remark, that the sure word of prophecy gives us reason to believe that we have not yet seen the brighter side of the divine administration towards it. God has been long showing what the tendency of sin is, what the evil of revolt, and to what measure man is depraved, and the necessity of grace to restore him to a holy state and to divine favor. When this has been done to the measure that God sees needful, that the pride of all mere human endeavors to reform the world may be brought low; then he will by his Spirit interpose in such manner, and to such measure, as he has yet never done, and this world for a long season will be a blooming paradise. The earth will yield her increase; it will be filled with inhabitants; they will dwell together as brethren, in unity. Sickness will be removed, or greatly alleviated; bolts and bars will grow rusty; prisons will fall into decay; the temples for divine worship will be numerous, and in good repair. The public, private, and secret worship of God will rise from every part of the world, and mingling, will ascend, as a vast cloud of acceptable incense before the throne of God and the Lamb. Cheerfulness will sit on every brow; tears will give place to smiles; and the millions of the human race, with few exceptions, will be truly, and to a high degree happy.

Now my young friends, I doubt not but that God, who delights to make his rational creatures happy in being employed in his service, will use very many of the rising generation, to bring forward, as instruments, this golden age. May the *little work*, I here present you subserve, with a multitude of others more worthy, the valuable purpose of assisting in qualifying you to put a hand to the great work in which God is about to reform the world.